POPE PIUS XII LIBRARY, ST. JOSEPH COL.
3 2528 06383 4925

WOMEN AND THE SETTLEMENT MOVEMENT

WOMEN AND THE SETTLEMENT MOVEMENT

Katharine Bentley Beauman

The Radcliffe Press
London · New York

Published in 1996 by
Radcliffe Press
An imprint of I.B. Tauris & Co Ltd
Victoria House
Bloomsbury Square
London WC1B 4DZ

175 Fifth Avenue
New York
NY 10010

In the United States of America
and Canada distributed by
St Martin's Press
175 Fifth Avenue
New York
NY 10010

A full CIP record for this book is available from the British Library

A full CIP record for this book is available from the Library of Congress

ISBN 1-86064-129-6

Library of Congress Catalog card number: available

Copy-edited and laser-set by Selro Publishing Services, Oxford
Printed and bound in Great Britain by WBC Ltd, Bridgend, Mid Glamorgan

TO FRANCESCA AND NED

Contents

Illustrations

Acronyms

ACUPA	Archbishop of Canterbury's Commission on Urban Priority Areas
AEW	Association for the Education of Women
AGM	Annual General Meeting
ARP	air-raid precautions
BA	Bachelor of Arts
BARS	British Association of Residential Settlements
BASSAC	British Association of Settlements and Social Action Centres
BASW	British Association of Social Workers
BBC	British Broadcasting Corporation
BCH	Bishop Creighton House
BRCS	British Red Cross Society
CAB	Citizen's Advice Bureaux
CBE	Commander (of the Order) of the British Empire
CCETSW	Central Council for Education and Training in Social Work
CCHF	Children's Country Holiday Fund
CEMA	Council for the Encouragement of Music and the Arts
COS	Charity Organization Society
DCH	Dame Colet House
DCL	Doctor of Civil Law
DD	*Divinitatis Doctor* (Doctor of Divinity)
E	Edward Talbot
ESA	Educational Settlements Association

ESOL	English for Speakers of Other Languages
FWA	Family Welfare Association
GB	Great Britain
GBS	Governesses' Benevolent Society
GDA	Girls' Diocesan Association
GFS	Girls' Friendly Society
GOM	Grand Old Man (W. E. Gladstone)
GWR	Great Western Railway
HMI	His (*or* Her) Majesty's Inspector
HRH	Her Royal Highness
ICAA	Invalid Children's Aid Association
IFS	International Federation of Settlements
ILEA	Inner London Education Authority
JP	Justice of the Peace
LBOH	Ladies' Branch of Oxford House
LCC	London County Council
LCSS	London Council of Social Service
LEA	London Education Authority
LMH	Lady Margaret Hall
LMHS	Lady Margaret Hall Settlement
LSE	London School of Economics and Political Science
MA	*Magister Artium* (Master of Arts)
MABYS	Metropolitan Association for Befriending Young Servants
MP	Member of Parliament
NACRO	National Association for the Care and Resettlement of Offenders
NALGO	National Association of Local Government Workers
NCSS	National Council of Social Services
NSPCC	National Society for the Prevention of Cruelty to Children
NUWW	National Union of Women Workers
OBE	Officer of the Order of the British Empire
OFV	Opportunities for Volunteering
OGA	Old Girls' Association

PA	Playgroup Association
SCREN	Southwark Computer Resource in Education Network
SPGSUSW	St Paul's Girls' School Union for Social Work
SSAFA	Soldiers', Sailors', and Airmen's Families Association
T & T	Time and Talents
TB	tuberculosis
Toc H	Talbot House
UGS	Union of Girls' Schools for Social Service
UGSM	United Girls' School Mission
USA	United States of America
VAT	Nickname for Violet Tritton
VSU	Voluntary Service Unit
WDA	Women's Diocesan Association
WEA	Workers' Education Association
WUS[S]	Women's University Settlement
WVS	Women's Voluntary Service
YWCA	Young Women's Christian Association

Acknowledgements

I am grateful for the help given to me by family and friends, including my son Christopher, Rosemary Peel of Lady Margaret Hall Settlement, Olive Chandler of St Margaret's House, and Oxford contemporaries including the late Ruth Bailey who put me in touch with the Talbot diaries and other papers at Keble College.

I am also grateful to Rosemary Toussaint-Giraud, Director, and Geraldine Xiberras, of Lady Margaret Hall Settlement, for their invaluable help in providing the selection of photographs.

Introduction

The settlement movement was started by university men in 1884 to help deprived inhabitants of inner cities. And women soon joined them; for when inner city problems first stirred the public conscience in the mid-Victorian years, the pioneers of social work included notable women. Both Canon Barnett and his wife Henrietta, key figures at the first settlement, owed much to their friend Octavia Hill. And while she helped to launch housing reform in London, elsewhere campaigning for social justice and women's higher education advanced often under one banner. Thus among Oxford lecturers for the Association for the Education of Women (AEW) in the Michaelmas term of 1879 was Ruskin's young disciple Arnold Toynbee of Balliol; he taught political economy in a room over a baker's shop in Clarendon Street as women were not then admitted to college lectures.

Democracy had only recently emerged as a new force in British life by January 1883 when Toynbee addressed a memorable meeting in London's East End. He asked those who heard him to accept middle-class help. Seven weeks later he was dead. But by then a new climate of thought was emerging, many believing with him that if educated young men, including the political leaders of the future, could experience the shocking social conditions in industrial cities, there might be more hope of changing them. For many contemporary women, however, as for the clergy, there was little novelty in the idea of helping disadvantaged people. The eighteenth-century religious revival, which placed service before doctrinal thought, had helped here. And Hannah More, Harriet Martineau, Elizabeth Fry, Florence Nightingale and Josephine

Butler were already among well-known figures to substantiate Dame Eileen Younghusband's twentieth-century comment that 'social workers, like cats, are traditionally feminine.'

The purpose of this book is to describe and evaluate the part played by women in the settlement movement from its start to the present day. In the early years some helped at men's settlements as well as starting their own. The practical schemes they initiated largely concerned women, children and young people. Their emphasis on the importance of training for those who undertook social work had long-term national and international implications. Moreover, university women were mainly responsible for leading public opinion towards a professional view of social work.

Women's settlements made a major contribution in both world wars as in the years between them. Among much else, they helped with evacuation, with maintaining morale during periods of heavy bombing and with staffing citizens' advice bureaux.

Then the advent of the welfare state, and particularly the youth work obligatory under the 1944 Education Act, brought an end to sex segregation in settlements. Meanwhile, social work training took a major step forward under the leadership of Dame Eileen Younghusband. 'Personalities have always counted for much in the history of Toynbee Hall – to such an extent indeed that its history is best written around them.' This view, expressed in the centenary year of the first men's settlement, certainly applies to those started by women.

Ruskin, with his passionate feeling for social justice, was early involved. This rich man's son, with no economic training, directed his powerful pen to social problems at a time when Chartism was moribund and the liberalism he so much disliked was in the ascendant. His statement that 'Government and cooperation are in all things the Laws of Life: Anarchy and competition the Laws of Death' appeared in what he considered his best book, *Unto this Last*, printed as essays in the *Cornhill Magazine* during 1860, after a first airing in *Modern Painters*. Still, under Carlyle's influence, Ruskin had also much to say on the right of the poor to education, but not till the start of the next decade would Parliament pass W. E. Forster's bill intended to bring elementary education within the reach of every English home.

During the 1860s there was only limited scope in industrial cities for the philanthropy of men who, whatever their religious views, might want some field of non-religious work for their professional life.

Young Edward Denison, son of the Bishop of Salisbury, having decided that while studying law he would also learn something of life among the poor and become an almoner for the relief of distress in Stepney, was soon convinced of the unsatisfactory results of giving 'doles', and in 1867 moved to the Mile End Road where he stayed for eight months, building and endowing a school and teaching adults there.

Clearly, other university men might like to learn about conditions in the East End, improve its culture and, as rate payers, serve on local boards while at the same time pursuing their own professions. Possibilities here were discussed in 1868 when Ruskin, shortly before moving to Oxford as Slade Professor of Art, invited Denison, with J. R. Green, serving at St Philip's in Stepney, the Revd Brooke Lambert and a few others, to his house in Denmark Hill. But Denison died within two years. Ruskin's influence on women social workers at this time was directed mainly through Octavia Hill.

Though settling among the poor was a new idea, visiting them in their own homes had for some time been the common aim of hundreds of visiting societies in metropolitan London alone. In the mid-Victorian years nearly every London parish church sponsored a visiting society and this usually included a ladies' committee, for women were obviously suitable visitors to enter houses where no man was likely to be found unless ill. The situation was complicated by the forbidding attitude of the poor law authorities towards admitting women visitors to workhouse wards; and Louisa Twining, after an education at Queen's College, as secretary of the Workhouse Visiting Society, fought a long campaign on this front before eventually being elected a guardian in Kensington in 1884.

The brunt of the work involved in administering charitable funds raised by Mansion House and other appeals fell on parochial clergy; and they, with an occasional almoner among them such as Edward Denison, helped to develop social doctrine through an experience of difficulties. Slum dwellers with a propensity to drink provided many a personal threat to those investigating their claim, as the Barnetts early discovered. Educated people with some leisure were clearly needed to watch over the actions of the poor law officials. This was provided when the Charity Organization Society (COS) was formed in 1869 after a cholera epidemic, its forerunner being a society called the London Association for the Prevention of Pauperism and Crime. Charles Bosanquet, first secretary of the COS, and his successor Charles Loch, who both wrote guides to visitors, were well aware that the vast majority of them were women. However, Octavia Hill considered it a major triumph when she was asked to serve on the first local COS committee in her own parish of Marylebone.

Doubtful visitors could refer any case to their local medical officer under the Public Health Act of 1848; and, when school boards were established in 1870, additional visitors were needed to discover and report the whereabouts of children. Moreover, a London County Council (LCC) education committee set up that year gave official opportunity to school managers to enquire into the needs of children and befriend them in a way that seemed suitable. Thus, by the start of the settlement era, school management and care committee work were part of the social welfare scene, providing an obvious field of service for educated young women keen to help in a poor neighbourhood.

In 1882 a spur to action was provided by the arrival in London of the American social reformer Henry George. His widely read book was criticized from a Liberal angle by Arnold Toynbee, who took its title *Progress and Poverty* for his own lectures to working men, and by the Marxist H. M. Hyndman, who helped to launch the Social Democratic Federation. Meanwhile, another group of people, seeking to impregnate society with collective ideals of equality and fraternity, started what within a year was to be known as Fabian socialism; William Morris had formed a Socialist League, and the Christian Socialists, long led by the charismatic F. D. Maurice and his friends, had brought new vision to the idea of voluntary cooperation in society, with intemperance, bad housing and the inadequacy of popular education as main targets for attack.

Ruskin was influential here. His *Sesame and Lilies*, published in 1865, is usually quoted as defining separate spheres of influence for the sexes. Less emphasis has been put on his view that women, like men, have both a personal work or duty relating to their homes and also an expansion of that, relating to the state, where 'order is more difficult, distress more imminent and loveliness more rare'. And so, as he told them, 'there is no suffering, no injustice, no misery on the earth but the guilt of it lies with you'.

The challenge was soon taken up, and not only at the universities. It had, however, been made clear when Lord Shaftesbury and Charles Kingsley helped to form a ladies' association for sanitary reform in 1859 that the ladies concerned would be asked to cope only, in Octavia Hill's words, 'with the minute and much of the practical work; the legislative and theoretical was to be done by men'. But at least women had scope here for work outside their homes. Ruskin was already learning from his young assistant, who wrote to a friend, 'We got at last upon the subject of education of women and he asked me much about it, seemed greatly impressed.' And education was to be a key purpose at the start of the settlement movement.

In the East End of London, where hard working artisans and their families struggled to make both ends meet on low pay and unemployed of all ages became 'paupers' dependent on the poor law, there were many large buildings, formerly residences of wealthy people but by then let out as warehouses or tenement blocks. As a few educated laymen had already jeopardized or given up promising careers to work in the neighbourhood and, in contemporary language, 'sup sorrow with the poor', given communal accommodation, owned perhaps by a college, why should not others join them?

The idea was put forward by the Revd Samuel Barnett, vicar of St Jude's in Whitechapel, at a meeting held in St John's College, Oxford, on 17 November 1883. Himself a Wadham man, he had brought his young wife to the university in 1875, shortly after their marriage, and subsequently hardly a term had passed without their going either there or to Cambridge. The seminal paper read by the vicar, called 'Settlements of University Men in Great Towns', was followed by the foundation of both Toynbee Hall and the High Anglican Oxford House in 1884. The same year Oxford for the first time opened some of its honours examinations to women.

The threefold purpose of Toynbee Hall, as stated in its memorandum of association, was

> to provide education and the means of recreation and employment for people of the poorer districts of London and other great cities; to enquire into the conditions of the poor and to consider and advance plans calculated to promote their welfare; to acquire by purchase or otherwise and to maintain a house or houses for the residence of persons engaged in or connected with philanthropic or education work.

Among 'splendid men' from both universities who came to support the new enterprise were future architects of the welfare state.

While the compassionate response of individuals to human suffering brought many voluntary organizations into being at this time, including the Metropolitan Association for Befriending Young Servants (MABYS) in 1877, the Children's Country Holiday Fund (CCHF) in 1884 and the Invalid Children's Aid Association (ICAA) in 1888, the settlement movement was unusual in covering a wide variety of needs. Women who had long devoted themselves to supporting those unable to live satisfactorily in the community without some help found there both scope to serve others and a career for themselves.

Octavia Hill had first met Ruskin in 1853, seven years before he roused the national conscience to the evils of the industrial age with his clarion call, 'there is no wealth but life'. She was then, aged 13, helping her widowed mother and sisters run the Ladies' Cooperative Guild, formed to give employment to women and Polish refugees. The Hill family lived above the shop in Fitzroy Square, where work in painting on glass was soon extended to toy making so that children at a nearby ragged school could be brought in. Octavia taught drawing and design while herself learning about life among the poorest families in Bloomsbury and something of business management before undertaking other responsibilities as pupil and then assistant to the famous art critic. Her first paid job, however, was as secretary for women's classes at the pioneering Working Men's College in Great Ormond Street to which she was steered by the Revd F. D. Maurice, an old family friend.

Maurice had at least as much influence on contemporary middle-class girls as had Ruskin on young university men. Only son of a Unitarian minister, he and his friend Charles Kingsley determined, while at Cambridge, to combat what they saw as the harsh economic doctrines of *laissez-faire*. After moving on to Oxford this leader of the Christian Socialist movement was ordained in the Church of England before settling in London to become, in due course, professor of English and modern history at King's College. A prototype of the modern sixth-form college, King's prepared young men of 16 and over for Oxford and Cambridge, and its atmosphere was orthodox Anglican, unlike that of the earlier established nonsectarian University College in Gower Street.

Largely through the influence of his sister Mary, one of seven and author of *Mothers and Governesses*, Maurice was soon involved with the lately reorganized Governesses' Benevolent Society (GBS), setting up its committee of education; and when in 1848 Queen's College in Harley Street was opened next door to the GBS home to provide education for young ladies over 12, he was appointed principal.

His adventurous leadership made a lasting impact both on general education and in fostering a spirit of social service among teenagers. Although Queen's College did not pioneer the admission of women to Oxford and Cambridge, as Emily Davies had hoped before she founded Girton College, by the time her brother Llewellyn became principal of Queen's College in 1873, the climate was set for a lasting link between it and the coming settlement movement. For among its pupils were Dorothea Beale, founder of the Cheltenham Ladies' College Guild, which started St Hilda's East in Bethnal Green, Frances Mary Buss, founder of the North London Collegiate School for Girls and a settlement named after her in East London, (Dame) Frances Dove, pioneering head of Wycombe Abbey, itself a leader in the United Girls' School

Mission (UGSM) and what is now the Peckham Settlement, and Edith Langridge, first head of the Lady Margaret Hall Settlement (LMHS), which still enjoys the support of Queen's College.

The last quarter of the century brought other major changes on the educational front. Between 1874 and 1876, quick on the heels of the 1870 Education Act, schools in Kensington, Notting Hill and Hampstead were started under the auspices of the newly formed Girls' Public Day School Trust, with several more in the provinces. But the education given there was nondenominational, and for many clergy families as well as for others, this was not good enough. 'I am very busy all day with one thing and another, schools this winter rather than hospitals,' wrote Mrs Francis Holland soon after her husband moved from Canterbury to be vicar in charge of the Quebec chapel at Marble Arch. 'I have been going about to some of the great High Schools to see their system of teaching. The whole education question is excessively interesting.' One sequel was the formation of a company called Church of England High School for Girls Ltd, with the Bishop of London as patron. Its first school, built on a site in Upper Baker Street, opened on 1 October 1878, to be followed soon afterwards by a sister establishment connected with St Peter's, Eaton Square. Then the founding in 1883 of the Church Schools Company absolved Canon Francis Holland from further responsibility on this front.

Miss Strong, an outstanding headmistress, who took control in Upper Baker Street in 1880, helped to link the Cheltenham Ladies' College Guild, where she herself was educated, with members of the Ladies' Branch of Oxford House (LBOH) at the opening of their joint settlement at Mayfield House in Bethnal Green; and the Francis Holland School in Graham Street in due course led to a settlement in Battersea, named after a former student, Katherine Low. Similarly, St Paul's Girls' School ran Dame Colet House (DCH) in Stepney for years before eventually linking up with Bishop Creighton House (BCH) in nearby Fulham. Other and perhaps less prestigious schools had also considerable influence. University women, however, led the way in 1887 with their settlement in Southwark.

Women also helped with men's settlements, as at Cambridge House. And the working partnership of men and women, characteristic of settlement life even in its pre-1944 days of sex segregation, was also evident in the private life of many pioneers. Thus, Octavia Hill provided Ruskin with much needed practical skills in his plans for social change; Canon Barnett accredited Toynbee Hall and other achievements to the steering that went on around Henrietta's tea table; Arnold Toynbee gratefully acknowledged his debt both to his sister and his young wife; and Beatrice Potter stated that she had married Sidney Webb mainly to make their working dreams come true. Moreover, in university circles couples concerned included the Edward Talbots, the Mandell Creightons, the Humphry Wards, the Arthur Johnsons, the Henry Sidgwicks and the Alfred Marshalls. And though T. H. Green, who with his wife had contributed much to the Oxford women's educational campaign, died in 1882, the influence of his idealist philosophy and theory of citizenship was long to outlast divisions in contemporary social thought.

Residents at the first 'settlement for educated women' were far removed from the popular image of affluent, irritating do-gooders, nor did they regard themselves as part of a single sex institution in the vanguard of female emancipation.

Settlers in Southwark and elsewhere mostly shared a common purpose, partly educational, partly to relieve poverty. Some helpers with wide social contacts might concentrate on money raising; others were involved in the hard slog of day-to-day work in the slums; and young visitors to Bermondsey, coming perhaps in the afternoons for regular collections of hospital or other savings at the Time and Talents (T & T) settlement, brought escorts who awaited them in the 'maids' room'. Fortunately, the maternal instinct cheerfully leaps over class barriers. And, as from the start of the movement the schools were the centre and origin of much of the work undertaken, the schoolchildren provided, as always, the best introduction to friendship with their families.

Settlement volunteers early found themselves welcomed visitors in infirmaries and workhouses. They taught children who missed school through illness, helped in the aftercare of boys and girls leaving the poor law schools, and did outstanding pioneering work for the mentally and physically handicapped excluded from the LCC schools. They brought reinforcements to COS offices and were in turn trained there for work in the field before more standardized training was introduced. Moreover, several settlements helped in apprenticing children, both normal and handicapped, to skilled trades. However, among a few outstanding personalities who loomed large in early settlement history, a division soon emerged between the majority who sought to improve local conditions by direct action and those who, like Beatrice Potter (Webb) and young William Betridge at Toynbee Hall, early campaigned for social reform through legislation.

The accolade for linking training with philanthropy must, however, go to Mrs Ellen Ranyard. Born in 1810, this daughter of a cement worker had long been visiting the poor in her neighbourhood of Nine Elms before the idea of Bible women occurred to her in 1857. Why should not people accustomed to life in the cuts and alleys be paid to give much needed advice in a variety of domestic matters while selling Bibles? By 1867 there were 234 such Bible women active in London's poorer districts and with no lack of applicants for the steady work. Thus it caused no surprise when in 1891 Miss Harington, secretary of the LBOH, proposed that her pioneering settlers should finance a Bible woman to work from Mayfield House in Bethnal Green with Miss Ingram, sister of the future Bishop of London. Moreover, Mrs Ranyard, sensing another yawning gap in current philanthropy, in 1868 signed up a staff of women to train as itinerant nurses, since her Bible women could give only elementary medical advice. Kate Newman, head of Mayfield House, was herself a trained district nurse, as was another of its residents who spoke on this work at an early meeting held to canvass settlement support in Oxford.

The reiterated point that settlers gained at least as much as they gave was made by the Bishop of Hereford, a founder and first president of Somerville, when he spoke to those in Southwark during 1901. He could look back to earlier days of the awakening of the richer classes to the sufferings of the poor when he worked as a young man in Whitechapel.

Christian social action takes many forms. Several settlements built a small chapel on their premises and at St Margaret's House, for example, regular services are still held there. The first head of LMHS became mother superior of a religious community for women in India; she was a bishop's daughter who was in charge of this Lambeth settlement before the First World War and, while there, made a major contribution to diocesan women's work. Another former LMH student worked at St Mildred's Settlement on the Isle of Dogs during the blitz and subsequently helped to steer it under clerical control before herself becoming a head deaconess. Thus, links mainly for training developed between religious houses and settlements of women started in the Toynbee Hall and Oxford House tradition.

These saw themselves also as forming a bridge between the churches and secular agencies such as the COS, while deciding perhaps that it was unnecessary to embark alone on any pioneering work. To many, indeed, there seemed already enough scope in supporting existing institutions and societies to help the aged, the sick and others in trouble. Thus, visiting families at the request of the newly formed ICAA was the first undertaking at the Peckham Settlement; and the CCHF, Henrietta Barnett's brainchild, is still a main commitment at several. But the Bloomsbury Settlement led by Mrs Humphry Ward soon went ahead with campaigning on a national front on behalf of children.

Like Westfield College, the first residential college for London University women students, which had opened in 1881, most settlements started modestly with accommodation for five or six volunteers. Even when adjacent terraced houses had been added to the original building, there was seldom accommodation there for more than 25. That the influence of the settlers over the years far exceeded what might have been expected from their numbers was largely due to the quality of the pioneers; and naturally the personality of the head was the determining factor in early developments. Several remarkable if little-known women, usually university trained and of a type no longer readily available for full-time voluntary work, soon put the movement in the vanguard of the effort to bring order out of the chaos then prevailing in the philanthropic world. To them, if not to their male contemporary counterparts, training was essential.

Social work training took a major step forward when the WUS, after collaborating with the COS and the NUWW, handed over its pioneering work here to the newly formed School of Sociology;

Edith Pearson, by then head of the LMHS, was closely involved as a member of the teaching staff of this school, which in 1912 became the social work nucleus of the London School of Economics and Political Science (LSE), dubbed by Lord Beveridge 'the favourite child of the Webbs'.

Despite this incorporation, WUS members kept in close touch through service on LSE committees; and, after the social services department there had been reorganized under a committee of London University in 1917, the WUS played a prominent part in drawing up a scheme of training for industrial welfare supervision. Miss Kelly, a WUS Pfeiffer scholar who graduated in 1905 from London University, became a founder member of the Association of Welfare Workers after spending 24 years as an industrial welfare supervisor; and, both then and later, as head of St Margaret's House between the wars, helped significantly on the training front.

A year before the outbreak of the First World War, considerably more women than men were attached to residential settlements. A list made at that time shows that 22 settlements were inhabited exclusively by women and 17 by men, while already six combined both sexes. Only about a third of these settlements stood in a direct relation with the universities; surprisingly, WUS was still linked with Toynbee Hall as 'irreligious', despite Canon Barnett's protests in 1884.

The influence of the Church, crucial at the start of the settlement movement, has lately been reinforced by the report of the Archbishop of Canterbury's Commission on Urban Priority Areas (ACUPA). 'You cannot keep social services in one compartment and Church activity in another,' wrote the Bishop of Woolwich in the mid-1950s when chairman of the executive committee of the Union of Girls' Schools for Social Service (UGS). Thousands of teenagers had by then contributed in some way to what is now the Peckham Settlement, and 'we hope to encourage many more to see for themselves what a fine thing Christian social service can be as a life's work. . . . The Settlement movement has always offered a grand opportunity here.' Though many settlements, including several started since the First World War, have closed, those throughout the country run in cooperation with Oxbridge or other universities are flourishing. Most pioneered by women now belong to the British Association of Settlements and Social Action Centres (BASSAC). Independent in character, these have developed along different lines though they are often engaged in similar work.

A historical approach here may throw light on the problems and tragedies of inner city life today, though now a key function of social work is helping individuals to use the available services effectively. Thus Ruskin might have predicted the report of a young Australian volunteers' organizer who recently attended a conference of 30 community workers in Lambeth: 'All the men tended to congregate at one end of the room talking about organizational problems and hierarchies in the Town Hall while the women wanted to discuss individual cases and human problems.' If the effort of J. S. Mill on behalf of civil rights for women was of small concern for most of the early settlement workers, equality of opportunity whether of race or sex is currently included in settlement campaigning for social justice.

Part I
Pioneers

1
Octavia Hill

Soon after Octavia Hill's widowed mother had moved her family to Marylebone and started a small school, their house in Nottingham Place became a local asset if not a blueprint for women's settlements. While the elder pupils were encouraged to befriend children living in local slums, particularly in arranging outings for them in nearby Regent's Park, Octavia started a work centre where women could learn how to cut out and make clothes as well as enjoy some social life. Helping home one evening a member who had fainted at a sewing class, she determined that something must be done about the damp, unhealthy, overcrowded building where the family lived. Had the time now come for her to pursue her grandfather Southwood Smith's work on East End housing? The way opened soon afterwards when Ruskin was left a somewhat embarrassing fortune by his father. Her campaign for better housing dates from 1864 when to his question, 'Have you a plan?', she could give a ready answer and, with her mother's school now well established, felt free to launch out in new fields.

By the following midsummer she had full possession of three cottages in nearby Paradise Place. This enterprise was soon followed by another in Edgware Road where nearly all the windows were broken when she took over. 'My work is daily more interesting,' she wrote in May 1866. 'Ruskin has bought six more houses and in a densely populated neighbourhood. Some houses in the court were reported unfit for human habitation and have been converted into warehouses, the rest are inhabited by a desperate and forlorn sort of people, wild, dirty, violent, ignorant as ever I have seen.'

From the first she had a vision of an indoor hall with garden or open space for each set of houses acquired, and was happy after one conversion to find 'an eager little crowed threading beads in the playground' for which Ruskin had promised some seats. 'I hope to teach them to draw a little. Singing we have already introduced.'

A prototype being thus established for later community centres and adventure playgrounds, the problem of involving charitably minded supporters soon loomed large. But disliking the slowness of committee work, only when an undertaking was nearing completion would she launch an appeal. Thus a letter describing one opening ceremony ended: 'Mr Maurice and Mr L. Davies came to the meeting, and numbers of ladies and gentlemen, and the whole place seemed to meet with such approval that subscriptions were offered and I hope to make the place really efficient. My girls are of course very helpful.' Clearly the work of training the young to expand her schemes in a practical way was at least as important as money raising.

Octavia was involved in the aftermath of the cholera epidemic of 1866 when nearly 8000 people died within six months, most of them in the East End. While Mrs Gladstone, then a regular visitor at the London Hospital in the Mile End Road, gave a lead to relief workers by setting up a home for orphans at her own home, Hawarden Castle, Octavia took action on another front. Shocked, as were many others, by the indiscriminate distribution of vast sums raised by the Mansion House appeal, she was soon gathering like-minded people, including the local curate, the Revd Samuel Barnett, to help put her ideas into practice, the main one being that sympathetic personal contact with large numbers of individuals in trouble is stimulated and controlled most efficiently through small groups. By 1869 her relief work was sufficiently well known for her to be invited to read a paper at a meeting of the Social Science Association on 'The Importance of Aiding the Poor without Almsgiving' and her dynamic unorthodox vicar in Marylebone, the Honourable Revd W. H. Fremantle, later dean of Ripon, impressed by her achievement, suggested that she should forward a report to the Local Government Board. Soon recognized as a driving force of charity reform in her neighbourhood, and the only woman member of the first local committee of what was soon to be widely known as the Charity Organization Society (COS), her experience of almsgiving led her to insist on providing employment instead of relief whenever possible, out of which came the COS pensions scheme, an important aspect of the work. As the aims of the society developed she became a member of its central committee when eventually local committees joined into a federation.

However, though she realized that friendship with such men as Mr Longley, secretary of the Local Government Board, and Mr Stansfield, president of the Poor Law Board, widened her scope for action, her work in Marylebone was particularly suited to women, whom she saw as a vast unused powerhouse ready for harnessing.

Voluntary social work on an organized basis, including the Women's Royal Voluntary Service, may look back for its origins to a letter she wrote in September 1871. After telling a friend of her sister Minnie's engagement to Edmund Maurice, son of the professor, she added:

> I am thinking of writing on women's work from their own home. You know how strongly I believe in its practicability and power. How I should like to talk to you on the question. I am under a promise to write some papers; and I am sure that this would be the most useful, though another about the houses would be the most popular. Of course, if I write, it would be with the definite scheme for making volunteers' work more efficient and available before people.

A born organizer, Octavia made a point of spreading around her good workers, whatever her own need of them. Mrs Nassau Senior, sister of the author Tom Hughes, was a case in point. She had already proved her ability in housing finance and with the Metropolitan Association for Befriending Young Servants (MABYS) when Octavia steered this friend into a pioneering appointment as the first woman inspector of workhouses.

Soon matrimony was to call another of her helpers. The following February her sister Miranda told a friend that:

> The curate who had worked with Octavia in St Mary's has just married Miss Henrietta Rowland, one of Octavia's best workers; and now they are going to live and work in the East End. Octavia thinks it is such a splendid thing to have such a man at work down there – she thinks it quite a nucleus of fresh life; and Mrs Barnett, of whom Octavia is very fond, is admirably fitted for the work too.

A common purpose had united the couple from their first meeting at one of Octavia's birthday parties. The somewhat uncouth curate was immediately attracted by the good-looking 19-year-old girl from Wimbledon with her Tyrolean hat and furs. But though they were soon working together in the parish, she was dismayed in February 1872 to have a letter from him proposing marriage. 'He looked so much older than his age, 27, that I had accepted his interest as that of a kindly elderly gentleman with small sensitive hands, a bald head and a shaggy beard. Indeed both in appearance and manner, he was far removed from a girlish idea of a lover.'

Even though Henrietta had already decided to spend her life among the East End poor, breaking away from a family circle of art-loving friends who, like her beloved parent, 'only considered the poor by the medium of the purse', these plans had not included marriage 'with its obedience and ties'. So she asked for six months' delay. The curate on his side knew that his love was for life. Soon after they were engaged, Octavia Hill went away for some time leaving them jointly responsible for much of her organization. Whether without the two women the Revd Samuel Barnett would have taken a different path in life at this point must remain an open question. Henrietta admitted that he was 'sorely tempted to accept a living offered him in the autumn of 1872 near his beloved Oxford'.

However, she was determined to get to east London and Octavia took the necessary steps. Through a friend of Edward Denison, who knew the Bishop of London, it was suggested that the living at St Jude's in Whitechapel should be offered to the St

Marylebone curate 'who would then marry a lady who had long wanted to take up work in East London'. It seemed almost a clinching argument that it was a parish 'inhabited mainly by a criminal population and one which has I fear been much corrupted by its doles'. The engaged couple went down to look at it and, standing in the rain outside St Jude's, they made their decision.

When that autumn Miranda had to rest for a while, joining an aunt in Florence, the already hard-pressed Octavia was in further trouble, writing in October 1873 to Mrs Nassau Senior: 'Miss Peters, my new assistant, has not yet come unfortunately. I almost pray that she may stay, as she seems so exactly all that I have long wanted.' The newcomer helped for two years until matrimony claimed her also. 'I wonder if you see the Charity Organization Report and noticed the appointment of Mr Loch as secretary. Did I tell you that he is engaged to Miss Peters?' wrote Octavia in November 1875. However, at least she acquired permanent allies in the two husbands.

Charles Loch and his bride's brother F. H. Peters had been at Balliol together, when Lock studied art under Ruskin. He was appointed general secretary to the COS at the age of 26. His predecessor in the job had been Charles Bosanquet, son of an Anglican rector and brother of the better known Bernard. A fellow of Balliol from 1870 and friend of Arnold Toynbee, Bernard Bosanquet resigned in 1881 in order to relate his ideas to more practical affairs in London, encouraged here in due course by his intellectual wife, the former Helen Dendy, whose father was a Unitarian minister in Manchester. Wielding much influence not only as editor of the *COS Review*, she argued that the aim of charity was to establish such dominant ideas as family responsibility, foresight and prudence. From its start in 1869 the COS had set out to coordinate and regulate all existing forms of philanthropy and not to become yet another among thousands of existing relief agencies. Scientific was the key word, Helen Bosanquet early insisting that in matters of social policy scientific principles must provide the guidelines. Settlement workers were soon to be involved here.

The Hills' house in Nottingham Place took on another aspect of future settlement life when an able young woman of independent means applied for residential training in social work for possibly two or three years. Kate Potter, elder sister of the future Beatrice Webb, arrived in the autumn of 1875. Soon afterwards Octavia wrote: 'She is very bright and happy here, extremely capable and has been through a good deal in her life, though she is young. She seems to fit in among us very well. . . . I hope to make way in the matter but it is a little difficult to know how to begin.' Three years later Kate moved on to join the Barnetts in Whitechapel, working there as a rent collector until 1883 when she left to marry Leonard Courtney, then secretary to the Treasury, who later fell out with Gladstone over Home Rule and became a Liberal Unionist. Kate was in due course to support the Women's University Settlement (WUS) and proved helpful also in political and court circles. Thus, having steered a petition, signed by many east London women asking for help in improving their streets, Henrietta was able to tell her husband, 'Kate is going to get it sent to the Queen.'

Octavia meanwhile was operating on an ever widening front. And, as life became increasingly hectic, in February 1877 she told a friend, 'The COS takes much of my time, though I have left all our local work to others. Then all the time I have 3500 tenants, and £30,000 to £40,000 worth of money under my charge.' A breakdown came later that year.

With a friend and helped by her sisters, she was able to plan some decentralization. Gertrude Hill had married George Eliot's stepson, Charles Lewes, in 1865 when the bridegroom's father commented: 'No one was invited to the wedding except Polly and I, the aunts, Gertrude's mother and sisters; yet there were many at the Church' (the Rosslyn Hill Unitarian chapel). By the end of that month of March, his Polly had begun a new novel, *Felix Holt: The Radical*. While engaged in her research for it, George Eliot did not forget the young social workers in Marylebone. Moreover, as her fame and fortunes grew, she gave sums of money both to Gertrude Lewes and to Octavia to distribute as they thought best; she also sent £200 to a fund raised in 1874 to provide an annuity for Octavia so that she could devote all her time and energies to plans for rehousing the poor. While others could teach, Octavia's most valuable work, as her friends now realized, lay in housing.

J. S. Mill's *Essay on the Subjection of Women*, published in 1869, hardly concerned Octavia, fully occupied as she was and certainly not hankering for a vote, unlike her friend Emma Cons. However, her rare involvement in politics included a crucial influence on the Artisans' Dwellings Act of 1876, the first housing act and foundation of all that were to follow. She was in the gallery of the House of Commons to hear the debate when, most unexpectedly, her own name was mentioned.

The bill was sponsored by Kay Shuttleworth, a 'brilliant young man' who, in her view, was typical of those for whom the early settlement movement was to provide an ideal educational experience. He had been closely associated with her in 1873 during the enquiry by a COS committee into the whole question of working-class dwellings in London. When a few years afterwards a COS committee was appointed to consider the working of the act, and how far it should be amended, Octavia and Lord Shuttleworth (as he then was) again worked together on that committee and he remembered gratefully the signal help she then gave. 'Miss Octavia Hill was pre-eminently fitted for contributing an exceptional amount of practical knowledge, experience and wisdom at the meetings of such committees and conferences on a subject which she had made her own.' He later remarked, 'She would quietly listen to a discussion of some point and at least say a few weighty words in her calm, impressive, tactful way, which would carry with her the general assent of all, or nearly all, and would thus promptly bring the debate to a sound conclusion.'

Octavia's interest in the early stages of the Artisans' Dwellings Bill, shared with the Barnetts, had coincided with harsh treatment on her own ground in Marylebone. A major row followed her publication of a report she had made on the plight of tenants placed in her care. The medical officer of health, stung by the criticism, immediately ordered the destruction of all tenants in the court concerned; and, though this drastic action was revoked soon afterwards, the majority of the vestry, to whom he worked, took his side, one of them loudly remarking that he hoped that they would now hear no more of Miss Hill and her houses. It seemed indeed that the tenants might even find themselves worse off than before.

However, in November 1874 Miranda was told by her sister Emily Maurice that 'Mr Bosanquet says the Vestry cannot condemn the houses. Octavia has called a meeting of B. Court tenants to consult as to how they can keep things in better order, keep the front doors shut etc.' But the start of tenants' associations, later an important part of settlement work, lay far ahead. Another helpful man had by now rallied to Octavia's help. When in 1873 building plans had threatened the fields around Swiss Cottage, scene of her childhood rambles, her campaign to preserve open country and fresh air for her poor friends in Marylebone, as dear to her heart as her housing schemes, had enlisted the sympathy of several well-to-do Hampstead residents. Among them was the altruistic, attractive Edward Bond and from now on he was much in her life.

He was one of the leaders of the COS, a founder director of the East London Dwellings Company and Conservative MP for East Nottingham from 1895 to 1906. Like Octavia, he never married, though they were engaged for a few months before her breakdown. Like other women pioneers on the social work front, Octavia used her pen to good effect, both financially and otherwise. Her article on 'Cottage Property in London' published in the *Fortnightly Review* was the first of seven she wrote on 'Homes of the London Poor'. There was no lack of material, as under her influence the housing movement crescendoed. Not, however, until 1884 would William Morris and H. M. Hyndham embark on a national appeal for an improvement in the living conditions of the poor. 'Such is the housing of the wage earners in our great cities and our country districts that even the leading partisans of our political factions at least are aware of the fact . . . that some steps ought really to be taken to remedy so monstrous an evil.' By the time this statement appeared, the pioneering Octavia Hill had helped at the birth of the settlement movement. This was complicated by the arrival of twins.

2

The Barnetts and the Toynbees

In 1875 Oxford had a memorable Eights' Week. 'Our party was planned by Miss Toynbee whom I had met when at school and whose brother Arnold was then an undergraduate at Pembroke,' wrote Henrietta Barnett when describing her first visit to the university since her marriage.

In 1869, at the age of 16, she had for four terms attended a school run by two sisters well ahead of their time in social outlook. 'Through their eyes I saw the degradation of the workhouse children and the possibilities of helping girls.' She did not forget the lessons then learnt. Gertrude Toynbee, on the other hand, came from a family long orientated to social work.

The Toynbee party was as seminal in its way to the settlement movement as Barnett's much quoted paper to be read at St John's College in 1883. For, after two years in the slums, it occurred to Henrietta that 'if men, cultivated young, thinking men, could know of these things they would be altered.' Thereafter, 'rarely a term passed without going to Oxford. Sometimes we stayed with Mr Jowett, sometimes we were the guests of undergraduates who got up meetings in their rooms and organized innumerable breakfasts, teas, river excursions and other opportunities for introducing the duties of the cultured to the poor and degraded.' They also paid several visits to Cambridge. 'We used to ask each undergraduate as he developed interest to come and stay in Whitechapel and see for himself. And they came, some to spend a few weeks, some for the long vacation, while others, as they left the university and began their life's work'. Arnold Toynbee was a frequent visitor to their Whitechapel vicarage during the years the Barnetts spent there before starting the settlement movement. Entertaining loomed large at St Jude's from the start, partly because, 'with the motherliness of a young wife', Henrietta decided that 'it would be good for her husband to have his ambitions fired not with ecclesiastical ambition – thank God neither of us ever descended to that – but with the desire for the power which, following recognition, would give further opportunities for service and influence.' With this in view, and always happy to spend time, thought and money in creating pleasure, 'I fearlessly invited to our Whitechapel vicarage all the most intellectual people we met.' Considering their close association with Octavia Hill, it was hardly surprising that plans for housing reform were among the first to emerge.

There was no provision at that time by building companies for unskilled labourers, daily workers at the docks and others who lived by casual employment; and, under the rules of the Peabody Trust, no tenant was accepted who could not give as reference a regular employer. Though George Peabody, who had died in 1869, clearly rendered a major service, as Queen Victoria recognized in her letter to him, another step forward was due, so a group of St Jude's workers, meeting in the little vicarage drawing room, formed the East London Dwellings Company. Delays seemed inevitable, but after a long wait of nine years the relevant act of Parliament was eventually amended. When in 1885 the East London Dwellings Company secured land on which to build accommodation for artisans and labourers, the completed block in Cartwright Street undertaken by Leonard Courtney MP was called Katharine Buildings after his wife, the former Kate Potter and pupil of Octavia Hill who had been working there. By then plans were already on foot for other buildings 'which are to be under the management of ladies'. Since their Marylebone days together Henrietta had considered Kate to be 'very bright, happy and extremely capable'. And she brought in her wake a host of other helpers as well as her two sisters (the future Mrs Alfred Cripps and Mrs Sidney Webb). Henrietta particularly admired the young Beatrice, who did not hesitate to plunge into Whitechapel slums 'fearlessly in her search for facts, working in sweating shops and living as a lone girl in block buildings'. She was to make her own distinct contribution to the settlement movement.

Henrietta's ideas on 'pictures for the people', developing as they did into the Whitechapel art gallery, grew from the fact that guests at vicarage parties had for some time been entertained by the display there of beautiful and interesting objects brought back from Egypt and other places visited by the Barnetts when on holiday. 'Why should not more people enjoy them?' asked an old soldier. So exhibits were sought from friends and museums, cases borrowed from the South Kensington museum and 'our humble schools turned into an oasis of beauty'. The vicar soon added a further dimension of interest by giving lectures and Henrietta explained that her husband's interest in art was basically religious. He might, as she said, be 'colour-blind' but was emphatic that 'the great want of the East End is beauty'. Soon the exhibition was occupying three large rooms built at the back of the schools with the financial support of many friends.

Henrietta's earlier contacts in the art world were put to full use. Pupil teachers in Stepney and other women's groups were among those whom she recruited to help.

Music was similarly encouraged. The Barnetts, blaming the forms of service for failing to express the religious needs of the people, sought an early remedy here, despite the fact that the vicar 'had no ear for time or tune', and as Henrietta remarked, 'neither he nor I were even quite sure of "God Save the Queen" until other people stood up.' When, as a result of their efforts, the *Messiah* was performed by a large choir during Advent, the vicar wrote in his first parish report that 'the effect was very grand, and in the solemn silence which followed each burst of glorious sound we felt that the people were indeed worshipping God.'

Among many musicians, both professional and amateur, who helped them were Clara Butt and Fanny Davies. Henrietta provided refreshments after the service for such friends to meet local people. It was an early example of that hospitality which the vicar was to credit as being the major influence in keeping together their vast body of supporters. 'St Jude's, Toynbee Hall and the Whitechapel art gallery were', as he said, 'all built on my wife's tea table.'

Fifty years later the Toynbee Hall opera club, like the Whitechapel art gallery, was well established. An amateur Faust, by profession an architect, and his wife, who was well able to cope with the part of Marguerite because of her early training as a musical comedy soloist, were among several enthusiasts who came to Aldwych East from the West End on Monday evenings to rehearse under John Tobin's baton; and, shortly before the outbreak of the Second World War, the young principals in Purcell's *Dido and Aeneas*, the opera chosen for the first performance after the King and Queen had opened a new hall at the settlement, found themselves playing the same parts at Glyndebourne, though the supporting chorus was no longer the local one from Whitechapel.

Henrietta's views on church services resulted in another innovation – she and the vicar had different views here. He approved the usual liturgy, though deeply grieving on the failure of the church to attract local people. She, on the other hand, 'could not find food in the old forms and time hallowed words which have to me lost their significance by a reiteration which pays no regard to changing circumstances'. So she instituted what they decided to call the 'worship hour', the vicar acquiescing with characteristic sympathy in the new service, which was held at a later time than other services so that he rarely attended at the end of a long working day. 'On the whole, Bartlett, I think the best thing I can do is to wink,' said Bishop Walsham How when consulted on the proposed service. Henrietta herself selected the governing thought for the day, chose readings and invited the singers.

If the Revd Samuel Barnett was called 'irreligious' by High Church of England contemporaries when he visited Oxford in 1883 to stir interest in his settlement proposal, clearly his wife was partly responsible. Her 'worship hour' was to continue in Whitechapel long after she and her husband had left; and 35 years later, to her delight, was revived at the new St Jude's on the Hill in Hampstead Garden Suburb.

Both the Barnetts were convinced of 'the equal capacity of all to enjoy the best, the superiority of quiet ways over those of striving and crying, and character as the one thing needful. These were the truths on which we take our stand.'

Whether or not to give outdoor relief was then a main issue. The

Barnetts made their own contribution to poor law problems. Anyone refused outdoor relief was directed to the local COS office and, after investigation by one or other of its group of voluntary workers, some help would usually be arranged. When Henrietta or the vicar visited poor homes or shelters, they often found that the claimant, then unemployed, had been a ratepayer and saw outdoor relief as his right. Other claimants stormed the vicarage, breaking windows there, and it was found advisable to make a hole through the wall into the church as an escape route. Not surprisingly, when the vicar asked his wife what she would like as a birthday present, she asked for a policeman to be posted locally. And this was done.

The vicar, like many others, felt strongly about the 'impertinence' of any judgement that had to be made as to whether anyone was 'deserving' and Henrietta's well-known nightmare about finding herself in the workhouse, condemned as one of the undeserving poor, was based on her own contributions here to what was essentially a woman's job.

A young mother or working girl might find herself in the underground wards of the Whitechapel Infirmary where no classification was attempted other than on medical grounds. Henrietta began visiting here to give confidence and to help restart patients in a difficult world. She 'plunged with ignorance and enthusiasm of 24 years dominated by the faith that no girls like being wicked. Slowly I learned the truth.'

One lasting result for the many girls whom the infirmary matron said 'are best left with you Ma'am' was the setting up of a domestic training establishment in Hampstead. 'Service' seemed then the only way of steering girls out of the Whitechapel environment. In 1877 the vicar became chairman of the MABYS, while his wife's imaginative kindness laid foundations for the CCHF, still a main concern of many settlement workers today.

The four years since marriage had been a gruelling time for them both. Neither was physically strong and when towards the end of the winter of 1876 the vicar again became ill, the doctor advised prolonged rest. As their usual holiday abroad was clearly impossible, they planned a period in Cornwall, including a duty temporary replacement for a clergyman at Wadebridge. Henrietta's invalid sister and her old nurse, who also lived at the vicarage, went with them, and they had many happy days out of doors, picnicking and bathing. Hospitable as ever, their early guests included Octavia Hill, then both ill and unhappy. Later Henrietta's sister and other friends came down 'bringing their horses and large carriage to add to the carrying power of the vicarage'.

But there were still so many to be asked, and one day Henrietta saw a woman standing by the door of a nearby cottage, watching with interest all the coming and going. 'Like a flash from Heaven came the idea to me. Why should they not go there instead of to us?' The vicar approved, adding that it would be cheaper in fares and so more could be asked if the guests came from the Home Counties. The *Guardian* was asked to take the matter up with the idea that country clergymen could suggest hosts and hostesses in simple homes. Out of the Children's Holiday Committee (East London) then formed grew in 1884 the CCHF, pioneer of similar societies in Europe and the USA.

Educational matters had a high priority for both the Barnetts, and one of their first acts on moving to St Jude's was to open the local church schools. They were both emphatic that children were largely educated by their surroundings 'to recognize beauty and to love order', and soon Walter Crane's coloured illustrations of *Aesop's Fables* were decorating the higher levels of school room walls, the Barnetts' friendship with this artist leading in due course to the start of an Art for Schools Association. Both set much store on gaining the cooperation of parents; mothers and fathers were invited to end-of-term parties and to meetings with school managers and teachers.

Options for school leavers were also given careful thought. Many parents in the parish were worried that their 13-year-old daughters had little choice between helping at home, idling their time away, working in a factory or going into service. Based on already existing rules for evening classes, similar afternoon ones were now started for St Jude's young parishioners. Many women teachers, both volunteers and professionals, gave a helping hand and, in due course, the indefatigable Miss Buss, head of the North London Collegiate School for Girls, was brought in to superintend them.

Meanwhile, the sudden death in 1873 of Dr Joseph Toynbee – a distinguished medical man called to Osborn in 1869 to treat Queen Victoria for earache – had brought his younger son and daughter even closer together. And Arnold said, 'I talk over early all my work with her. Indeed I hardly do or say anything that I don't tell her of – our lives are almost one.'

They had both been brought up to admire Ruskin, and Gertrude would certainly know that her brother, soon after coming up to Oxford, had written to ask the Slade professor if he would give the undergraduates a lead in matters other than art. Arnold's letter was remarkably opportune. Answering from Naples in 1874, Ruskin acknowledged that his energies were concentrated where his heart no longer lay.

> But my error was partly the result of my desire to keep as far as possible for some time from the work I was appointed to do. But I am certain that it is my duty now, and a much more serious one than any that are directly official. I hope that when I return to Oxford we may have little councils of friends both old and young in my rooms at Corpus, which will be pleasanter for us than formal lectures and will reach many other needs of thoughts than any connected with the arts.

The Ruskin School of Art, which he had started in 1871, might attract young women in Oxford, including in due course Maggie Benson of LMH, but there were few undergraduates at Balliol or elsewhere who wanted thus to spend their free time.

Before going up to Oxford in 1873, Arnold, always dogged by ill health, had spent a year alone at a quiet seaside resort, developing his interest in religion, metaphysics and the philosophy of history. His subsequent ten years at the university began quietly at Pembroke College where he took no active part in physical or intellectual contests, though exercising a profound influence on a small circle of friends.

After his appeal to Ruskin, which resulted in various idealistic if impractical activities, including the well-known undergraduate road making at Hinksey with himself as foreman, Jowett invited him to Balliol as lecturer and tutor, and in October 1878 he began a career of intense development and social activity. Like Professor T. H. Green, he became a poor law guardian as well as a co-operator and Church reformer and followed with close interest and practical sympathy the development of friendly societies and trades unions. Moreover, he was deeply involved in pioneering better housing, open spaces and free libraries. His permanent value is in the impulse and direction he gave to the aspirations of men and women in all walks of life for social reform.

Deeply religious, like his father, he felt the need to spend his life in active usefulness. As a fellow of Oriel wrote, 'He was never so great as when he showed the smallness of differences among Christians compared with their points of union, or as when he sketched the future of the Church as it might be in a time of Christian toleration and yet of Christian zeal.' This added irony to the coming controversy in the early settlement movement over the use of his name.

His marriage while at Balliol gave him a happy home life with a devoted wife who sympathized with all his work. Arnold had met his 'Charlie' soon after he came up to the university and in the five years before their marriage they were able to see much of each other. Henrietta Barnett was among many who sent congratulations in 1878 and Arnold wrote to her that December, 'May I thank you for your affection to me. I shall always strive to be worthy of it. I do not think I will say that you have too high expectations of me – that would be treason to my love.' And Gertrude appreciated that this new happiness 'was an immense strength' to her brother in the last ten strenuous years of his life.

It was Gertrude, however, who was with him on 18 January 1883 when he rested before giving his historic lectures to the working men's club in east London.

> We – the middle classes I mean, not the very rich – we have neglected you. Instead of justice we have offered you charity, and instead of sympathy we have offered you hard and unreal advice. But I think we are changing. If you would only believe it and trust us, I think that many of us would spend our lives in your service.

His characteristic vitality and intensity had not left him, but that day, in their last talk together, he told his sister, 'You have never seen me as ill as this.'

Oxford was shocked by his death seven weeks later as it had not been since its loss of Professor T. H. Green from an epidemic the previous spring.

That Toynbee had tried to fill the gap left by the older man is clear from many letters sent to his wife and sister. The chairman of the Oxford Board of Guardians wrote to Charlotte on 28 March 1883, 'During the three years that he was a member of this Board your husband gained the respect and confidence of all who met him here.'

And Gertrude heard from the master of Balliol that:

> His loss is to me and many others one which cannot be replaced. There was no young man in Oxford who was exerting so valuable an influence. He was full of ideals and perfectly disinterested, and had gracious and charming ways which gained the hearts of others. He showed the type of character which they might imitate. Two things used to strike me about his intellectual gifts. First he had a quality which young men rarely have – moderation; secondly he was impatient of abstract thought and always sought to clothe his ideas in some practical form. . . . I am sure that he was one of the best persons I have ever known. Hoping that you will come and see me sometimes. I remain dear Miss Toynbee,
>
> Yours most truly,
>
> B. Jowett

For the rest of her short life Gertrude was bitterly to regret that, at a time when she was herself desperately ill, she had destroyed many of her brother's intimate letters to her. Arnold's young widow, like his sister, had many friends in Oxford, including Mrs Talbot and Mrs T. H. Green, and Charlotte's interests in due course centred on Lady Margaret Hall (LMH). Practical and efficient, she served as its house treasurer for 37 years, until 1920, and was elected an honorary fellow in 1926. The Lady Margaret Hall Settlement (LMHS) long had her support as a council member, but she declined an invitation sent her to become head of the WUS.

3

Toynbee Hall and the London School of Economics

The settlement idea, which took definite shape in Oxford, had been floated five months earlier in Cambridge. In June 1883 some undergraduates at St John's College there appealed for help to the vicar of St Jude's. Roused, as so many others, by the writing of Ruskin, Hyndman, Henry George and 'the bitter cry of outcast London', they wanted 'to serve the poor', but were not prepared to start a college mission. Had the vicar any other suggestions? Their letter arrived when he and Henrietta were leaving for Oxford and was slipped into a pocket. But engine trouble on the journey caused a long hold up and, as they sat on a railway bank with other passengers, an answer was written, advising the young men to hire a house in some industrial quarter where they could come for short or long periods and 'learn to sup sorrow with the poor'. He did not, however, advise a college mission.

Such missions were then popular, but a main objection was that they tended to operate only within the recognized parochial organization. Members of a college would adopt a poor district in a large town, find a clergyman for it and associate themselves in his work. He began with a hall, which he used as a centre, gathering a congregation into it and, as Barnett said, 'many districts thus created in east London now take their place among the regular parishes, and the income of the clergyman is paid by the ecclesiastical commissioners'. But such a college mission excluded the Nonconformists and Barnett was often asked, 'How can I help when I'm not a member of your Church or creed?' While acknowledging that such a mission 'might bring devoted workers into the service of the poor', it was not, he thought, the form most fitted to receive the spirit which is at present moving the universities.

Barnett was 40 and in the prime of life when he addressed the well-known gathering of undergraduates and others in Sidney Ball's rooms in Oxford on 17 November 1883. As on other occasions, he surprised his audience by his quiet common sense. '"Something must be done" is the comment which follows the tale of how the poor live', was his opening remark, followed soon by '"What can I do?" is a more healthy comment.' And 20 years later the prime minister's daughter Helen Gladstone, then chairwoman of the WUS, asked Professor Arthur Sidgwick to tell members how in the small crowded room in St John's College, after Arnold Toynbee's death, Mr Barnett read his plain, quiet, reasonable and well-reasoned plea for a small settlement of men in the East End. 'Those who like myself were present are not likely to forget the scene. His bare facts, his earnestness, his calm and carefully moderated hopes, impressed those who heard him far more than any decorated picture would have done. But no one could have then foreseen the wide spreading of the idea.'

Another meeting was hosted by Cosmo Lang (the future Archbishop), a committee was formed, an association started and money invested. Then a head must be sought who would turn the ideal into the real and to this end the vicar wrote an article which appeared in the *Quarterly Review* in February 1884.

But no suitable candidate emerged. Now the Barnetts found themselves in a dilemma. They had already spent 11 years in Whitechapel, they were neither of them physically robust and changing family circumstances had given them opportunities for the travel they loved: the vicar's beloved mother, to whom he wrote almost every day, had died in 1880 and his father three years later. As Henrietta put it, 'If this child though was not to die, we must undertake to try and rear it.' They went to the Mediterranean to consider the matter, and on a Sunday morning sitting at the end of a quaint harbour pier at Menton, made their decision.

Then they wired home to obtain the refusal of the big industrial school next to St Jude's, which had recently been vacated and 'we thought to be a good site for the first settlement'. They were to stay there for over 20 years.

But some months went by while the Barnetts sought more financial and other support before their settlement could open. Meanwhile, the High Church party in Oxford had been pursuing similar ideas. Octavia Hill was involved here. Aged 46 and by then a national figure in housing reform, she was invited to address an East End of London meeting to be held at Keble College in the first week of March 1884; the Bishop of Bedford was the other main speaker. She stayed the night with the warden and Mrs Talbot after the decision had been taken to start a High Church settlement in Bethnal Green to be called Oxford House.

On 10 March, a memorial service was held at Balliol College to mark the first anniversary of Arnold Toynbee's death. The Barnetts were present and afterwards a proposal was made that their settlement when it opened should bear his name. 'The Keble people are very vigorous and it will strain charity to be in spirit their fellow workers', wrote Samuel Barnett to his brother the same month. Feelings were running high and, as Henrietta later remarked, 'that men should think it necessary to start another settlement because Toynbee Hall was not in their opinion religious was a deep, a very deep pain to Mr Barnett.' This was hardly surprising in view of what they had already achieved together at St Jude's.

Charlotte Toynbee, like Arnold's close friend Alfred Milner, at first opposed the idea of a settlement in London as a memorial to her husband, preferring the alternative suggestion of a series of university extension lectures. But eventually she fell in with the majority view and became a member of Toynbee Hall's first council, chaired by Philip Lyttelton-Gell.

Soon enthusiasts from universities came to work at Toynbee Hall. This was hardly surprising as the accent from the start was on attracting people of different political parties and religious outlook who appreciated its spiritual methods, its aims to permeate rather than convert and its trust less in organization than in friends linked to friends. The attraction has proved permanent.

The main accent was on education and the vicar straightaway set on foot his Education Reform League, both he and Henrietta campaigning as always to provide 'the best for the lowest'. Excellence as an educational aim combined without difficulty with their brand of neighbourliness. The league was the most important of the methods adopted to help Toynbee Hall realize its own potential. Every resident was invited to bring friends among the artisans, tradesmen and teachers, and thus 'a splendid body of working reformers was gathered together'. The league, which had subcommittees in other parts of the East End, also served as a class on education for university graduates with the warden as their teacher. Henrietta could in due course draw back, though she would still occasionally lend a hand at the male-run Toynbee Hall in times of domestic crisis.

Meanwhile, Mrs Edward Talbot and other women supporters of the High Anglican Oxford House had begun work there, mainly on the domestic side. However, after deciding to function as the Ladies' Branch of Oxford House (LBOH), they soon joined the Cheltenham Ladies' College Guild for social work at the nearby newly opened Mayfield House. They were, however, described as 'the residents' by Cheltenham Ladies' College Guild members in written reports.

The long-standing division of men's settlements into 'religious' and 'non-religious' hardly concerned the women, who had largely ignored similar problems at the university when starting women's colleges. Octavia Hill's reputation as a national authority on housing was further established a few weeks after her Keble visit when she attended a conference of the ecclesiastical commissioners to advise them on the management of property in south London. She was the only woman at this meeting, which included two archbishops, two bishops and the Lord Chancellor. The Southwark property, inherited by the commissioners and intended to provide for the maintenance of the clergy, contained some of the worst slums in London, and the work gave Octavia scope for more large-scale planning than had previously fallen her way. Her battle to preserve Parliament Hill, which led to the formation of the National Trust, also opened in 1884. Miranda wrote that year, 'It has come to a point where two peers and a Cabinet minister call and consult her in one week. She had Fawcett here yesterday, Lord Wemyss the day before to ask what he should say in the House of Lords and the Duke of Westminster on Wednesday to ask what the Prince of Wales could do in the matter.'

Then, in December 1885, Octavia told Emily Maurice: 'I have an offer of £2000 for houses. As a gift or investment I think I shall use it and the Bishop of Rochester's £1000 to buy a house in Southwark to keep our workers together.' She took one in Nelson Square, Southwark, a few doors away from where the WUS would start its long life in 1887 with help from both her and Henrietta Barnett.

Henrietta meanwhile was increasingly concerned with issues relevant to her main work as a manager of the Forest Gate schools. Despite seeing herself as 'one of the women who are not fit for public work and dislike and distrust all forms of conflict', she was soon involved in a major fight on a matter of national concern.

Two disasters at pauper schools brought matters to a head. In 1890, after a teacher at Hackney had been sacked for ill-treating the children the school suffered a devastating fire, and four years later widespread poisoning at another school was attributed to bad meals. One sequel steered by Henrietta was a 'monster deputation' to the House of Commons.

Her efforts were not in vain and much had happened on this front by the time the Barnetts went to Oxford in December 1896 so that Henrietta could read a paper to an audience of women, many of whom were already involved in the settlement movement.

'My wife has been very busy with poor law work', wrote Barnett in January 1897, shortly before the opening of the LMHS. 'She has seen Lord Peel and her new State Children's Association committee is to meet for the first time on Wednesday.' And in March of the following year, 'At this moment my wife, under the leadership of Sidney Webb, is attacking the Asylum Board. Her bill was introduced yesterday and looks as if it would pass. It is down for a second reading on Thursday.'

If Henrietta's influence on both social legislation and the settlement movement continued long after H. H. Asquith had dubbed her 'the unofficial custodian of the children of the State', surely none of her initiatives produced as much lasting good as did the CCHF. Beginning in a small way and run by a committee at Toynbee Hall after the curate who had been organizing it left in 1881, three years later it became a national society and prototype of many similar ones abroad. A considerable machinery had to be kept oiled and running, as well as the money collected, new workers enlisted and the necessary reading matter produced on such principles as the scale of parents' contribution and the selection of children. The work commended itself to all sorts of philanthropic minds: it was economical; it began and finished each year; it had measurable results in children's pleasure and health; and people as usual sank their differences while helping children.

Among early secretaries for this and other Toynbee Hall groups were 'men who usually lived with us at Toynbee Hall', and by 1903 the CCHF secretary was a Balliol graduate, R. H. Tawney, a close friend of William Beveridge, also at Balliol, whose sister he married. Barnett offered Tawney the job with a salary of £200, and he spent three years until 1906 as resident CCHF secretary, and subsequently another five years from 1908. G. E. Gladstone and E. T. Urwick were among other well-known Toynbee Hall figures who similarly 'began their official lives in the service of children'.

Soon after being appointed canon of Westminster in 1906, Barnett gave up the wardenship of Toynbee Hall and became its president. But though he died seven years later, Henrietta's involvement there long continued. She attended the Toynbee Hall reunion dinner in 1919 at the start of J. J. Mallon's memorable 40 years as warden. And when she spoke at a party given at Toynbee Hall in 1932 to mark her eighty-first birthday, she asked 'has the effort failed? Let the answer be in the swarming men now in high places in this country who owe all their knowledge of the working classes to their Toynbee days. You find them everywhere.' The middle classes had certainly been given their chance.

Cosmo Lang had known both the Barnetts since the early days of the settlement movement and when, as Archbishop of Canterbury, he spoke at her funeral service in 1936, he clearly felt that this 'perfect partner' in their marriage had also provided most of the ideas. As he put it, 'the ideals and plans which glowed in the fervent imagination of the wife were clarified and defined and disciplined as they passed through the mind of the husband.' Her book on the canon's life and work has long outlived them both.

Meanwhile, as she wrote it, that intellectual offspring of the Webb partnership, the London School of Economics and Political Science (LSE), was fast growing up.

Beatrice Potter had joined the Barnetts' circle of friends in Whitechapel shortly before the settlement movement started. She was then a good-looking intelligent young woman in her mid-twenties.

Unlike her sister Kate, who took up charitable work with Christian conviction, her motivation came from intellectual sympathy with the mid-Victorian enquiry into why, in the midst of so much plenty, when British trade throughout the world was at a high peak, there should at home be millions living in mean streets, unable to make a decent livelihood. After deciding to investigate the causes of poverty among COS clients in Soho, trying to sort out the 'deserving' from the 'undeserving', she came to the conclusion that normal working-class life was a closed book to her. Nothing if not thorough, and well aware of her family roots in Lancashire's world of cotton mills and Nonconformist chapels, in 1883 she went up there, hiding, with some amusement, her wealthy Potter background under the disguise of a 'Miss Jones'. She was thus able to gain first-hand information about the cooperative movement and some respect for the possible benefits to be had from government interference in industry, as through the Factory Acts, in the same year that Arnold Toynbee was debating with undergraduates about 'Why are the Poor Poor?' and appealing to his East End audiences to accept middle-class help.

'Another day in Whitechapel,' wrote Beatrice in 1885. 'Met Mr Bond there and looked over fittings. Stove suggested by architect a failure; the management fails to go straight to the best authority and find out whether what is proposed is likely to succeed. Afterwards talked with Mr Barnett.'

Samuel Barnett, trying to steer this ardent young worker, wisely suggested that she should spend any unoccupied time in getting more general information, and 'find out particulars about medical officers, sanitary officers, relieving officers, school board visitors, and voluntary sanitary committees, their powers and duties'. The possibility of combining all agencies for housing into one body was soon put forward for Mr Bennett's consideration. 'Had not thought this one out and was rather astounded at the way he took it up and wanted me to elaborate a plan and become the moving spirit.'

Her idea of a housing association, when analysed to herself in November 1885, produced a further idea that she must 'do a survey of all the inhabitants of Katherine Buildings, dead and alive; occupation of all members; actual income from work, charity or private property; race; whether born in London; if so, belonging to London stock? If not, reason for immigration, and from what part of the country; religion; as much of previous history as obtainable.' Others were already in the field here.

> Yesterday I again went to Whitechapel, and dropped into the Barnetts to lunch. Mr Barnett is very full of an idea of a conference which should result in an association of the agencies for housing of the poor. About 160,000 persons live under the superintendency of these bodies; it seems a pity there should not be some intercommunication and exchange of valuable experience and a sifting of it for public purposes. But the whole thing wants thinking out. Miss Hill was dining there that night to discuss it. Mr Barnett thought she would be adverse to it. But it seems that the lady collectors are deteriorating as a body and that some stimulus is wanted to attract stronger and finer women into the profession; and Mr Barnett evidently grasps at any plan likely to furnish this.

Beatrice's impatience is evident in her criticism not only of the standards approved for the new blocks going up in Deptford, which were in accordance with views expressed by Octavia Hill when she gave evidence before the Royal Commission on the Housing of the Working Classes in 1884, but also of the older woman herself. In July 1886 Beatrice wrote in her diary:

> I met Miss Octavia Hill the other night at the Barnetts. She

> is a small woman with a large head finely set on her shoulders. The form of her head and features, and the expression of the eyes and mouth, have the attractiveness of mental power. A peculiar charm in her smile. We talked on artisans' dwellings. I asked her whether she thought it necessary to keep accurate descriptions of the tenants. No, she did not see the use of it. Surely it was wise to write down observations so as to be able to give true information, I suggested. She objected that there was already too much 'Windy Talk'; what you wanted was action; for men and women to go and work day by day among the less fortunate. And so there was a slight clash between us, and I felt penitent for my presumption. But not convinced.

The clash was to come to a head in 1907 when they served together on the Royal Commission on the Poor Law.

If Beatrice, living and working fearlessly among the local drunks and criminals, was exhausted at the end of each day, her vitality soon reasserted itself and she enjoyed evenings in the Barnetts' drawing room discussing problems with other social workers.

Deciding that Henrietta's campaign for 'pianos and pictures' was inadequate, even if bolstered by municipal welfare schemes with a vision of the best things made free so that everyone 'may have a public library or a picture gallery in his drawing room', she soon embarked on what seemed to her the deeper problem of how men and women were to become the thrifty workers approved by the COS when they could not find jobs. Nothing could help them to a satisfactory life, she concluded, but the removal of poverty.

Her easy pen now led to discussion beyond the Whitechapel circles of social workers. During weeks fully occupied in nursing her invalid father, she read of charitable gifts to unemployed men in the docks and reacted with an article called 'A Lady's View of the Unemployed', which was published under her name in the *Pall Mall Gazette*. Two major results were the start of Joseph Chamberlain's deep interest in her and a suggestion from Charles Booth, a Liverpool shipowner who had married her cousin Margaret Macaulay, daughter of the historian, that she should help him with his vast work to appear in due course as *The Life and*

Labour of the People of London. Pamphlets such as *The Bitter Cry of Outcast London* were fashionable, and Beatrice found that her descriptions of life in Whitechapel were just what her cousin Charlie needed to make his facts and figures come alive to the general public.

Beatrice was now set on a path which was to make her a parallel influence with young men working in the Toynbee Hall team and soon to include the future educationist (Sir) Robert Morant and (Lord) William Beveridge, architect of the welfare state.

Beveridge first visited Toynbee Hall in 1900 and was appointed sub-warden there three years later. He heard about the job, carrying a salary of £200, from the Balliol College chaplain when he was 24 and held it from September 1903 to November 1905. During this time he was in charge of the settlement when the Barnetts were abroad with the Toynbee pilgrims. He also served as an East End school manager. Booth had by then led the way in social research and, like Beatrice Potter, Beveridge was determined to find the solution to social problems. However, he left Toynbee Hall before the resignation of Balfour as Conservative prime minister had brought in a Liberal government and his next experience was as a journalist on the *Morning Post*. Beatrice Potter meanwhile had met, a few months after the great East End dock strike of 1889, the 29-year-old civil servant with socialist views who had written what she considered 'by far the most interesting article' in the recently published *Fabian Essays*. His patient devotion, comparable to that of Samuel Barnett for his similarly outspoken Wimbledon bride, had its reward and in 1891, shortly after the publication of her book on the cooperative movement, they were married in St Pancras vestry despite the disapproval of many of her own family and friends, including the Booths. She was proud that Sidney Webb, who had joined the Fabian Society in 1885, was considered by Bernard Shaw, another of its leading lights, to be 'the ablest man in England'. The society, described as 'intelligence officers without an army', and formed in that autumn of 1883 when the Barnetts visited Oxford to launch their settlement ideas, took its title in February 1884 a month before Octavia Hill spoke on settlements at Keble College.

In the great work for the unification of London education,

which soon occupied the Webbs, Beatrice was mainly concerned with 'our devoted nursing of that delicate infant, the LSE: its rapid growth and admission into the University of London, as part of the Faculty of Economics and Political Science, a new faculty on which Sidney had insisted'. Thus, after returning from a world tour lasting nine months in 1899, their social environment changed through the need for wire-pulling in connection with the proposed London Education Act.

The LSE grew from a legacy left in 1894 to five trustees, with Sidney Webb as chairman, by an 'eccentric old gentleman' Henry Hutchinson, who had long helped to finance the Fabian Society. 'We desired that the lectures and investigations held at the school should be representative of all branches of economics and political science, and no differentiation against persons was to be allowed on the grounds of sex, religion, or economic or political views.' Premises for the school were soon found at 10 Adelphi Terrace, and a wealthy young woman, Charlotte Payne-Townshend, was roped in to help as a socialist and radical.

The newcomer took rooms over the school, subscribed £1000 to the library, endowed a woman's scholarship, became bored with Graham Wallas and married Bernard Shaw. Then Passmore Edwards, who had recently given Mrs Humphry Ward considerable sums to start her settlement in Bloomsbury, contributed £10,000 when the school needed more room before finally moving to Houghton Street: he had also given large sums to help Canon Barnett's library projects at Toynbee Hall.

The Webbs were now involved in a pattern of educational advance on three fronts, national, municipal and Fabian, complicated by a network of friendships in which the Conservative A. J. Balfour, later responsible as prime minister for the Education Act of 1902, proved far more in harmony than, for instance, the rising young Liberal barrister H. H. Asquith, particularly after he had, in Beatrice's eyes, 'ruined himself by his marriage to the silly Margot Tennant'. By January 1897, she was able to write cheerfully that 'the London School was progressing. Sidney has contrived to edge it into any possible London University. It is still a speculation in money, students and output, but it promises well.' Then in July 'Sidney and Haldane are rushing about London trying to get all parties to agree to a Bill for London University.' The LSE's future now seemed secure and its development, as envisaged in controversies surrounding the sale of LCC premises nearly a century later, would have distressed both the Webbs. In August 1992 *The Times* wrote, 'the LSE has remained true to the objectives of its founders. When Sidney and Beatrice both founded the school in 1895 they wanted to create a high-powered think-tank specializing in the social services. They would have understood immediately Professor Ashworth's modern vision of a "European Social Services Party".'

Social activities and money-raising were only part of Beatrice's work on its behalf. Despite having had no university training, she enjoyed a position as both counsellor and don. Thus, in October 1897, when Sidney was lecturing in Oxford:

> I stayed here for my usual Wednesday afternoon at home. This is rapidly becoming a series of interviews with members of my class at the School of Economics. I enjoy lecturing every Thursday; the preparation of my lecture takes the best part of two mornings either in actual preparation or in resting so that my brain may be clear. The weekly class brings me into close connection with the work of the school; I see some half dozen students every week and talk over their work with them. I am glad that our life becomes every day more that of students and teachers.

In 1897 the LMHS had opened in Lambeth and its pioneering settlement members, keen to promote training for social work, had here a firm ally.

Meanwhile, Beatrice had not lost contact with Anglican and Conservative circles whose leaders, including the Creightons and Talbots, were then campaigning for religious education in schools. When she attended the Manchester conference of the National Union of Women Workers (NUWW) in October 1897 several delegates there had recently been involved with the Lambeth conference, and the Bishop of Rochester's wife with launching women's 'religious settlements' in Lambeth and Peckham. 'There was the usual gathering of sensible and God-fearing folk dominated by the executive of bishops' wives, who gave to the proceedings an atmosphere of extreme decorum and dignity.' But she resigned from the executive owing to their persistence in having prayers before all their business meetings, which, she considered, was wanting in courtesy to those of other religions whom they wished to serve with them. 'Some of them agree but say that the Union would lose membership if it were not understood to be deliberately Christian.' It was a dilemma to be faced years later by many Anglican educationists in areas with large ethnic minorities. Moreover, she admitted that 'the bishops' wives are a nice lot' and regretted parting company with them. 'Possibly it is the predominance of the Lyttelton family that gives the governing body of the conference such a sweet and wholesome flavour – there being at least three Lytteltons on the executive, whilst the subcommittees swarm with younger members of the family. The Lytteltons and Louise Creighton are the presiding spirits of the conference.'

Under Mrs Creighton's leadership the NUWW was soon to be responsible for starting 'religious' settlements in Liverpool and Birmingham which, unlike others, included in their arms the 'study of industrial conditions'.

Beatrice's contribution to the settlement movement was mainly in her emphasis on the need for professional standards when researching into social problems, with facts and documents being regarded as at least as important as opinions gathered from interviews; and in helping to provide through the LSE a means for students to train both in practice and theory. Following the path blazed by Cobbett with his *Rural Rides*, when he collected evidence contrary to that produced by a select committee on agriculture in 1821 in favour of imported corn, Beatrice and her friends, many with settlement experience, became in due course freelance partners with the government official machine in the field of social investigation.

Her continuing demand for preventive measures for social evils was highlighted in her brilliant campaign for the break-up of the poor law; and her Minority Report on the findings of the Royal Commission set up by Arthur Balfour in 1905 was only possible because by then, with her cousin Booth's help, she had mastered the technique necessary to ensure that members of an official enquiry had control over its agenda. While the Majority Report, signed by Octavia Hill, C. S. Loch, Mrs Bernard Bosanquet and other COS supporters, sought only to improve on existing practice and was soon forgotten, Beatrice's recently revived ideas, well ahead of their time, heralded the legislation of the welfare state, and she was to live just long enough to see the publication of the Beveridge Report.

The honorary degree conferred on her by Manchester University in 1909 was in recognition of the Minority Report, sponsored by her and written by Sidney, but did not alter the status of the LSE as the Webbs' 'favourite child'. The Canning Town Women's Settlement, started in 1892 with 15 women as residents, was by then providing LSE students with their own base for practical training in social work, though it was later to close.

One result of Beatrice becoming better known was a request from Mrs Henry Fawsett that she should withdraw her opposition to women's political enfranchisement. Having long regretted her support of Mrs Humphry Ward's manifesto in 1889, she now wrote to say so, giving her reasons for the change.

Millicent Garrett Anderson sent this reply to *The Times* on 5 November 1906 adding: 'Those who have been working for many years for women's suffrage naturally regard with extreme satisfaction the adhesion to the movement of two of the ablest women who have hitherto opposed it, Mrs Creighton and Mrs Sidney Webb. Mrs Creighton's change of view was chronicled in your columns about a week ago.'

It was then 45 years since young Mandell Creighton had first met his bride in an Oxford already enchanted by Ruskin.

4

Young Wives at Oxbridge

'The best strength of a man is shown in his intellectual work as that of a woman in her daily deed and character.' This was Ruskin's view when *Sesame and Lilies* was first published in 1865 and there is no reason to suppose he changed it after being appointed Slade professor at Oxford four years later, though a new preface in 1882 mentioned 'colleges for women'. His popular influential lectures on art were open to both sexes, with predictable results.

When coming away from one of them in 1871, good-looking 25-year-old Humphry Ward, newly elected fellow and tutor of Brasenose College, was asked by his friend Mandell ('Max') Creighton, fellow of Merton, to introduce him to a young woman in the audience who was wearing 'a beautiful yellow scarf'. She was Louise van Glehn, daughter of a London merchant well known to the Ward family. Max proposed a few weeks later. In academic circles only professors and heads of houses were expected to marry, but the climate of opinion was changing. The more impetuous Humphry Ward not only declared his love at this time for Dr Arnold of Rugby's granddaughter, Mary Arnold, who was also attending Ruskin's lectures, but married her within the year.

Early remarkable for a vivid imagination, high spirits and decided character, Mary's early life had not been easy. When her father, newly converted to Roman Catholicism, came home from Tasmania with a family and no job, it was her aunt Jane, wife of William Forster, the future minister of education, who largely helped them. In 1858, the seven-year-old Mary was sent as a boarder to Miss Anne Clough's school in Westmoreland, spending the holidays at Fox How, her grandmother's large country house nearby, while her father taught at the Catholic University in Dublin before moving to the oratory in Birmingham. However, he again changed his ideas on religion, not for the last time, and by 1865 was settled with his wife and growing family in Oxford, hoping to support them all by taking pupils. Two years later Mary left school to enjoy life in university circles still recovering from Newman's conversion to Rome. She was soon a popular guest at the Lincoln College parties, at this time preferring Dean Pattison's friends committed to scholarship and research to the Balliol protagonists of public service. After producing a learned thesis on west Gothic kings and bishops, her vision of herself as a woman of letters was bolstered by a comment from the historian Creighton to whom she had submitted it: 'There is nobody but Stubbs doing such work in Oxford now.' But Humphry Ward now intervened and, after being married by Dean Stanley in 1872, the couple enjoyed Oxford life together for the next nine years, during which their three children, Dorothy, Arnold and Janet, were born.

A pointer to the future was the leaflet Mary wrote on *Plain Facts on Infant Feeding*, which she distributed in the slum areas of Oxford. Her happiness at this time is caught in a portrait painted by her friend Bertha Johnson, daughter of Professor Todd of King's College, London, who had studied at the Slade before settling in Oxford as the wife of the chaplain of All Souls College.

Mrs Arthur Johnson was among those who attended Ruskin's lectures in November 1873 and, as she recalled:

> It was after one of these that Mrs Creighton, then a remarkably handsome young woman in the aesthetic costume of the period, came up to me and asked me to join a committee of ladies for providing a system of lectures and classes for women in Oxford. Having always been an enthusiast for equal rights to education I joyfully assented and found myself with an interesting little company of organizers.

They included Mary Ward, Mrs Edward Talbot, who had come as a bride to Oxford when Keble College was opened with her husband as its first warden in 1870, Mrs. T. H. Green, wife of the most influential philosopher then in Oxford and sister of the author John Addington Symonds, and Walter Pater's sister Clara. Afterwards Mary Ward, Clara Pater and Bertha Johnson met to send out circulars in the Creighton's house, Middlemarch, where equal rights were pursued to the extent of Max undertaking to baby-sit his year-old first child. Bertha's husband was a lecturer when the new group's first series was held in the Clarendon buildings in spring 1874 and he arranged a 'collections' examination at the end of the course. There was then much interest in the welfare of elementary schoolteachers and pupil teachers, and several were invited to the lectures. These were held each winter until 1879 when the committee expanded to meet a new situation.

Louise Creighton's colleagues also met regularly at Lincoln College, both as members of the Browning Society and to inaugurate a trade union for women working in Oxford; both the rector and his wife were ardent supporters of women's rights, not only in education but also in political and industrial matters. To Bertha Johnson 'Mrs Pattison was a complex character – he declared she was the cleverest woman he had ever met – but to us there was a sense of strain in her talk at one time and a provoking frivolity at another often when you specially wanted her to be serious and helpful. Still she was devoted and kind in working for others.' There was clearly some lack of harmony here. After the rector's death in 1883 and his widow's marriage the following year to Sir Charles Dilke, she became a main financial prop of the Women's Protective and Provident League, founded by Emma Paterson in 1874 and supported by such friends of the labour movement as William Morris and the industrialist Thomas Brassey. Mrs Creighton meanwhile pioneered elsewhere as founder president of the NUWW, a grouping of women's organizations, largely middle class and Anglican, forerunner of the National Council of Women and largely responsible for spreading the settlement movement outside London.

Lavinia Talbot was another young wife who had much influence on her contemporaries and not only because Keble College had been a rallying point for churchmen since its foundation three years after John Keble's death. When she and her husband visited Cambridge early in 1878, they called in at Girton and, impressed by what they saw, felt, as Dr Talbot remarked, 'that here was a form of new development in education which was bound to expand. Why should not the Church be for once at the front instead of behind in its development? We came back to Oxford with the thought in our minds of starting a small residential enterprise.' Rival claims of denominationalism and nondenominationalism were then constantly being debated, and at a meeting at Keble that June it was hoped that a Church of England women's college would be founded, though one not representing any particular section in the Church. As this idea was not generally acceptable, it was decided to form an Association for the Higher Education of Women (AEW) in Oxford to be entirely responsible for the educational side and finance, with Professor T. H. Green as secretary. There should be two halls of residence, only one of them denominational, and a scheme for students who for various reasons did not wish to reside in a hall. Thus LMH and Somerville came into being in 1879, followed shortly by the Oxford Society for Home Students (later St Anne's) and then St Hugh's College, sponsored by LMH. St Hilda's College, linked with Cheltenham Ladies' College, was the last to join the group.

Among those who attended the early AEW lectures was Elizabeth Wordsworth, who surprised no one by coming top in the examinations. She frequently visited Oxford at this time, her brother John, later Bishop of Salisbury, being then a fellow and tutor at Brasenose. After Dr Talbot's suggestion of having two halls of residence had been adopted, she was appointed principal of the High Church one in November 1878, being at the same time told that she might admit some members of other religious bodies. Dr Talbot wrote:

> The appointment was extraordinarily fortunate, it brought us not only the lady's own distinction of intellect and character, but the cachet and warrant of a name second to none in the confidence of English Church people. None could have been a greater protection against any charge of

> rashness in our attempt. Within the Hall she was quietly supreme; and outside her social and intellectual distinction won a place for the Hall in Oxford society which might have been long in coming to it.

She was to remain principal for 30 years. It was she who suggested that the hall should be named after Margaret, Countess of Richmond, mother of Henry VII and a considerable benefactor of both Oxford and Cambridge, whose effigy in Westminster Abbey had deeply impressed her young mind when her father was canon there and who later called forth her well-known remark: 'a gentlewoman, a scholar and a saint, and after having been three times married, she took a vow of celibacy. What more could be expected of any woman?' Miss Wordsworth also suggested the crest of three daisies with the motto *ex solo ad solem*, which, on a large brass plate, was in due course to adorn the LMHS front door in Lambeth.

Humphry Ward claimed responsibility for naming the nondenominational hall. He had met the distinguished scientist Mrs Somerville while on holiday in Naples and his wife, an active member of the AEW, joined the Somerville committee, serving for some time as honorary secretary and remaining on it long after she left Oxford. She was also largely responsible for the teaching arrangements, all lectures for women students being then controlled by the AEW in consultation with the college principals. When in due course her settlement needed its first woman warden, the candidate appointed was a former student of Somerville. Mrs T. H. Green also joined the Somerville supporters, while Mrs Arthur Johnson, opting for LMH, was well qualified to ensure that no friction arose, at least among the women, between the denominational and nondenominational camps.

Lavinia Talbot made a distinctive contribution here, in some ways personifying the settlement ethos of progress in social welfare across the barriers of politics through friends linked with friends. Her Lyttelton family connections with the Whig element in public life through the marriage of her mother's sister Catherine Glynn to the young Gladstone was offset by the Conservatism of the Talbot family, later reinforced when her sister Lucy married

Lord Frederick Cavendish. Her 'Uncle Willie' was then living quietly at Hawarden Castle having resigned the Liberal leadership in 1875 after, as he said, '42 years of laborious public work', despite the opposition of his wife, Lavinia's beloved 'Aunt Pussy', who could not envisage him staying quietly in the country writing learned books about the past.

The political climate of that time had much in common with that of today. Irish troubles were soon to culminate in terrorism and after Disraeli's departure a ginger group in Parliament, mainly Conservative, whose members included Sir Stafford Northcote, Lord Randolph Churchill and Arthur Balfour, seemed as determined as were the Irish nationalists on obstructive tactics. Lavinia Talbot was closely in touch with Arthur Balfour and, though her sister Nora had married Henry Sidgwick, brother of the Oxford professor, the Talbots frequently stayed with the Sidgwicks on their visits to Cambridge. In both universities Lavinia's tact and common sense soothed many ruffled feelings and her diary lights up the current scene.

Henry Sidgwick had risked his whole career by resigning his fellowship at Trinity College because he no longer held the religious beliefs professed when accepting it, a gesture which largely brought about soon afterwards the abolition of religious tests for such appointments in the university. He then took up the cause of women teachers as his form of social work, and was one of a joint board of Oxbridge representatives whose deliberations in London resulted in the first higher local examinations for women being held at Cambridge in 1869.

Both Emily Davies and Anne Clough had pressed the needs of girls as well as boys on the Schools Commission Enquiry in 1864, and Miss Clough had carried on the campaign as secretary of the North of England Council for Promoting the Higher Education of Women, presided over by Mrs Josephine Butler, and supported by the Yorkshire Ladies' Council of Education. Henry Sidgwick had corresponded with Miss Clough about the possibility of an examination to test teachers and governesses at a standard higher than that fixed for the 'local' examinations for pupils under 18 in the schools, and in 1871 he persuaded her to leave her educational work in Liverpool and take charge of a house he had rented in

Cambridge so that some at least of the aspirants might prepare themselves adequately for the new higher local examination. He was one of a group of dons who had offered them free lectures and among his pupils was Mary Paley, soon to marry the economist Alfred Marshall and help start the women's settlement movement. In 1872, Arthur Balfour, a former pupil of Henry Sidgwick, had persuaded his sister Nora to leave the family home at Whittinghame and take charge of his newly set up establishment at 4 Carlton Gardens. Already enthusiastic for the women's education movement through the influence of their mother, Lady Blanche Balfour, Nora soon became a shareholder, with Miss Clough and Henry Sidgwick, in a company formed to promote a women's college; when a site in the Newnham district was acquired from St John's College she made in 1874 her first gift to the foundation of £500, writing at the same time to Mr Sidgwick that 'I should like to offer a scholarship to Miss Clough's Ladies' College.' He and Miss Clough had signed an appeal for funds. Newnham Hall was opened for 30 students in 1875.

Almost before its walls were dry Nora Balfour went to stay with Miss Clough, who had moved in 'regardless of comfort'. After her marriage to Henry Sidgwick in 1876 the couple lived at Newnham till their own house was ready, the professor even having his meals in the dining room there after a period of eating in Trinity. However, by October they were installed at Hillside and involved in much entertaining; while Newnham business engaged her, his work for women took its place as part of general university reform. A year later the Gladstones' daughter Helen came to stay at Hillside as a Newnham out-student and soon afterwards was appointed secretary there. In 1879 the lecture committee and the Newnham Hall committee merged as the Newnham Hall Association, and Newnham College came into existence the following year with Mrs Sidgwick, a born administrator and trained mathematician as its treasurer, destined to guide its fortunes either as vice-principal or principal for 39 years. She was a keen supporter of the settlement movement largely because of the possibilities it offered her students for social work training and jobs.

Meanwhile, Emily Davies had taken charge of five girls with educational aspirations during 1869 and, after obtaining Octavia

Hill's supporting signature (among many others), had moved her Hitchin women's college to Girton in 1873. She had frequently found herself in disagreement with Henry Sidgwick, being insistent on the need for women to take the same examinations as men and opposing any suggestion of 'girls' subjects'. They also disagreed over religion and Girton, unlike Newnham, had its own chapel.

Miss Davies was a member of the London School Board for three years from 1870, helping in the campaign which resulted in degrees being granted to women by London University in 1874. When she retired from her Girton post in 1875 she was succeeded by Miss Bernard, who welcomed the Talbots on their visit four years later. Thus, in May 1879, Lavinia recorded:

> Off again to Cambridge to visit the Sidgwicks. Just saw our hosts and then drove off to 'lionize' Girton where we liked Miss Bernard so much it has given us a prejudice in favour of the whole place. There are 43 girls in the huge building – they seem to be clever, good pronouncee [*sic*] and easily managed, a deal given to free-thinking but less than formerly. Take more to Miss Bernard than Miss Clough. Back to Cambridge to Newnham; little interview with Miss Clough and then had snug tea in Helen's room and no end of jabber. Some rest before dinner at Nora's to which came besides A. J. B. and Eustace (both in house), Gerald and Alfred. Somehow overwhelmed with shyness at start of dinner; no one talked but H. Sidgwick and me, and what was said was caught up Balfourwise and quizzed. However, after the Selwyn College matter was disposed of, got on easier and the evening was very pleasant. Eustace looks the picture of a big happy man.

On Saturday they saw the site for Selwyn College, 'a fair spot big and wide which pleased us much', and on Sunday they went to Trinity chapel and King's College where there was 'plenty of talk about Lightfoot and Westcott. It seems strange that in spite of this fine school of theology here, no younger man could be found to succeed Lightfoot. E has interviewed both divines, much interested.' In 1896 her husband, by then a bishop, would collaborate with Bishops Westcott and Selwyn and other members of Cambridge University in founding Cambridge House, with its adjacent Talbot House, in Southwark, comparable with Oxford House in Bethnal Green and intended as a centre for the social and mission work undertaken by the university in south London.

Ruskin had recently left Oxford, a sick man, and on 25 May the Talbots dined at the deanery to meet his successor. Lavinia had 'a very pleasant dinner twixt Dean and Mr Richmond but was not impressed favourably. Mr Richmond very affected I thought in manner. One cannot believe in him as a teacher of men whatever his painting may be. Lots of singing. Came away late.'

The run-up to Oxford's autumn term of 1879 brought 'very busy days, E over his 71 men up for matriculation, I over L[ad]y Marg[aret] Hall, which has to be scrambled into shape by Saturday. Also two young women are quartered here.' And a few days later:

> The excitement beyond all others now is the start of L[ad]y Marg[aret]. By much contrivance the house was ready on Sat[urday] 11th, and enter Miss Wordsworth and four students, and on the 13th four more. There have been some presents of pictures and with Mrs Johnson's clever taste I must say the house is extremely pretty, the girls very pleasant and good-natured.

Then on 16 October:

> We had a nice little bright service at LMH as an opening by the Bishop. All the committee there and a good many others. The service held in the drawing room. The Bishop spoke excellently. One had many hopes and fears, the hopes predominate. Somerville starts well too, with 11 or 12 girls as against our 9. Miss Lefevre very taking, but is less *en rapport* with her Committee than Miss Wordsworth, that is pretty plain.

Though the university now provided a higher examination for women, there was still a long struggle ahead before women would be admitted to any university honours examinations or to lectures in men's colleges.

Lavinia had three brothers at the university as well as her cousin Herbert Gladstone, and visitors that term included her sister Lucy and Lord Frederick Cavendish, who were followed by Mr Gladstone and his daughter Mary. Young Edward Lyttelton was staying at Keble while preparing for Eton and, early in November when Lavinia was reading German with him:

> Thomas said a gentleman wanted to see me outside; the card showed it was Cardinal Newman. We came into the drawing room where Lucy and I received him, an old man rather tottering in gait but his face full of life and gentleness. He had the little red skullcap on, long cloth cassock cloak sort of thing and a check necktie. He brought with him a postbag holding the last lot of Keble's letters to him, which he wanted to deliver up himself to the Warden of Keble College. He wanted to explain to E (which he did when E came in) that the erasures he made were not passages to his own advantage or disadvantage, but simply all those of Keble's own self-deprecatory remarks, which he said were painful, and which he could not allow to go down to posterity. For instance Newman said he blamed himself exceedingly 'that I became a Catholic'. In the year [18]45 he said with a pathetic look he received no letters from Keble. We also talked of Pusey and his power of amassing knowledge. Freddy came in and as he got up to shake hands with him he didn't sit down again but went away E walking with him to Bo. Price [*sic*]. He told E that he thought Keble College was the hopeful thing about Oxford now. It was full of interest to us and we quite burst when he went away.

Since John Keble had delivered his famous assize sermon in 1833, which had launched the Oxford Movement, and Newman, then aged 34, had written the first of the tracts that called on ordained clergy to choose their side in the ecclesiastical debate that was to split the Church of England, liberalism had come to stand for more than one attitude of mind.

Gladstone, with other politicians, travelled to Oxford in 1845 to vote in the hebdomadal council in the decisive battle between heads of houses and the Newmanites, though the victory of the latter had not prevented Newman's secession from the Church of England four years later. It was at this time that Gladstone was elected to Parliament as junior member for Oxford University, to emerge in due course as the leading layman of the High Church party as well as leader of the Liberal Party. Soon after becoming prime minister in 1865, he had persuaded Richard Church, who had always remained a friend of Newman since their youthful days together at Oriel, to leave his country vicarage in Somerset and come up to London as dean of St Paul's. And the two men, in many ways so different, worked together as intellectual allies determined to save the Anglican Church as it was, being helped here by Dr Talbot who, with Lavinia, often stayed at the deanery on visits to London. Gladstone took immense care over ecclesiastical appointments, relying much on the dean's wise judgement and helped in the vast secretarial work involved by his daughter Mary, who controlled the special cupboard in 10 Downing Street needed for her father's ecclesiastical patronage. Meanwhile, at Oxford the Broad Church philosophical liberals, soon to be led by Dr Jowett at Balliol College, remained poles apart from the High Church Anglicans based at Keble.

The term ended for the Talbots with a visit from Mr Balfour, who came from Hatfield and was 'full of Midlothian', for in November 1879 Gladstone 'had set off for a campaign in view of the coming election', setting up headquarters at Dalmeny where 'Lord Rosebery's position and money helped matters in the effort to win the seat from Lord Dalkeith.' Other visitors soon arrived:

> [including] the Freddies, who made a fine set of ears. I heard Uncle W calling Dizzy a chartered liar (to F). Edward came from Penrhyn, giving an amusing account of the flock of Mesdames and Misses Pennant, and the Sidgwicks came on Saturday; his stammer is a drawback with Uncle W who has barely the patience to listen through a long sentence. Helen came too and I had much Newnham talk with her and Nora.

Lavinia Talbot had just celebrated her thirty-first birthday when she met Arnold Toynbee and his wife in February 1880. 'Professor Seeley and his wife came for Sunday, viewing a movement for lectures to working men. He is a shrewd not showy man, much amused with things. He thought us very unlike Cambridge. He and Ed had two long theological talks which unfortunately I missed.' Lavinia was showing Mrs Seeley round Oxford at the time. 'We had some history people and others to meet him after dinner. Next day several for luncheon – a charming Mr and Mrs Toynbee, etc. Mr Seeley talked a great deal, mostly on social matters.' She was to see much of Charlie Toynbee in the year ahead.

Mary Gladstone looked in at Keble on her way back to London after her father's second Midlothian campaign, and when Mr Balfour came to stay shortly afterwards there was naturally 'much political talk'. Whig landowning aristocrats easily predominated in Gladstone's next administration, which was to last five years and prove a watershed in political life, including as it did such radical leaders as Joseph Chamberlain and Sir Charles Dilke, and bringing in Home Rule for Ireland.

A pointer to the future came at the Leicester congress that September when 'the Bishop of Bedford talked of both country and S. London poor very interestingly and received quite an ovation'. The Talbots had travelled with 'dear old J. Wordsworth who was nearly as funny and charming as in '72' and who read a paper on the three schools of thought in the Church. Bishops Lightfoot and Benson and Dr Farrer also spoke, then 'Ed led off on the Wednesday morning with a capital paper well received on education and the upper middle classes.' The following month he preached at Radley on 'losing one's life to gain it. Boys very attentive'; and soon afterwards she went to the school to be 'the medium for distributing ambulance certificates to the boys'.

A devoted mother, Lavinia 'minded leaving my little sweet trio who . . . took the goodbyes cheerfully' when she and the warden set off for Rome during the Christmas vacation, having as usual more than one family home at their disposal – 'May goes to Hawarden for a fortnight and the little boys to Falconhurst.' On their way home in February Mary Gladstone met them at Charing

Cross and took them to Downing Street. 'There was excitement because Uncle W had made a wonderful speech and the upshot of the evening was the suspension of 35 Irish. They all came in quite late, Uncle W to my eyes not so tired looking as any of his sons, and so dear and composed and vigorous and simple.' Then March brought news of the Boer War settlement: 'England is left in a dignified position though giving the Boers self-government in the Transvaal.' Later that month when Mr Balfour came to stay 'there was a good deal of talk on the Fourth Party which is now defunct.'

The Barnetts' work in Whitechapel was by now attracting attention in political circles, and soon afterwards Lavinia was again in London 'mainly to attend an Art Exhibition Lord Rosebery opened in Commercial Road for the poor'.

But the summer term was overshadowed by family tragedy. In the ever worsening Irish situation, policy had veered from coercion to conciliation. When Parnell agreed to cooperate with an appeasement policy he was released from gaol on 2 May 1882, whereupon the Lord Lieutenant, Lord Cowper, and the Chief Secretary, Forster, resigned, to be replaced by Lord Spencer and Lord Frederick Cavendish. Lord Frederick reached Dublin on 6 May and the whole nation was shocked by what followed. Lavinia was never to forget the day when

> E came in to tell me that dear Freddy, who had gone to Ireland for one or two nights, had been stabbed while walking in Phoenix Park with Mr Burke, the Permanent Under Secretary. Freddy had not an enemy in the world. 'I have come to do what good I can' he said during his one afternoon of work. How wonderfully darling Lucy has stood it is a thing to be thankful for on our knees. Lady Louisa Egerton and Meriel broke the news to her and Uncle W was with her directly afterwards.

Dr Talbot took the funeral service at Chatsworth. Lady Frederick Cavendish was to devote much of the rest of her life to social and educational work as president of the Yorkshire Ladies' Council of Education and with settlements in London.

In September another funeral brought Gladstone to Oxford. Dr

Pusey, the spiritual leader of the early Tractarians, died peacefully with full mental powers up to the last few days. Lavinia 'raced off alone to Cambridge' later that month for the opening of Selwyn College, and heard much talk afterwards on 'the equality of women on which Professor Stewart has pronounced views'.

Dr Jowett, who had recently 'preached spitfire at Dr Pusey', was now vice chancellor at Oxford, and at a dinner party Lavinia held that autumn in his honour, Miss Wordsworth from LMH was among the guests. 'Then about 81 people came in the evening which went off well with much spirit and *noise*. I sang with the violin. Success.' On 3 November she 'dined with the Somerville world; bright and pleasant but oh so ugly'; and later that month 'dined also Lady Margaret Hall, prettier girls, more silent, very pleasant and bright atmosphere too. Long talk with Miss Wordsworth.' Then on 13 November 'Mrs Johnson gave an address to large meeting in our Hall, over which I had worked hard, on the prevention and the spread of infection, which had been successfully done in Hastings. Dr Acland in the chair. Good meeting though abruptly ended.' It was only six months since little Cuthbert Acland and Professor T. H. Green had both died in the scarlet fever epidemic that swept through Oxford in 1882.

Soon afterwards Bertha Johnson took over secretarial responsibilities for the AEW, helped by Arthur Sidgwick. Working closely with Elizabeth Wordsworth she had already become secretary for LMH in 1880, an honorary post she was to hold until 1914. She was also in charge of the Oxford Society for Home Students for ten years from 1883 and thereafter their principal until 1921. Like her friend Mrs Arnold Toynbee, Mrs Johnson was made an honorary fellow of LMH in 1926 at the same time as were Miss Wordsworth, her two successors as LMH principal and two men.

Eleanor Benson, the Bishop of Truro's elder daughter, who had come up to LMH in 1881, was well into her second year when Archbishop Tait died and Lavinia entered in her diary for December: 'The Bishop of Truro has been offered Canterbury.' Eleanor then left Oxford to live at home and it was in memory of her and the work she did for the poor in south London that the warden of Keble was in due course to suggest that the proposed LMHS should be located in Lambeth.

The spring term of 1883 brought Ruskin back to Oxford as friends, thinking him fully recovered from his mental breakdown, had arranged that he should be reinstated as Slade professor of art. On 9 March vast crowds gathered outside the little museum room for the first of a series of lectures on 'The Art of England'. Among them were some with memories of his lectures ten years earlier, which had been followed by the meeting at the Creightons' house. Now on a 'glittering cold day', Lavinia Talbot found 'there was no getting near the doorway'. Next day she tried again and

> got in to hear dear old Ruskin after standing ages outside the door. His grey beard and lapses among his teeth alter him a good deal, but when he began to speak, there was the same Ruskin. Full of grace are the lips. A beautiful description of a new Holman Hunt picture which is just coming out, a clever analysis of Rossetti with Holman Hunt, a dead outspoken bit about the Resurrection and Christianity were the chief features. He had some fascinating little drawings with him.

On their way through London soon afterwards, the Talbots stayed with the Humphry Wards in Russell Square – 'lovely house, furniture, fittings. Mr Ward less tiresome in his own house and Mrs nice as always. An agreeable little dinner to meet us including A. Milner and Mr Buckle of *The Times*.' They then spent a night with the dean of St Paul's and Mrs Church, arriving at tea time and going on to dinner at Lambeth Palace. 'The first time I have ever been there; no one there hardly; E very glad of a business talk with the Arch B. . . . Mr Randall Davidson much to the fore and so capable. E found it curious going from the Dean, who might have been Archbishop, to Lambeth.' Afterwards they went on to Hatfield. Then in December the Talbots 'got a delicious six days at blessed old Hawarden' and Lavinia came home 'more awe-struck over the GOM than ever – detectives came down in shoals as there was alarm over the results of O'Connell's hanging.'

Later that month she met Mrs Josephine Butler at Arthur Butler's house and was 'much struck. She looks old and worn but beautiful.' They had another talk together soon afterwards 'before a meeting in Holywell for women only, when she spoke perfectly. Formed an Association and hope to do something.' Both in Oxford and later in Leeds and Southwark Josephine Butler's campaign for moral welfare had the support of the Talbots and Gladstones. And the three daughters of the first headmaster of Harleybury were all to be involved in the settlement scene, the eldest, Olive, becoming warden of the LMHS and the youngest, Christina, who lived to the ripe old age of 98, ending her distinguished academic career as secretary for social work training courses at Barnett House.

The educational and settlement themes already interwoven in Lavinia's diary are highlighted in 1884 and on 7 March that year she records an historic event not included in the official archives of Keble College: 'We had a marvellous East End of London meeting in our hall. About 800 undergraduates to hear [the] Bishop of Bedford and Octavia Hill speak. They stayed with us and were both very interesting and edifying. I shall never forget the impression of O. Hill — a little brown skimp woman with splendid eyes.'

Keble had shown itself aware of the housing and other needs of working people, out of which the settlement movement was mainly born, and taken action. But Lavinia does not mention the memorial service for Arnold Toynbee held that week in Balliol College, and it was not until two months later that she took the opportunity offered to ease 'the very deep pain' felt by the vicar of St Jude's in Whitechapel by what he saw as the start of a rival settlement. Meanwhile, on 10 March, she 'went to a debate in college on the Women's Examination question. Very funny was Mr Lefroy when he declared in my eye that it was an accepted fact that all men deteriorate when they marry.' On 11 March 'Congregation again passed the W Exam but in lessened majority, 35. Sir W. Anson spoke well but slightly against.' Elizabeth, sister of the warden of All Souls, was soon to help start the Ladies' Branch of Oxford House (LBOH). Then, on 14 March, 'Mr Knight Bruce came to talk to our men about the Univ Settlement. He is Bp of Bedford's Chaplain, and after a bit much to be liked and admired.'

Early in April the Talbots were in Cambridge and, while travelling there with Arthur Sidgwick, they had much talk about F. D.

Maurice as 'E was now hard at work over his review for Macmillan. However, it was sent off on Thursday.' Lavinia's half-sister Sarah came to stay that month, 'a tall plain girl of nearly 14, extremely clever and docile in her pretty obedience to the oldies' and destined in due course to be the first organizing secretary of the LMHS and chairwoman of Bishop Creighton House (BCH).

The Bensons were her next guests at Keble, involving their hostess in 'a great luncheon at All Souls, after which the Archbishop was DCLd in the Theatre amid acclamation'. Lavinia found that Mrs Benson was 'keener than keen over the women's question and attacks everyone right and left . . . the Archbishop far brighter than when we were at Addington. . . . I went to the station to see them off after a very bright little visit.' It was followed by 'a few more hectic days canvassing on the women; hopes and fears alternating, during which the Bishop of Exeter and his wife came to stay on 27 April for the Bampton lecture; he must weigh 15 stone and is a very big man altogether, sometimes reminds me of Uncle W'; then directly they left 'Mr Moberly came to vote the right way.'

'The voting is over and in Convocation of nearly 800 MAs the majority in favour of the Statute was 143. Intense relief' was Lavinia's jubilant entry for Tuesday 29 April. And it was perhaps not surprising that at a dinner party in the evening at University College there was 'much cackle over the women'. Thus a month after Oxford House was conceived and Toynbee Hall named, classical and mathematical moderations and the Final School of Modern History and Science were now open to women. But not until 1890 were they allowed to take all final honours schools of the BA course at Oxford. Cambridge was even more dilatory.

On 4 May 1884 Lavinia, up in London again,

> came straight to St Paul's to go thence with E and Mr Campion to Bethnal Green (St Andrew's parish) where the Oxford Settlement is to be. After walking down Whitechapel a long way, turned left and at Bethnal Green station met Mr Knight Bruce, who showed us [the] church, empty schoolroom and all the capabilities. It is excellent in many ways, perhaps too close to the church and vicarage for quite

> the right independence, and too close I think to Mr Barnett and Whitechapel. District crammed with people but it is wide and airy and not like the hideous squalor of Soho, etc.

Later that month, after spending some time at the British Museum, they went by underground to Whitechapel where another of Henrietta Barnett's picture exhibitions had recently opened.

> Found ourselves there at last – went to the church service, or rather, music, all seats bright red, pots of lilies on the altar. Mr Barnett appeared and his nice curate Mr Gardiner and took us into the Exhibition. A very striking sight, heaps of *really* poor and a very fine set of pictures. About 35,000 will have thronged there. Liked Mr B – his wife very indifferently – not sure she isn't affected. Mr Gardiner very nice. All three *very* modern. Spent an hour with them in the Rectory. Discussed fully all *our* E and Mission scheme, and what Mr B fears over it. Felt the atmosphere clearer in consequence.

But, as his wife recorded, the vicar of St Jude's 'could not help minding when the followers, if not the leaders, of the Church party tried to influence earnest men, who had arranged to come to Toynbee, to withdraw and join the religious Settlement'. And the Barnetts' offspring, which never acquired a ladies' branch other than Henrietta herself, was to be listed as 'irreligious' up to the start of the First World War.

During a visit to Ireland in September the Talbots drove from Vice Regal Lodge to where in the Phoenix Park the roads divide 'and then [we went] on foot to the spot which has been before me all these weeks. *How could they?* We stood reverently by the wooden cross. Came away ... as if a great shadow over us.' Travelling home via Chester they called in at Hawarden where 'Uncle W and E had a fine franchise and House of Lords talk' and she had 'talks with Mary and Helen on Girton matters and Lucy'.

Though the autumn term, busy as usual, was overcast by illness, accounts of entertaining include such entries as 'Miss Wordsworth dined here and was most pleasant.' Ruskin had tea at Keble on 7 December after a visit to LMH. He had already been to Somerville and, as Miss Wordsworth wrote to her sister, 'We were all very jealous. However, Maggie Benson caught him at the School of Art and made him promise to come.' Ruskin enjoyed the occasion, writing afterwards to the principal, 'I was so lifted up and carried off both my head and my feet last night, that today I venture to ask place on the Library shelves for all the books I've written that I'm proud of.' And he also sent some volumes by Maria Edgeworth, little knowing that her three Butler great nieces were to play an important part in the life of both the hall and its settlement.

'Sweet May', the Talbot's eldest child, had her ninth birthday that term, and she, with her two young brothers and baby sister, took up much of their mother's time. Moreover, by the end of term 'E is tired and longing for silence and books.' The long illness that was to haunt him for three and a half years had already started, and for her it meant constant anxiety as she nursed her husband through it.

However, before the end of 1884 they were able to visit the newly started Oxford House in Bethnal Green. It was

> most interesting and wonderful to see the devoted work there. E preached in St Andrew's, quite a congregation who have to be told where the collects and prayers are, and sing delightfully like street singers. They want men, women, books, pianos, woodwork, clubs, houses, rooms, *everything*. Stopped at Lucy's who has had a grand and beautiful time at the Mission in the East End, and has never looked so much herself.

The great feature that term had been the start of Pusey House and Mr Gore's lectures. And although 'the knee threatens to come to some real mischief', her husband was more comfortable, 'and by moving from his bed onto a couch in the morning room, was able to see something of the East Enders while they were in Oxford'.

It was clearly no time to enlist the warden's help in a new project for women. Then, early in 1887 Edith Langridge talked with

Eleanor Benson and Mary Talbot about starting an LMH settlement at the time that the scheme for the WUS was being put forward, 'and we concluded that joining in that need not do away with our cherished hopes of having an LMH and definitely Church settlement later, provided that, knowing also clearly about our hope in that direction, the other colleges still wished us to share in the united project.' And this of course they did.

Lavinia meanwhile was keeping life at Keble as near normal as possible despite a house full of guests during April 1887, including Miss Yonge and Dr Bright, 'who flirted like anything', and delegates to a university extension scheme conference, when 'E kept quiet'.

The Oxford Mission to Calcutta was now competing with London's East End for support in Oxford among both senior and junior members of the university. Miss Milman, sister of the Bishop of Calcutta, was treasurer for LMH, and close links were to develop between the Oxford Mission and the LMHS. 'A big Calcutta Mission of ladies was held in our drawing room with great success, Mr Gore speaking so well,' wrote Lavinia on 18 November 1887. And the next week she was again in London selling at a bazaar for the mission which was opened by the Princess Christian.

Lavinia also kept an eye on progress in Bethnal Green. Thus in December 1887, she went with Lucy

> to dine at the Oxford House and see the Clubs. Very interesting. Messrs Sewell and Campion to the fore mostly, also Messrs Eye and Laing. At the House itself things might be more comfortable and will hope be made so by Mr Henson. Saw four or five Clubs and sang at a very smoky one to unkempt but civil men. Liked the whole thing.

The warden, however, was able to go up with her in February 1888 to the opening of a

> great Club at Bethnal Green. At the Oxford House found many worthy clergymen and laymen, and the luncheon just over. Mr Henson has improved the comfort of the house

> amazingly. The Archbishop came and we all streamed off to another parish close by the Museum where the new Club is – a huge Hall splendidly adapted and built. Ed was in the Chair. Hall full. E spoke excellently – so did the Archbishop who was well received, and much more at the end than at the beginning of his speech. T'others were mighty dull. The Hall is next to the lovely house of the Buchanans (a tea merchant come to live in GB) with a ballroom, lecture room etc.

This house, overlooking Victoria Park Square and the London Museum for Children, was soon to become well known to the LBOH. 'The only wretched misfortune was that E had his glorious old watch stolen – picked right off. The repeater his father was given by the GWR as a thanks for his great services. A real life long trouble in its way.' However, on 19 February, her husband's forty-fourth birthday, 'the dear Dons here *and* the undergrads separately have decided to give E another watch. He is so pleased.' She felt at this time 'there was much to be thankful for – but still there is anxiety – and then the mist over the future'. On Palm Sunday Mr Balfour came to stay.

> Three years ago he was here reading poetry to E in his fever and weakness – and how many Palm Sundays before! He has gained confidence and hopes to a great extent as to Ireland, and feels he can win if he has time. He declares two-thirds of the police stories and such are fabrications. Mary Ward has brought out a new novel, *Robert Elsmere*, dedicated to T. H. Green and darling Laura. A philosophical Unitarian story I gather.

Laura Tennant, wife of Lavinia's brother Alfred Lyttelton, had died on Christmas Eve 1886. The book, which caused a sensation not only in settlement circles, was to be reviewed at length by Gladstone.

By October 1888 it was settled that the warden of Keble should become vicar of Leeds. After a final meeting at LMH in December, and a dinner with Miss Wordsworth and her vice-principal Miss

Argles, shortly to become head of the WUS, the Talbots bid farewell to their university friends. They moved to Leeds the following March and later on Lavinia gave as a main reason for her devotion to the LMHS the link it provided with the life she had loved in Oxford. And here she was not alone.

Part II
Some Settlers, Social Work and Training

5

Blackfriars Women's University Settlement in Southwark

Three years after Oxford had launched both Toynbee Hall and Oxford House, the first women's settlement emanated from Cambridge. The ground there had been well prepared by the Talbots and Barnetts, though when describing the difficulties surmounted and 'the settlement's splendid work which has been for many years a household word' Henrietta added, 'With all this Mr Barnett had nothing to do except – and it is a large exception – the inexhaustible sustenance of his sympathy for whatever I was caring about.'

Cambridge had heard about the settlement idea six months before it reached Oxford. And in July 1853 the vicar of St Jude's took the first party of 150 excursionists from Whitechapel to Cambridge, the visitors including Beatrice Potter and her sister Katherine Courtney whose husband was a senior fellow at St John's. But when in May 1886 the vicar spoke to undergraduates at Trinity College about starting a settlement, Henrietta commented, 'The meeting was large and took, I think, the proposition well. There was, however, an absence of Oxford enthusiasm, and there were but few questions.' The Barnetts stayed with the Montagu Butlers and next day lunched with Miss Clough at Newnham. 'We are delighted with her. She is old, but evidently still in the box and driving. The girls seemed intelligent and proud of rooms full of knick-knacks. Miss Gladstone was there and we had a long talk. Mrs Sidgwick was the finest of the lot.' The writer added that 'One of the new lady guardians caught me but she won't succeed, she is too earnest.'

Soon afterwards the women's settlement movement embarked on life under the umbrella of the Ladies' Discussion Society, recently formed in Cambridge to spread interest in social work and related subjects to speakers directly involved. Henrietta was one of two guests asked to address its second meeting. Miss Clough, when inviting her on 15 February 1887 to stay at Newnham, wrote, 'Mrs Marshall and I think that if our students are interested in what you tell them of Toynbee Hall, a separate house might be set up in a poor neighbourhood, and some of our students might join in the work. Mrs Sidgwick would favour a scheme of this kind.' The possibility that it offered of careers for her students was a main attraction here for the wife of the so-called 'Father of Newnham'. That night

> the weather was awful, foggy and cold, so as Miss Clough could not go out to the evening meeting she asked me to read to her my paper. Alone in her room I read it to her and I can see her now with her white hair, penetrating dark eyes and rather forbidden mien, listening to every word. When I finished she leant forward and, to my astonishment, kissed me and said 'God bless you, dear, and all your hopes.' I have rarely received a blessing I value more.

After Henrietta had read her paper again a few hours later to an audience that included Blanche Athene Clough (about to become secretary to her Aunt Jemima and already vice-principal and tutor in charge of Clough Hall), Katherine Stephen (another future Newnham principal) and about 20 students, a second paper was contributed by Alice Cruner. This qualified teacher, formerly a student at Newnham, described an experiment she was making in south London based on a house she had taken there and for which she needed financial support. Both papers roused considerable interest and the speakers agreed to have an informal meeting next day with anyone keen to hear more.

Henrietta then developed the settlement idea at some length and, after promises of donations and subscriptions had been recorded and it was clear that no immediate action on a large scale would be financially viable, Miss Cruner's enterprise was put forward with her consent as a basis on which to build. Girton was consulted and before the end of the Lent term a further meeting was held at Newnham. A joint committee of ten was then formed, the Girton members being Miss Ward (vice-mistress of Girton, later Mrs Claud Montefiore), Miss Gavin (later headmistress of Notting Hill High School), Miss Lowndes, Miss Latham (later principal of St Mary's College, Paddington) and Miss Best. The Newnham representatives were Miss B. A. Clough, Miss Katharine Stephen, Miss Tuke, then a resident lecturer, Miss M. Gardiner, later headmistress of St Felix School, Southwold, and Miss M. Powell.

The joint committee met twice a week during the summer term when Henrietta Barnett helped to formulate the objects of the settlement as subsequently stated in its memorandum of association: 'To promote the welfare of the people of the poorer districts of London and especially of the women and children, by devising and promoting schemes which tend to elevate them physically, intellectually and morally, and by giving them additional opportunities for education and recreation.' Clearly those at the university could not themselves take an active part except by raising money, electing representatives onto the executive committee and rousing interest among students.

The first executive of seven was composed of two representatives from Girton (one former and one present student), two from Newnham, two from LMH and Somerville (Oxford having by then agreed to join the scheme), and Octavia Hill who joined the first general meeting. A joint association of Oxford and Cambridge colleges supporting the project approached various London colleges, including the London School of Medicine for Women and University College, which replied favourably as a first step towards joining, by which time energetic Miss Gruner had already taken further action. She would certainly have been pleased by Helen Bosanquet's somewhat misleading statement in her *History of the COS*, published in 1912, that 'the Women's University Settlement was founded by Miss Gruner.'

On 27 June 1887 she met four Cambridge friends in London, at 48 Mall Chambers, and talked about the origin and progress of the scheme before 'stating the conditions under which she was willing to accept the position of head worker'. These included the provision of paid secretarial help, but unfortunately, as it turned out, no steps were taken in this direction for over a year.

The other women – Mrs Bradby, a Girtonian then living at St Katharine's Dock House in the East End and subsequently for many years a pillar of the settlement, Mrs Carmichael, Miss Gardiner and Miss Frances Gray, high mistress of St Paul's Girls' School – thanked Miss Gruner 'for the harassing and protracted work she had already done, expressed their entire satisfaction in her and unanimously ratified her appointment'. It was decided that subscribers should be asked to guarantee support for three years, and Miss Gruner was to keep control for the time being of money already entrusted to her.

Eleanor Benson, the archbishop's elder daughter, was now asked if she would serve on a subcommittee to run the house. She lived conveniently near, having left Oxford in 1883 (after only two years at LMH) when the family moved from Truro to Lambeth Palace. A brilliant classicist and in many ways the most normal member of the family, she threw herself wholeheartedly into making the settlement a success. Constance Elder, a Newnham friend of Miss Gruner who had just returned from abroad, was also lined up, together with Miss Gray.

Further LMH involvement came in November when Edith Argles asked to stay for eight weeks early in 1888. She had been one of the original intake at the hall and was by then its first fellow and vice-principal. Miss Wordsworth sent parcels of clothing and an LMH chapel collection, no doubt approving Mrs Bradby's suggestion in April 'that the following be added to the suggestions of work – Sunday school classes, Bible classes, religious teaching of any kind in connection with the churches and chapels in the neighbourhood'. In May, another LMH supporter, Edith Langridge, came to stay for a week to help during the resident's temporary absence.

MABYS was the first charity to ask the new settlement for help. In August 1887, when the committee met at Miss Elder's home,

Campden House Kensington, before the opening of 44 Nelson Square on 12 September, a letter was read from Miss Bonham-Carter, honorary secretary of MABYS, asking if one or two bedrooms could be reserved for one or two nights a week for ladies working in Southwark under that association, and also if such ladies could be provided with a midday meal. Not to appear discouraging, this was agreed conditionally, but university women would have priority. By the mid-1880s MABYS was placing over 5000 pauper girls in domestic service each year, about a quarter of the number coming out of the London poor law schools, some being not more than ten years old. Clearly someone must keep an eye on them, and the Barnardo Homes, the Waifs and Strays' Society and the Salvation Army were all concerned here.

By the end of October the settlement was collaborating also with the London Pupil Teachers' Association, the COS and the CCHF. Volunteers were also preparing themselves to work under Miss Argles for the Recreative Evening Classes Association and some began a course of training, starting a tradition that was to colour women's contribution to the settlement movement: a piano had been bought and the settlement library was in working order under Miss Elder, Mrs Henry Sidgwick being among those sending books from Cambridge.

Early educational work was directed mainly at local schools and the school board authorities soon granted free use of the local schoolroom for children's entertainments. Three reading parties, debating and music clubs and dancing classes had been started for pupil teachers; expeditions had been made to the National Gallery; an invitation to a party in Kensington had been received from Mrs Rathbone, secretary of the Chelsea branch of the Pupil Teachers' Association; Miss Gifford had been nominated as a school board manager; and help had been provided at the Pocock Street schools nearby.

Moreover, Miss Argles had given seven lantern lectures for the Girls' Friendly Society (GFS); many cases had been undertaken for the COS; five workers were helping with MABYS; over 500 children had received some special treat during the Christmas holidays; and a mothers' club had been started in the New Cut, just across the main Blackfriars road from Nelson Square.

If such activity hardly measured up to Toynbee Hall ambitions of becoming a university in the East End, the Oxford and Cambridge women were certainly welcomed to the neighbourhood. Mrs Alfred Marshall presided at the settlement's first AGM, held in June 1888 at the Temperance Hall in Blackfriars, when over 80 members attended as well as the full committee. As Mary Paley, then 'a tall pretty girl', she had unofficially taken honours in the Cambridge moral science tripos in 1874, the candidates being watched over by Dr Kennedy, Regius professor of Greek, in his own drawing room while friendly tutors, including Henry Sidgwick, 'ran to and fro with our papers'. Two years later, and by then a young lecturer for Professor Marshall, she and a friend had daringly gone up to London for the night to attend the wedding of 'their beloved Mr Sidgwick' to Nora Balfour, whose friendship Mary was to enjoy for over 50 years. During her speech at the AGM she quoted Charles Booth's book, which had put Southwark (if not joined with Newington) in the second poorest class, with Whitechapel. Various papers were then read and Miss Gruner spoke on the general work and answered questions. As there were then only four resident volunteers to cope with nine branches of work, more nonresidents were urgently needed and there was general regret that the settlement had to close during the summer when boarding schools were shut for three weeks, policy here being subsequently changed.

At a meeting later that week it was agreed that the printed report should be headed *Women's University Settlement for Work in the Poorer Districts of London.* Though 'WUS' soon became the accepted abbreviation, the settlement was referred to at this time as 'WUSS', stressing the connection with Southwark. In July 1888 Miss Bruce, a Cheltenham old girl who had gone on to Cambridge, came to stay for a month, one of several future heads of settlements who were to be trained at Nelson Square. In October Mrs Buss wrote from Shoreditch vicarage, Hoxton, asking for workers there, but none were available. Not until the following spring did Miss Beale tell Eleanor Benson that the Cheltenham Ladies' College Guild was thinking of starting its own settlement.

Octavia Hill, already a national personality on the housing front, now joined the scene at Nelson Square. After the ecclesiastical commissioners had handed over to her in December 1884 the management of their property in Southwark, the extent of the area involved gave her scope for more large-scale planning than had hitherto come her way, and most of her time was now spent in south London. She realized that the high value of London sites made it financially expedient to pull down cottages and replace them with blocks of flats, but after disposing of a disused warehouse, she created a garden on the site for tenants of the new blocks in Red Cross Street, and that they might have somewhere to meet indoors a hall was built after an appeal had been launched in *The Times*. The local authority was cooperative, but Octavia, wishing to keep control of the letting, collected enough money to endow the new building, she herself becoming one of the trustees, and Red Cross Hall was opened in June 1888 by the Archbishop of Canterbury.

Octavia's impression of her new neighbours, and the welcome she gave them in a part of London where she was herself so closely concerned, are clear from her letters. 'They are all very refined, highly cultivated (all I fancy have been at the universities) and very young. They are so sweet and humble and keen to learn about the things out of their ordinary line of experience. I much delight in thinking one may link their young life with the house and hall and garden in Southwark.' And taking the initiative here, early in October 1888 she wrote to the head worker at No. 44 enclosing tickets for a performance of *The Pilgrim's Progress* at Red Cross Hall and inviting her to undertake the management of a group of houses containing about 30 dwellings: 'the time occupied would be 12.00 to 2.00 on Thursdays.' But when Miss Gruner reported to her committee that she had agreed to the proposal 'and they were at liberty if they wished to accept it as settlement work', the accent of independence preceded a crisis.

By 26 November the committee members were having to deal with a long and bitter complaint from an overworked head reacting to criticism about Miss Gruner's 'abrupt manners and the way she made life at the settlement unnecessarily depressing'. Her problems were considerable. She was already secretary of the Southwark branch of the Pupil Teachers' Association, manager of a group of board schools, organizer of an independent CCHF fund, and now a house property manager for Miss Hill. To help her she had only two long-stay residents, most of them coming for only two or three weeks at a time, and was herself housekeeper and general secretary, responsible for the health, supervision and training of all at the settlement. She was working till 11.00 p.m. most nights and often till 1.00 a.m., while on Saturdays she was often hard at it for 15 or 16 hours, partly because ten sets of accounts had to be kept, involving 18 books, five of them concerned with the pupil teachers. She had indeed one resident maid-of-all-work, but was clearly herself another. No doubt the committee should have shown more imagination, but it was a situation unfortunately only too likely to occur at a residential settlement with little money behind it.

Faced with this quite unexpected outburst, five of the committee, which by now included as the Newnham representative Margaret Sewell, honorary secretary of the COS, met at Mrs Bradby's house and afterwards a letter was sent to Miss Gruner referring to 'the terrible strain you have had to bear'. However, she insisted on resigning and, though refused permission to return the £50 given her for expenses, continued to attend committee meetings until 17 March 1889, when Miss Elder left with her. There was a considerable stir in Cambridge circles, but the crisis was weathered. The lease of No. 44, which had been taken in Miss Gruner's name, was transferred to Miss Sewell, and Miss Benson was given a mandate to go ahead with her suggestion that the settlement be incorporated under the Companies Act, following the example of Toynbee Hall. With help from Lord Thring, this was arranged by 22 March 1890.

Miss Benson, besides acting as treasurer and undertaking to cope with the income tax papers, also chaired several meetings during the difficult months when a search was being made for a new head worker. When, on 25 March 1889 during a meeting held at 21 Cleveland Gardens, Miss Sewell reported Octavia Hill's keen interest in the settlement and her offer to appoint a worker there as rent collector with a salary of £40 if a suitable one could be found, a delighted committee responded by asking the new supporter to join them and also if there were any chance of her becoming head worker. However, Miss Hill replied cautiously that she could not at present undertake any closer connection than as a member of the executive. Her impact there was immediate.

When she attended her first committee meeting on 27 April 1889 it was agreed that Constance Bartlett, a senior member of LMH who gave the Benson sisters as her referees, should work under her while living at No. 44. It was a wise appointment and for the next 17 years Miss Bartlett remained at the settlement, becoming responsible for the management of the whole of Octavia Hill's property in Southwark. Combining outstanding practical ability with a sympathetic approach to her tenants, she proved a steady and reliable helper, not only in practical matters such as troublesome drains but also in solving personal problems. Her memory was long cherished after she retired to the country in 1907 for health reasons. Octavia Hill, meanwhile, served on the executive committee for 11 consecutive years and again from 1903 to 1906. Several of its meetings were held at her house in Nottingham Place, and her influence and experience proved invaluable to the young settlers.

In the search for a head worker, Miss Benson wrote to Mrs Arnold Toynbee and Mrs T. H. Green, both now living as widows in Oxford, but neither was prepared to leave home. When Edith Langridge, who had taken on the responsibility of treasurer of a new MABYS lodging house as well as running a woodcarving class for boys, and Marion Bruce, soon to move to Bethnal Green, also proved unwilling to accept even temporary responsibility, the job fell for a few weeks to Miss Tuke, who had family links with the Trinity Mission in Camberwell and was also prepared to take on housing work accepted for Octavia Hill in Dyers' Buildings. It was not until June 1889, just before the AGM, that an executive chairwoman, Eleanor Benson, was able to tell the committee that Edith Argles of LMH had accepted the post of head, at least for a year, and would be coming at the end of September. She also gave the good news that Miss Spooner would act as temporary head if required for the late summer months, an offer eagerly accepted, particularly as Dr Spooner of New College was already closely identified with LMH.

News of WUS had by now reached the USA. Margaret Sewell reported in May 1889 that Miss Coman of Wellesley College,

Boston had applied to come for a fortnight to get information that might be useful to a settlement then being organized in the USA. Though No. 44 was full and the visitor could only be invited to take lodgings in the square while boarding at the settlement, five months later an account arrived there of the opening of the university settlement in New York. Meanwhile, Miss Sewell had been asked to address a meeting of London University students who were considering whether they should join. Then Octavia Hill agreed that the AGM in 1889 should be held in her Red Cross Hall.

Soon the volunteers in Nelson Square suffered what Miss Sewell described as 'a great and irreparable disaster' with the death in October 1890 of Eleanor Benson. Unsparing of herself in local social work among slum dwellers in Southwark and Lambeth, her memorial was to emphasize the growing voluntary commitment to public health projects, including the improvement of sanitation and of medical and nursing services for the borough.

As other agencies were already in the field here, WUS played only a subsidiary role, but in 1892 a notable contribution was to be made when, in collaboration with the metropolitan and national nursing associations, a home for district nurses was established in St George's Road in her memory. Meanwhile, her sister Maggie was elected as LMH representative on the WUS committee, Mrs Benson being co-opted soon afterwards. The growth of specialization and the rise of the salaried worker were now at hand. A policy of working wherever possible with public authorities or established philanthropic societies meant that the settlement worker was trained in business methods. By the end of 1890 the departmental idea was established at this settlement when Octavia Hill persuaded the executive committee to pay £50 a year to a worker supervising the house-to-house collection of savings. Soon the WUS executive was represented on various departmental committees, largely for financial reasons, and by 1912 modest salaries were to be paid to nearly half of the settlement's nine heads of departments. By then it was widely acknowledged that 'the growth of a permanent body of those who organize tends to draw in fresh recruits and enlarges the field of this employment.' Meanwhile, amateur helpers grew in numbers and a few substantial bequests kept settlement finances in balance.

Octavia Hill now made another valuable contribution. Following the resignation of Edith Argles in 1891 as head worker, for the second time she refused the post herself but suggested that Margaret Sewell, elected chairwoman in 1889, should take it on. So Miss Sewell now became head worker at the settlement, a post she was to fill with honour for nine eventful years until ill health forced her resignation in 1900. However, she stayed on the committee and resumed the chair in 1901, retiring eventually in 1934 only three years before her death.

Her friendship with Octavia Hill added much to local life in the pioneering days. They shared a love of natural beauty and the countryside, the new head of the settlement proving a generous supporter of the National Trust, and both felt strongly about the need for training of all social workers whether voluntary or professional. Thus Octavia wrote of the settlement in 1892: 'I look upon it not only as a great added strength to my management of houses in Southwark but still more as a promising centre for that training of workers to which must be devoted so much of the energies of those who would see wiser methods of work among the poor prevail.'

Margaret Sewell was already a distinguished figure when she took up the new job:

> tall, commanding, gracious and a born leader. Unlike many of her generation she welcomed with open arms modern changes in method and outlook. She was one of the first to discern the great possibilities for good in an alliance between the statutory social services which were taking shape and the voluntary personal effort of which she was a staunch supporter.

And, as Elizabeth Macadam, a Pfeiffer scholar, added: 'Those of us who were privileged to come under the influence in the late nineties were fortunate indeed.'

Miss Sewell was soon spreading further afield her ideas on training. In a paper read at the Bristol conference of women workers in 1892 she emphasized that 'for effectual work vigour and knowledge seem to me of special importance' and 'to enjoy work one must not overdo it. Holidays are essential.' Poor Miss Gruner had clearly proved this point in Nelson Square. 'As for special knowledge, one must understand the working of the Poor Law, the School Board, the County Council and the Vestry, all of which bear directly on the life of the poor. My experience is that the ordinary visitor practically ignores the existence of all these.' Besides some grasp of voluntary charitable organizations, 'a great deal of local knowledge is also needed for good work, knowledge of local clubs and charities as well as of what people are already doing for themselves, for example in Friendly and Trade Societies.' She added that 'I do not speak of better things still, of Faith, Hope and Charity, because all agree that these are the very root and spring of good work.'

Red Cross Hall had by now been made available for four lectures on Friday evenings by Bernard Bosanquet and it was no surprise to the WUS committee, when Miss Hill chaired its meeting on 9 December 1892, to hear that she had been asked to write on 'Training of Workers' in the next issue of *The Nineteenth Century*. Then, early in the new year, she asked if an assistant housekeeper could be appointed to free Miss Sewell to help the settlement 'in ways in which it would be impossible to replace her', and one started work in February who was prepared to give service in return for board and lodging. The training initiative now quickly got off the ground on a broad front. After the head worker had been asked to get in touch with possible lecturers and draw up a prospectus for a training course, to be sent to all members, colleges, the *COS Review* and elsewhere, Miss Sewell gave two lectures, at 4.00 p.m. on Thursdays, as an introduction to the course. Octavia Hill lectured in March and Bernard Bosanquet promised two informal talks on 'The Duties of a Citizen', starting what was to be a major preoccupation of settlements as they came to stress community work in the postwar years.

Another women's settlement had by now started in Bethnal Green, whose workers were able to draw on experience gleaned in Blackfriars. The Honourable Meriel Talbot, a CCHF enthusiast in Nelson Square, went off in February 1891 to become honorary secretary to the LBOH committee, of which her mother was chairwoman, working from Mayfield House. However, she was back again at Nelson Square the following month to learn, on one day a week, about MABYS's work and something of house management, taking on Miss Sewell's responsibilities here in Williams Place. Then Miss Jourdain of St Hugh's College at Oxford, also soon to be involved in Bethnal Green, came as a resident for a few days at this time, St Hugh's applying to join WUS in June 1892. Moreover, several schools, including the South Hampstead High School, were already giving their support, chiefly in providing entertainments at Christmas. Fees for rooms were now raised to 16/– for a front room, or £1 if only part-time work was given.

As the settlement widened its borders under Miss Sewell's leadership, 'she presided over a process by which one house grew into several and the several were compounded into one; new branches of work have been started and old ones developed; the numbers of workers both resident and non-resident have swelled in amazing fashion and the feature of training for social work has become a characteristic of our settlement.' Miss Sewell welcomed particularly Octavia Hill's close interest in the settlement's own housing problems and her offer to lend offices at No. 35 to the settlement; also, several WUS committee meetings were held at the Hill's house. Negotiations with trustees and existing leaseholders of Nos. 44, 45 and 46 opened early in 1894 and that April, when it had been decided to take the freeholds of these three houses, purchase money was provided by debentures of £100 each, the agreement being signed by Octavia Hill. She also signed the receipt on 7 December 1894 for £250 received from the Pfeiffer bequest, a windfall already allocated for repair work on No. 45.

News of the bequest for women's work made by a benefactor of Newnham College, Mrs Emily Pfeiffer, author of a book on *Women and Work*, had reached the settlement through Miss Ewart, one of its 'ordinary' as distinct from 'college' members. However, it was not until nearly two years later that Eleanor Powell, by then chairwoman, heard of the grant of £2500, to be spent 'for the endowment of scholarships, studentships, fellowships or lectureships under the title of which the name of Pfeiffer should be associated . . . and the erection of buildings with which the name of Pfeiffer shall be permanently connected'.

The title deeds for the purchase of No. 44 were in Mr Cobb's strongroom by February 1895, Mrs Sidgwick and Miss Powell being co-signatories with the solicitor for a further £520 payable under the bequest. Then, in April that year he wrote, 'I think the plan you propose of calling the house "Pfeiffer House" and placing the inscription at the entrance hall will be sufficient compliance with the terms of the Trust.' The plaque is still there. The major part of the grant went to endow the Pfeiffer scholarships at the WUS, which were to consolidate its reputation as a leader in social work training. Early beneficiaries included Minnie Sharpley, sister of Mrs Sidgwick, devoted secretary at Newnham and soon to be deputy warden at WUS.

As the settlement approached the end of its first decade, its work still followed the lines laid down in Miss Gruner's day, with some pioneering, much emphasis on cooperation with established agencies, including the London School Board, the COS, ICAA and MABYS, and with one settlement member accepting responsibility for each branch of work. There was also as much movement as heretofore among those staying in Nelson Square, nine of the 31 residents during 1896 being collegiates and the others including three Americans.

The settlement's rules were now broadened so that more honorary members of the association might be elected without pledging themselves to any direct work, these including Mrs Sidgwick (representing colleges) and Charles Loch (the COS), Mrs Arthur Johnson of Oxford, secretary of the Association for the Education of Women (AEW), Miss Swanwick and Canon Scott Holland. Thus valuable guidance was provided by onlookers, including men.

Then, in 1896, important developments took place on the training front. A Joint Committee for Lectures was set up on which the NUWW (represented by Mrs Creighton and Miss James) collaborated with the COS (Bernard Bosanquet and Charles Loch) and the WUSS (Miss C. E. Collett of London University and Miss Powell as honorary treasurer) to give lectures on charitable and social work both centrally, at the Portman Rooms in Baker Street, and locally, as occasion arose. Helen Bosanquet was also involved here and Minnie Sharpley was appointed as salaried lecturer. The lectures were immediately crowded out and the *25th COS Annual Report 1895* (published in March 1897) emphasized that this was the first organized attempt to train social workers generally in the field, placing an emphasis upon teaching theoretical methods, combined with practical work in agencies. It also stressed the collaboration of WUSS with the NUWW and the COS.

However, the COS, not satisfied with these arrangements and spurred on by one of its district workers, Mrs Dunn Gardner of Lambeth who had earlier written a paper on social work training, in June 1897 set up its own special committee on training composed of six men and two women, Margaret Sewell and Marion Bruce, and a statement was soon issued that the committee 'believe that the Society as a training society is as yet in its infancy and that it is capable of almost boundless development. They would like to see in the society the nucleus of a future university for the study of social science, in which all those who undertake philanthropic work should desire to graduate.'

These ambitions of the COS, voiced particularly by Charles Loch and E. T. Urwick, led to the dissolution of the Joint Committee for Lectures in 1901, mainly because the WUSS's articles of association confined its work to London. That this sequel had not been anticipated is suggested by a statement in the *33rd Annual Report of the COS* that 'it was with the greatest regret that the Joint Committee found itself obliged to accept this decision as final and acquiesce in the loss of the help of the body to which the lecture scheme owed its origin.' The connection with the NUWW was severed at the same time. However, the COS committee on training, still including its two women members, was now reconstituted as the more prestigious 'committee on social education'.

Mrs Creighton had her own perspective on the matter. In 1894, when taking the chair at the annual meeting of the settlement, she had spoken of its importance as a centre for teaching and training, and suggested that 'the experience gained ... might be profitably transmitted by means of lectures and leaflets throughout the provinces'. Her husband was then Bishop of Peterborough and, 'as a resident in the provinces, she had felt what might be done by those who had the opportunity of being abreast with new movements and inspired by new ideas, if only they would not confine their work to London'. By 1895 the NUWW had been founded under her presidency. However, no one was likely to dispute the statement on social work training made in 1925 by Elizabeth Macadam, a Pfeiffer student at WUSS before her appointment as warden of the Victoria Settlement in Liverpool, that 'the movement began, in this country at least, in the classes organized by Miss Sewell for workers at the university settlement of which she was then warden and with which she is still associated.' Miss Sewell had in the meanwhile been to the USA and Canada.

WUS had early directed its educational work in the community to local schools. Then, in 1893, it started the Acland Mixed Club for boys and girls, hoping to attract to evening classes the rougher children among school leavers. It was called after Sir Francis Acland, Minister of the Crown responsible for including evening institutes in the national scheme for education. The curriculum was made as practical as possible and included hand work, drill, recitation and music classes, as well as ordinary school subjects, games and swimming.

In 1896 this mixed club, with about even numbers of boys and girls, received a government grant of £26. It was highly successful and many developments over the years included the Acland Women's Club, which eventually linked up with St Mary's Girls' Club, and buying two houses in Nelson Square for which the settlement was trustee.

Work for sick children, begun soon after the settlement started, was helped forward in 1889 when contact was established with the central organization of the Invalid Children's Aid Association (ICAA). Seven years later this work was recognized as a north Southwark branch of the parent society, which in 1927 amalgamated with the south Southwark branch of the association. The aim of the association, which is primarily to help doctors and hospitals by seeing that the prescribed treatment is carried out, provided scope for considerable numbers of volunteers and particularly for those prepared to hold classes for invalid children.

WUS was also a pioneer in seeking employment for these children. A crippled boot-making shop was started in 1896; and some years later evolved into St Crispin's workshop. Housed in premises on the Southwark Bridge Road, this lasted until 1921 when the boys were transferred to the British Red Cross Society (BRCS) to complete their training in a world which by then fully recognized the need here. Moreover, a registry, begun to help invalid children, was to develop into the settlement's influential registry and apprenticeship department, set up in 1902.

Helen Gladstone, the prime minister's daughter, was warden in Nelson Square from 1901 to the autumn of 1906. She had already given much encouragement to the work there while vice-principal of Newnham, but left Cambridge in 1896 to be with her father, whose life was then drawing to an end. She took on the new responsibilities when Margaret Sewell returned as chairwoman and had the support for several years of Octavia Hill. It was a strong team, though Miss Gladstone was often abroad. Later a block of flats in a modernized Nelson Square would be named after her, as well as a room in Bishop Creighton House (BCH). Miss Sharpley (who had already proved her ability as lecturer, then as deputy head) succeeded Miss Gladstone, and for the next five years there was further collaboration in training matters with Octavia Hill.

Octavia Hill died on 13 August 1923, 25 years after she had helped to start the settlement, and there were many of its workers among the crowds who thronged into the cathedral church at St Saviour's, Southwark, to hear Canon Rawnsley give his memorial address on 'The Power of Personal Service'. The preacher had known her for nearly 40 years, 'from the time when as a young layman in a London slum, I helped her colleague Miss Cons, as a rent collector, until the last day when I saw her in the committee room of the National Trust'.

He quoted Canon Barnett's words that 'all help must be co-operative. Helper and the helped must be partners', and Ruskin figures largely in the address, which included the Archbishop of York's statement that 'I have always had the deepest veneration for her character and work' and a similar one from the Archbishop of Canterbury.

Two years later the outbreak of the First World War found the settlement geared to make a valuable contribution to the welfare of women and children in Southwark, particularly through its CCHF work. This was pursued with vigour through the next four years, as well as infant welfare and other long-term commitments.

Though the first public appeal for the settlement, launched in 1912, was abandoned in 1914, £4000 had by then been raised. This sum, with several generous gifts and legacies, enabled the settlement to carry on until 1925, when the fourth house, 47 Nelson Square, was bought.

6

From Cheltenham and Oxford to London's East End

The pioneering educationist Dorothea Beale had just completed 25 years as head of Cheltenham Ladies' College when Oxford undergraduates first heard of proposed settlements in London's East End. During her 'silver wedding' celebrations held at the college in July 1883 she suggested the formation of a 'Union of Workers with the primary object of strengthening each others' hands whether they ever met or not'. Emma Patterson and others were then much loved with the women's trade union movement, though the birth of the non-political NUWW, of particular concern to the settlement pioneers, lay still 12 years ahead. The Cheltenham Ladies' College Guild, based on the principles of cooperation, culture and service, took shape during 1884, Chaucer's modest 'dayes-eye' gazing steadfastly on high being chosen as its emblem. The image of the daisy chain appealed to many besides the Bishop of Sydney, who preached at the college that year on 'working together and working together with God', and Ruskin, who was entertained there shortly afterwards before giving 64 books to its library.

The guild's president was herself a product of Queen's College, Harley Street. 'I think the foundation of Queen's College in 1848 was an era memorable in the history of our country,' she was later to tell settlement workers. 'It was by earnest, deeply religious thinkers and believers – Maurice, Kingsley, Plumtree, with the sympathy of Tennyson and other like-minded [people] – that the foundation of the first college for women was laid. It was there as the first lady Mathematics Tutor I went through seven years' apprenticeship in teaching.' She had then gone on to Bedford College before taking charge of the first proprietary school for girls, founded in 1853 as the Cheltenham College for Young Ladies. And emphasizing the value of education as an equipment for social services she asked: 'How can girls be prepared for such work as falls to them as heads of great schools, and hospitals and settlements, as doctors in foreign lands, if their education was, as I found it, minus mathematics and science, and concluded at 17 or earlier?' Something had to be done, but the country's need was still for women 'thoughtful, disciplined and self-controlled, with the confidence and persistency of faith; not a few but a great army, to contend with the evils that are undermining the foundations of society'.

It was hardly surprising that when the guild held its first biennial meeting in 1886 its founder should talk about education. By then there were 50 professional teachers among its members and, in her view, 'the training of cultured ladies as teachers in elementary schools was work of incalculable importance in bridging over the separation of the classes.' Moreover, every board school should, she said, have evening classes connected with it. Guild members could help here and 'should do for the poor what some women have done for the daughters of the middle classes in bringing education and culture into their lives. . . . I want the Daisy Guild to feel that they have not really helped any unless they have called forth in them the desire to work for others.'

The vast majority of the 226 who had by then joined it had no paid job and she accepted this prevailing pattern of life, giving such encouragement as, 'It is wonderful what quite young girls can accomplish from their own home.' Many indeed were already involved with the GFS, the YWCA and MABYS as well as in hospitals and clubs. 'Evening Homes' for working girls had been opened in Nottingham in 1879, the Leeds Girls' Club, where one guild member was working, in 1881 and the Union of Girls' Clubs as recently as 1885.

Charitable work in connection with the college itself had begun in 1876 when Margaret Newman, one of a family closely connected with it, made plans to open a house nearby for students wishing to attend classes but unable to afford the normal fees, an initiative which led to the start there in 1887, as a memorial to her, of the first training college for teachers above elementary school standard; its name, St Hilda's, reflecting Miss Beale's admiration for the patron of learning and renowned abbess of Whitby.

Miss Beale, however, though later on keen to promote an elementary school staffed by her own pupils, at first vetoed any such corporate undertaking by the guild. Apart from other objections it would involve fund-raising which, with rare exceptions, was against the college tradition. Rather than spending money on 'some hazardous experiment', she thought that members would be better advised to give to charities already known to them. However, after a four-year build-up of opinion, at the biennial guild meeting of 1888 she fell in with the unanimous resolution to embark on some corporate work, though asking that her previous opposition should be recorded. Many suggestions for schemes were then circulated and a decision was reached the following spring that 'the Corporate Fund be devoted to starting and supporting a Mission in one of our large towns, the place to be decided by the vote of Guild members'.

Fortunately, Miss Strong, a music teacher and formerly a pupil at the college, who was soon to be head of the high school in Upper Baker Street, could give cogent reasons why the proposed venture should be in St John's parish in Bethnal Green. 'The vicar earnestly desires that the corporate work of the Guild benefit that parish. And besides being first in the field he is the son of Bishop Bromby, one of the prime movers in starting the school which has developed into our Ladies' College. Three of his daughters have been pupils there and two are Guild members.' One indeed was on the management committee. 'Active work has been going on in St John's and the neighbouring parishes for some years. The consequence is that the people are all aroused and anxious to be taught. They crowd into classes and meetings and there are not enough workers to satisfy their wants.'

Further reassurance came from May Wolseley-Lewis: 'I think

many know that if Bethnal Green is chosen, Miss Kate Newman has most generously offered to undertake the management of the work gratuitously, and also to pay her own expenses.' Besides being a member of the guild, she had been connected with the college for some time as a member of the council, was a trained nurse and 'having taken the direction of the District Nursing in Cheltenham, she has had experience of work among the poor'. Kate Newman was a younger sister of Margaret, who had recently died.

Miss Beale then read a paper written by the vicar describing St John's as 'a typical East End parish of the better sort. In a population of nearly 13,000 there are but few of the depraved and dangerous classes. It is a two-roomed and not a one-roomed parish.'

The main worry was now over finance. Though the guild's treasurer already had promises of subscriptions amounting to £112 for three years, 'it is impossible to begin under the most favourable circumstances with less than £150 or £200 guaranteed.' But help was at hand.

Financial problems were to be solved largely by admitting as residents certain members of the LBOH already at work in the nearby parish of St Andrew's. Kate Newman had moved into Mayfield House, the chosen residence overlooking Victoria Park Square in Bethnal Green, before it was formally opened on Saturday 29 October 1889, when several members of the LBOH were present.

Oxford House in the nearby parish of St Andrew's had been relying to some extent on women's help, especially on the domestic side. The Honourable Mrs Edward Talbot became involved here after her first visit to Bethnal Green in 1884 and now, within the year, three separate initiatives were taken on its behalf. The Revd A. Winnington Ingram, recently appointed head, was intent on rallying the support of academic wives, daughters, sisters and aunts to help, spurred on by his sister at Oxford and three of her friends who wanted to live in Bethnal Green and undertake work at Oxford House, 'which it is thought only women can do'. It was common knowledge that a ladies' branch was already supporting Cambridge men in their non-residential mission work south of the

Thames. Cambridge House and the nearby Talbot House in Southwark were not to start until 1896.

Another group of Oxford women, led by the warden of All Souls College's sister, in 1889 circulated a printed form headed 'A Ladies' Settlement in East London'. This explained that the Cheltenham Ladies' College Guild had set the scheme on foot, but it was thought possible that Oxford ladies and their friends might like to join and that a decision had rapidly to be made as to whether to take a house for four residents or one for 14. 'If the ladies of Oxford could guarantee the sum of £100 annually for three years, or a succession of two residents paying for board and lodging, the settlement might start in October in the larger and more suitable house' and supporters of this combined venture were asked to communicate with Miss Anson at All Souls College. In any case the settlement would be in the parish of St John's, not far from the Oxford House in St Andrew's parish with which the Oxford ladies might work; the reassuring fact was also stated that Kate Newman of Cheltenham, known in Oxford circles as her brother was a distinguished classics scholar of Balliol, had undertaken permanent residence and the management of the house. The required financial guarantee was soon sent from Oxford to Cheltenham and a lease was then taken of 'a comfortable and substantial house with 15 rooms. . . . Mayfield House is in a square which is built round the museum green; the green is well kept by the Kensington museum to which it belongs, so that the house has a pleasant outlook and is in a healthy situation with an open space in front.' However, a report on satisfactory sanitary conditions would, it was agreed, be necessary, though there seems to have been a slip-up here.

A third initiative came from the Honourable T. Allnut Brassey, son of Lord Brassey, first Lord of the Admiralty in Gladstone's second administration and known to his many Balliol friends as 'Tab'. On 20 July 1889 he sent out a notice stating that a meeting was to be held four days later at the family home, 24 Park Lane, to form both a West End committee to raise subscriptions and find workers for Oxford House and a ladies' branch on the model of that working with the Cambridge mission in Camberwell. This brought an immediate reaction from Miss Anson, who wrote from

Hawkhurst, Kent on 23 July: 'I hope your meeting will bring much support to your scheme for a ladies' branch of work, but till your offer of large support came it seemed expedient to merge ourselves in the Cheltenham enterprise to begin with.' But clearly some confusion might result and she added: 'Do you not think if the Oxford ladies' share in the settlement takes the title of Ladies' Branch of Oxford House it will solve all difficulties?' This title, or its shortened form LBOH, was to be used long after the parting of the ways between Oxford and Cheltenham.

The Bethnal Green Ladies' Committee was the name used at the formation meeting held on 19 October 1889 at 10 Great George Street, the West End home of Lavinia Talbot's elder sister, the Honourable Mrs John Talbot, who then began her long association with the settlement. Revd Winnington Ingram presided until she was elected chairwoman and her daughter Meriel Talbot and Lady Idina Brassey, daughter-in-law of Lord Brassey, became joint secretaries. Bertram Talbot was the only other man present, though H. F. Hussey soon took on the job of treasurer.

Elizabeth (Ella) Anson had come up from Oxford for the meeting with Beatrice Harington, daughter of the principal of Brasenose College. After a proposal had been made that the London and Oxford committees should amalgamate, she said that no Oxford committee yet existed, though she and her friend were acting as treasurer and secretary of the one about to be formed. Kate Newman then explained the arrangements made at Mayfield House and the work already started there before Ingram, supported by Mrs Talbot, proposed that a Mayfield House girls' club should be formed. A subcommittee was accordingly set up to furnish a room at the settlement for this purpose, with Miss Ingram, who had already moved in, taking on responsibility here with Lady Idina Brassey and the Honourable Maude Lawrence. Bertram Talbot then proposed that Miss Newman should become a member of their committee; and that its functions should be to repay the sum of £150 guaranteed annually for three years, to enlist workers and disseminate information.

At the next meeting, held at 24 Park Lane, the Honourable Mrs Charles Egerton, Lord Brassey's daughter, began here many years of devoted service to settlement work in Bethnal Green, to be followed soon after her death in 1927 by her daughter Phyllis. The Honourable Mrs P. Lyttelton-Gell, who belonged to a family already closely involved with Toynbee Hall, joined Miss Anson and Miss Harington to form a contingent of three from Oxford. Other newcomers were Mrs Spencer Follett, the Honourable E. Gathorne Hardy and Lady Gwendolen Cecil, who was soon to move over to the new and prestigious general committee headed by the Duchess of Westminster and including Lady Frederick Cavendish. With HRH Princess Marie Adelaide, Duchess of Teck, as president and 11 patrons including the Duchess of Cleveland, the Duchess of Portland, Lady Edward Cavendish and Mrs Gladstone, a dimension of support hardly anticipated by the Cheltenham Daisy Guild was thus secured for the new settlement. A small group had already visited Mayfield House and Miss Newman's draft circular was amended to include the information that 'Ladies living at the West End may assist by taking an interest in special branches of the work, district visiting, sick nursing, collecting hospital letters and convalescent tickets, collecting books, games and flowers, and working with the guild.' Various members of the committee agreed to supervise these different departments and Mrs Egerton, Miss Harington, and Mr T. A. and Lady Idina Brassey were appointed to draw up a circular. It was further agreed, as Miss Anson had suggested, that the new London and Oxford group involved in Bethnal Green should be called 'Ladies' Branch of Oxford House' (LBOH).

Soon the Oxford side, with Mrs Lyttelton-Gell as president, was able to report a gift of 80 volumes to the Mayfield House club library from a society called the 'Utopians'. As a result of this the Honourable Sarah Lyttelton, Lavinia Talbot's young half-sister, joined the LBOH committee as the Utopians' representative, thus gaining useful experience for her later settlement responsibilities in Lambeth and Fulham.

Kate Newman was already living at Mayfield House when it was formally opened on Saturday 29 October 1889. With her were Miss Winnington Ingram, Miss Noar, a Bethnal Green enthusiast who had given up early ambitions as a singer to devote herself to social work, and three Cheltenham Ladies' College Guild members, one of whom wrote:

> For those of us who were staying in the house and friends who were near enough, the day began with a celebration in St John's which is just across the square. When we came back the parcels had arrived and the hall table was covered with boxes of flowers. Few gifts are more acceptable in the East End where flowers are hardly known.

A council meeting of the Cheltenham Ladies' College Guild was held there at 3.00 p.m. that day when it was formally agreed that 'the Oxford people be told that the committee gratefully accepted their offer of help to the amount of £50 per annum, and half the rates, taxes and lighting till 29 September 1890'. In return they were to be 'allowed' a certain number of rooms in Mayfield House and would carry on their own work there.

Miss Beale's team clearly felt in control at this point. After a short service in the church at 4.00 p.m., attended by the head of Oxford House and addressed by Bishop Barry, former Primate of Australia who later became chairman of the college council, most people returned to Mayfield House for tea. Among others from London and Oxford they included 'Mr Brassey and Lady Idina Brassey, and Lady and Miss Anson'. That there was ample scope for the newcomers was shown next day, when:

> One or two of us who were unable to stay in the house spent a most interesting Sunday at Bethnal Green. It happened to be a Quarterly Church parade Sunday of the University Club for Working Men, of which there are 1000 members, and whose buildings are in the same square as Mayfield House. In the evening we went to a Mission service in the large hall attached to the Club.

A month after the opening ceremony the 26-year-old Cheltenham Ladies' College Guild member, Marion Bruce, moved into Mayfield House as a 'permanent resident', hardly imagining she would stay with the settlement for the rest of her working life. At first she was mainly identified with the COS, serving both on its central committee and council while also acting as branch secretary, and Miss Selby, a trained nurse who had joined Miss

Winnington Ingram on the Oxford side, was soon helping Kate Newman with a nursing class held once a week for local mothers.

Dr Buchanan, a guild member's father who had recently retired as medical officer of the Local Government Board in London and who lived in Victoria Park Square, was a tower of strength on this front. His daughter Lily, soon to marry the Revd George Adam Smith, in due course became the mother of another public-spirited old Cheltonian.

While other work continued under the auspices of the CCHF and MABYS, pioneering came mainly from Miss Beale's imaginative interest in technical education. Though popular with guild members, 'industrial work' had less appeal to the Oxford contingent, which by 1890 was already taking an independent line. An offer from the guild in July 1890 that two members of the LBOH should join the Cheltenham House committee was declined.

A year later, when the renewal of the lease for Mayfield House came up for discussion, the LBOH committee decided unanimously to start an independent settlement provided a suitable house could be found. This raised a problem for the Cheltenham side, as Miss Newman's health was giving cause for anxiety. However, after a temporary move to St Bartholomew's Mission House in May 1892, a lease for seven years was taken that October by the Oxford group of 4 Victoria Park Square. 'The house is eminently suitable for our purpose. It has accommodation for eight or nine ladies, at a rent of £90 with three living rooms and suitable offices.' When the question of a name cropped up, St Margaret's House seemed a happy choice. Much of the work would be done in St Andrew's parish, and this sister of the Saxon heir to the English throne, who had become a beloved figure, was renowned for her piety and concern for the poor.

A letter was sent to Kate Newman thanking her 'for her courtesy and friendliness to the Oxford residents during their connection with Mayfield House'. Though different versions of the parting were given in letters to the press (Miss Beale writing in December 1896 to the *Guardian* that a statement by Mrs Lyttelton-Gell and Miss Anson in *The Times* of 19 December 1896 'did not convey an altogether accurate impression ... Mayfield House was taken originally in 1889 by the Guild of Cheltenham Ladies' College'),

Miss Newman was *persona grata* to both sides. And she became first president of the newly formed federation of settlements before her early death in 1893. Meanwhile, persistent drainage and other problems at Mayfield House had left their mark. Moreover, the Oxford group was still hard at work nearby.

At the Cheltenham Ladies' College Guild meeting held in June 1896, Miss Beale suggested that the time had come to leave Mayfield House (to be demolished later) and start elsewhere. But where should they go? Options were discussed at St Hilda's Hall in Oxford at the end of that year, east London winning by 15 votes against five for south London. After the possibilities had been further reduced to Stepney, Shoreditch or Poplar, Canon Barnett helped to sway the decision in favour of the boundary area of Shoreditch, then notorious partly through the novel *A Child of the Jago* published by Arthur Morrison some months earlier. The author gave vivid descriptions of rat-infested slums where people were sleeping ten in a room, crime was rampant and the death rate four times higher than anywhere else in London. Such was the pressure of public opinion that early next year in 1897 the LCC started a clearance scheme between Shoreditch and Bethnal Green in preparation for building its first housing estate.

Encouragement to settle in that neighbourhood had also come from the vicar's wife, Mrs Septimus Buss, well known in Cheltenham circles and a friend of Miss Beale, who had been struggling there for years. 'When we first came to Hoxton Street fights were a daily occurrence,' and several former pupils of Miss Buss's North London Collegiate School had helped in parish work there. 'One lived with us at the vicarage for five years.'

Negotiations were soon on foot between the guild committee and the Artisans' Dwelling Company about a piece of ground set apart for a coffee house in the Boundary Street area, near a factory employing factory girls who clearly needed a club. Then at a meeting held at Shoreditch vicarage on 18 March 1897, with Miss Beale in the chair, the decision was taken that 'we must build for ourselves with money raised by debentures and shares.' A circular was issued with her signature and on a wave of enthusiasm the necessary £3000 was forthcoming within a fortnight.

In 1898, the *annus mirabilis* which saw the enlargement of St

Hilda's College in Cheltenham and the recognition of St Hilda's in Oxford as a hall of the university, St Hilda's East, an attractive four-storey building in Old Nichol Street, was opened by the newly appointed Bishop of London, Dr Mandell Creighton. 'We are now famous as being the only women's settlement which has built itself a house, and it really is a delightful house,' remarked the guild's president on that occasion. Miss Beale's vision of the path ahead was already clear.

> There are two sides to the work at St Hilda's East. Like the St Hilda's of Cheltenham and Oxford, it is a place of training. I want it to be a place where under the direction of our Lady Warden, and in cooperation with the COS, social problems may be studied and the necessary support given to those prepared to devote themselves to working out reforms among women and children Then help must be given to enable people to help themselves.

Both these aims were soon to be realized. Moreover, the Bishop of Stepney, shortly after becoming visitor to the settlement, was told that 'our lady warden is classed Al by the COS,' for on Miss Beale's recommendation Marion Bruce had already taken up the post, which she was to hold at St Hilda's for 32 years. Under her influence this settlement exerted a major influence in the evolution of the trained social worker.

In 1903, William Booth, author of *Life and Labour in London*, wrote, 'The Women's Settlement known as St Hilda's East seems to be a very active and well conducted organization. The Settlement becomes a national training school for those who desire to learn best how to serve the poor.' That year a resident attending the first course of the School of Sociology and Social Economics, recently founded by the COS, carried out her practical training at St Hilda's, setting the pattern for the years ahead. At the school's examination in 1908 two of the four candidates gaining distinctions were residents at this settlement, while a third was a Cheltenham Guild member who had begun her training there. Then in 1920 the Board of Education recognized the settlement as a hostel for students wishing to train as teachers in continuation schools.

After leaving Cheltenham, Marion Bruce had enjoyed life at Cambridge before training for social work at the Women's University Settlement (WUS). In temperament she met Miss Beale's earlier expressed wish that the proposed settlement should be in the charge not of a committee but of a commander-in-chief. Indeed she took the post only on condition she be allowed full independence, being in a position to refuse any salary and pay for her board and lodging. The hospitality offered there soon reflected her wide sphere of interests at home and abroad. Besides students and local people she welcomed many foreign visitors to London's East End. France, Sweden, Germany, Switzerland, Belgium, Japan, Egypt and the USA were all concerned here. In due course she was to take a leading part in organizing an international congress of social workers. 'It was at party times that one saw what the Warden was and meant us to be to our neighbours,' remarked one early resident. 'Her quick sense of humour, her power of seeing the amusing side of little everyday things, helped to keep life sane and sweet. She always had a sense of proportion in the things that matter. She understood the essentials and wasted no time in getting to grips with them.'

The local Skilled Employment Committee, based at St Hilda's East, and replacing earlier thrift clubs, was one of her main interests. This committee was to guide more than 5000 local boys and girls to skilled jobs before being shut down in 1952, by which time its pioneering had contributed to the formation of the Juvenile Advisory Bureau for the Ministry of Labour and the later Youth Employment Committee under the Education Committee.

Volunteers coming to St Hilda's were often surprised at the confidence the warden placed in them.

> She took it for granted that we wanted to give of our best to the people who needed our help. . . . How easy it was made for us – the beautiful, inspiring prayers in the Oratory, the quiet library with its well-chosen books, the orderliness of the house, the cheery social life and all the old residents so willing to help a newcomer.

Among these was the music-loving Miss Noar who, after

moving with Miss Bruce and others from Mayfield House, became the mainstay of the club's work at St Hilda's East, the devoted members of her girls' club continuing to meet regularly as her 'Married Girls' Club' long after many had moved from the area. Robert Mayer was among the many musicians whom she attracted to the settlement and, like the warden herself, Miss Noar lived to be 93. Cosmo Gordon Lang, as Bishop of Stepney and visitor to the settlement, spoke at St Paul's cathedral during the memorial service held there for Miss Beale in 1906. Among those who heard him was Lillian N. Faithful, then vice-principal at King's College women's department, which under her leadership had grown from a 'centre for ladies' into a women's college of London University. Appointed principal of Cheltenham Ladies' College shortly afterwards, she proved herself a staunch friend of St Hilda's East. Having strong views on the need for students of social science to 'get practical knowledge of all details of their work by service of their own', she herself lived for a short time in Shoreditch, working afterwards to improve the wretched housing conditions there. A year before the outbreak of the First World War about 14 women were living at this settlement.

> The house was always full and we each paid £3. 3*s*. a week for a little room with a gas fire. There were three students, including me, taking the LSE social science diploma, and some postgraduates. When we were not doing practical work or attending lectures, we studied in the long library on the first floor, though I also recalled writing essays for my tutor in the basement, while keeping guard over hats and coats belonging to members of the girls' clubs.

As well as the residents, there were men and women, experienced people in various walks of life – one was a barrister – who came part-time. Some also worked in the surrounding boroughs of Dalston, Hackney, Stepney and Hoxton.

> Two of us were Church workers and visitors; others were at the local offices of the COS. Most of our work was organizing but there was also much laborious pen-pushing

> to be done. And we were school managers. At the age of 23, with no knowledge of social work, I was made a manager of a big school in the Bethnal Green Road. The warden's comment to me was 'Oh, you will learn if you do that.'

She arranged the work of all residents and then left them free, although available in her downstairs sitting room every evening to give advice to anyone who needed it.

> She liked us to attend prayers which she took in the Chapel each morning before breakfast. The Clubs at St Hilda's were all run by residents, we students were there to help and to learn. Another resident and I who had both previously been art students, ran a Saturday Club for crippled boys who learned woodcarving. Our neighbours came to us, many and often, for help and advice of every kind, for all knew that 'the ladies' were there to help if they could. They made us feel that they liked and respected us.

Clearly Henrietta Barnett's complaint about some 'young ladies at Toynbee Hall who made her "long to shake them"' was now out of date, as the ground was prepared for CABs.

The dire poverty in Bethnal Green and the neighbouring districts was seen as the chief problem,

> and of course dirt and ill health, often caused or exaggerated by poverty and bad housing. Tuberculosis was rampant – a terrible scourge. Mostly people lived in what had once been decent little houses but were then let out in one, two or three rooms to a family. But alas the grannies had to go to the workhouse infirmary, a sad dreary place indeed at the top of Hoxton Street.

In August 1914 the warden recalled those on holiday to St Hilda's to help organized meals for families with no income when the men joined up. 'There was such a rush of recruits that it was some time before the regular pay came through and meanwhile it was chaos. All day long there were queues of wives and mothers at the Post Office, waiting for the War Office allowances.' Settlements at Peckham and elsewhere were similarly involved. Though no large-scale evacuation faced London at this time, the influx of Belgian refugees brought its own problems. Miss Bruce soon added Red Cross work to her many other commitments, as secretary of the BRCS Bethnal Green branch, and she also took on a night job at the Enfield arms factory. Later this formidable and influential woman became one of the founder members of the Bethnal Green and Shoreditch Housing Association.

Pioneering between the wars included the opening in 1925 of The Bookshop in the Bethnal Green Road. This joint effort of Oxford House and St Hilda's East was a bookshop-with-club experiment in further education for young school leavers. In due course it became the sole responsibility of Mabel Warburton, in college from 1895 to 1897 and 'one of St Hilda's most inspiring and beloved workers'. Eventually in 1935, on resuming her job of inspecting schools in the Middle East, she handed over control of The Bookshop to the settlement, providing at the same time the salary of a leader for the boys' club, which flourished until the Second World War.

A new training initiative marked Miss Bruce's last year in office. In 1931 the College of Nursing asked the settlement to arrange an intensive course on social work for five of its students, all trained nurses, who were hoping for appointments as health visitors. Two of the senior residents were able to help the warden here. The usual settlement week for London University students was held that year in March, foreign students including one each from the Berlin, Geneva and Paris settlements. When the warden retired there seems to have been general pleasure that she moved to a small house nearby, where she stayed for 18 years, before dying at Oxford in 1956 at the age of 93. 'I count it one of my greatest privileges to have known her,' wrote a guild member at that time. 'St Hilda's East is what it is today largely because of the traditions she inspired.' During her years in office residents worked on a wide front in Bethnal Green, acting as settlement representatives on many public bodies, and helping with care committees, skilled employment work, the ICAA, infant welfare centres, the CCHF, Guides, nursery schools, hospitals and elsewhere.

Meanwhile, Beatrice Harington of the LBOH and head of St Margaret's House had steered her settlement along a somewhat different path. Church work for her had priority.

* * *

St Margaret's House was formally opened at 4 Victoria Park Square, Bethnal Green, on 21 March 1893 by HRH the Duchess of Teck, president of the LBOH, whose daughter May, then about to be married, would visit the settlement in 1931 as Queen Mary.

Soon afterwards Oxford support was stimulated by an influential meeting held in All Souls hall, when Mrs Lyttelton-Gell, vice president, 'dwelt on the responsibilities of upper-class womanhood to their less fortunate sisters,' though neither group as yet had votes or degrees. Miss Harington, head of St Margaret's House, described the various schemes already undertaken by its residents 'to brighten the colourless life of East London'. These included clubs of various kinds, Sunday school teaching, musical drill, Sunday teas for old ladies from the workhouse, befriending young servants under the auspices of MABYS, COS work, district and hospital visiting and 'a needlework scheme for giving employment to very poor women throughout the winter'. Then Miss Selby, a trained nurse whose work lay chiefly in St Bartholomew's parish, spoke on the difficulties of nursing patients in their own homes. After an associate member living in Oxford had said how helpful temporary residents could be in giving the long-term ones a few days rest, Miss Anson, secretary and treasurer for LBOH, wound up the meeting.

Though the special expenditure incurred by the move into St Margaret's had been largely met by generous donations and would be cleared off by drawing room meetings and sales, there was need of an assured annual income of about £80 in excess of subscriptions already promised. She asked sympathizers with St Margaret's not to consider a subscription of five shillings too modest before thanking all who had enabled the committee 'to turn their philanthropic dream into a substantial reality'. A similar subscription was to prove popular at other early settlements.

In the autumn of 1894, when outstanding bills had been paid, the committee agreed that expenses amounting to £3. 10*s*. 0*d*. should be given to delegates from St Margaret's House attending the conference of the NUWW to be held next year in Glasgow. Then, as it was found before Christmas that a larger house in the square could be leased which would accommodate five more residents, Miss Harington offered to be responsible for the rent during her lifetime, Mrs Talbot and Miss Selby agreeing to be joint trustees. The move was accordingly made. It was also decided that the head should have an assistant, with board and lodging provided.

Hardly had they all settled into No. 24 during the autumn of 1895, than the Revd A. Winnington Ingram, by then rector of Bethnal Green as well as head of Oxford House, strongly urged the committee to rent the nearby university house, also overlooking the square, especially in view of 'the removal of the Cheltenham people to Shoreditch, and the benefit to east London of the excellent work done at and from St Margaret's'. As two of the residents at St Margaret's were willing to take on the remaining six years' lease of No. 24, furniture there was carried along to what became known as No. 17, the Oxford House council, 'our landlords', having by then paid for some structural repairs. They were also to receive a rent of £75.

Ingram was now asked to accept the title and office of warden of St Margaret's, Mrs John Talbot continuing to hold office as chairwoman and Miss Harington as head, and the large rooms at No. 17 were soon in demand for classes and other social gatherings run jointly with the women's branch of the adjacent University Club for Working Men.

St Margaret's now began to assume the character of mother house for other women's settlements in the East End. In October 1896 St Helen's House at Stratford was opened by HRH Princess Helena, Duchess of Albany, widow of Queen Victoria's son Leopold who had died in 1884. Its purpose was to support Oxford's Trinity College Mission, while being worked on the same lines as St Margaret's, with Miss Harington as head and one of her volunteers as resident sub-warden. It was the forerunner of the present-day Albany settlement in Docklands.

In 1897 Miss Harington's sister, who had been living with her at

St Margaret's, was made head of St Mildred's Settlement, founded by Winnington Ingram in the Isle of Dogs, a bulging promontory from the Thames's north bank associated with Henry VIII's hunting expeditions.

The same year saw the start of the LMHS and that autumn, when the LBOH held a public meeting in the Oxford town hall, Miss Wordsworth, principal of LMH, Miss Harington and the Revd A. Winnington Ingram, by then a canon of St Paul's, were all billed to speak. Soon afterwards St Margaret's committee decided that 'the Oxford ladies' colleges should be told of any house vacancies' and five years later past and present students at St Hugh's had formed what was to prove an enduring link with Bethnal Green, while others at LMH 'supplemented by funds from the LBOH, invited as usual a large party of club girls for Whit Monday'.

The end of 1897 brought evidence of further university and London support in the formation of a North Oxford Association, largely organized by Miss Anson, and a West End Association, with Lady Idina Brassey and Miss Meriel Talbot as joint secretaries. Soon increasing demand for accommodation by prospective new residents was met by taking two rooms in a nearby private house. But a major change was at hand. In April 1899 the LBOH committee, meeting at All Souls College, decided not to renew the lease expiring that autumn, but to seek a larger property to accommodate 20 residents. When, in December 1900, 21 Old Ford Road, belonging to the Female Guardians' Association, came onto the market with immediate possession, arrangements were made to find the necessary £3600 to buy this house of character and charm, reputedly built in 1705 by a Huguenot merchant whose rear garden included a mulberry tree attractive not only to his silk worms. The LBOH committee met there for the first time in January 1903.

On St Margaret's day in June 1904, attended by the new head of Oxford House, the former warden, by then Bishop of Stepney, came to dedicate the small chapel built by the residents and soon to be given stained glass windows representing St Mildred and St Cecilia, as a memorial to Alice Margaret Harington, who had died in 1901, and the link she had established between St Margaret's

House and the daughter settlement. Fortunately, like the main building, the chapel was to come unscathed through the bombing of two world wars. The religious commitment of this settlement has been strong from the start.

For some time new settlement undertakings were restricted to girls' and children's clubs as 'every parish priest is full of energy and it is clear that to strengthen existing organizations and not to waste time and thought in planning and carrying out new schemes is by far the greatest service we can render.' This was one way to 'draw our people nearer to that influence which it is our desire to see paramount in their hearts'. Such words were characteristic of Beatrice Harington and it was not surprising that Dr Winnington Ingram, when Bishop of London, wrote, 'It was a happy day when I induced her and her sister to leave the riches of Oxford for the life of Bethnal Green. She loved the people and they loved her.' Her endearing sense of humour was not the least of her assets.

By 1912 residents were working in six local parishes, requests from further afield having to be refused, and also helping at COS offices in Whitechapel, Bethnal Green and Hackney. Several were school managers and care committee workers for six groups of elementary schools. The Workhouse Girls' Aid, the Refuge and Public Welfare Committee and the National Council of Girls' Clubs had each their representative from the settlement, one resident was secretary to the East Bethnal Children's Holiday Committee and Miss Harington was deanery representative on the Mothers' Union council, local secretary for the Women's Holiday Fund and lady president of the League of Mercy for Bethnal Green.

Oxford links proved strong at this time, so holidays for club members that year included the usual Whit Monday outing when 45 girls were entertained delightfully by LMH and St Hugh's College students. They dined in hall at LMH for the first time, the programme for the day being 'as kind and charming as ever'. Another outing was to Falconhurst, where club members were entertained by the president of St Margaret's and Miss Evelyn Talbot, and other invitations included one to Scotney Castle from the Honourable Mrs Edward Hussey, whose daughter Gertrude was to help for over 30 years at St Margaret's before dying there while on a visit in 1921. There was also a drive and tea for 28 elderly and infirm people in Kensington Gardens. Moreover, '45 of our small children have benefited enormously by that wonderfully kind provision of Lady Plymouth, whereby four at a time spend one, and often more, months in the country at the bare cost of the railway fare.' At the same time other CCHF work went ahead, the settlement dealing with over 1500 children directly or through the east Bethnal Green committee, while many of their elders were sent away through the girls', women's and St Margaret's own holiday funds.

At Christmas time, since rich parishioners were scarce to the point of non-existence, St Margaret's had to look elsewhere for its appeal funds. The settlement, like the LMHS in Lambeth, was fortunate in enjoying royal support. HRH the Princess Christian of Schleswig Holstein became patron in 1911 and that year the list of donors was headed by the King, who sent a brace of pheasants from Windsor, and the Queen, 'who did us a like favour . . . a little later besides sending her yearly gift of primroses'. Packages of clothing came up three times a year from the LBOH work scheme in Oxford and provident collecting brought residents into regular contact with a large number of people every week, with an increase of £70 in the sums paid in during 1912 (to a total of £462) resulting from collections in a new but poor district.

The stated object of St Margaret's at that time was 'to provide a centre in Bethnal Green at which ladies can reside for religious, social and educational work among the women and girls of St Andrew's and of the surrounding poor parishes', and a tribute from the Revd H. V. S. Esk, the new rector of Bethnal Green but one who could look back nearly to the beginning of settlement work there, bore out that the objective was being achieved.

> Bethnal Green owes more to St Margaret's than I can say. The willing, loyal, constant help given so ungrudgingly in so many of our parishes, the refining and uplifting influence where the St Margaret's resident has often been the only lady in the parish, to say nothing of the extra parochial work, are debts which the clergy can never repay.

But now came a period of anxiety following the death of Sir William Anson, warden of All Souls College, as 'to the Oxford House and St Margaret's this national loss has meant the removal of a very foundation stone.' Soon afterwards Miss Anson, Lady Warren, asked if the Oxford committee meetings could in future be held at Magdalen, her husband's college.

The outbreak of war in 1914 brought various crises to Old Ford Road. There was difficulty in getting some children back from their summer holidays; soon residents were in short supply with consequent financial trouble; and the club membership fell, with girls working long hours in factories and few wanting to venture out in the blackout. But at a time when visiting took on a new importance, 'our knowledge of homes and individuals is of real help to the SSAFA ladies.'

Then in 1917 a major financial crisis, characteristic of the settlement world, nearly caused the closure of St Margaret's House. 'Repayment of loans' and 'interest on loans' had been a regular feature on the balance sheet since the premises were bought in 1900. The largest loan was for £3200 from a committee member, the Honourable Mrs Whittuck, who died in 1915. Two years later her executors had no choice but to call in the balance of the debt, amounting to £2750. Consternation ensued, for the chances of large-scale contributions to non-war work seemed remote. The Home Office was stressing the importance of youth clubs and it seemed probable that the work involved would eventually qualify for government grants. But that was in the long term.

Then, in January 1918, an anonymous donor, known to the clergyman brother of a council member, Miss Sawbridge, who had already contributed £10,000 for the work of training volunteers through the Church Council for Service, promised to clear off most of St Margaret's debt in an arrangement by which St Christopher's College in Blackheath would also benefit. The balance of £450 was made by other gifts and Brigadier H. E. Montgomery of Chester Square, related by marriage to the Anson family, now felt able to continue as treasurer, though he was away on active service and his son Arthur would eventually take on the job.

An important change, however, resulted from the emergency. By May 1918 the need to place the settlement on a more adequate financial footing pointed to incorporation, with its objects and machinery embodied in memorandums and articles, as in the case of Oxford House. The main question now was whether St Margaret's should have a separate incorporation and be registered as the owner of the property, or continue to exist as a voluntary organization relying on the fact that Oxford House was incorporated, and asking its council to sign a declaration that it held the legal estate in trust for St Margaret's House.

Mrs Talbot thought it advisable to keep as much in touch as possible with Oxford House, so the second course was unanimously approved. However, the constitution still needed some alteration, including replacement of the committee by a council. The settlement's purpose was at the same time broadened to include help for students to equip themselves to cope with current social problems both at home and abroad.

The settlement now lost two good friends. Miss Harington had said in 1914 that she wanted to leave at the end of the war. Her charm, tact and sense of humour, combined with a broad outlook on life, while attracting workers of varying opinions, had contributed much to the smooth running of the house, clubs and committees. She continued her service on the council and help with the CCHF until 1933, and when she died three years later a bursary for students and a memorial to her in the chapel of St Margaret's were subscribed by many friends. Then Mrs Talbot, the president, also resigned in 1919, after 30 years at the helm, having perfectly combined and represented, as Miss Anson remarked, 'both Oxford and London interests, while unfailingly and efficiently steering us along'.

Another of the devoted pioneers, Lady Mabelle Egerton, after wartime canteen service at Dover, now became president though soon retiring in favour of her sister-in-law, Lady Brassey. With the appointment of a second salaried member of staff to work as bursar, both local and wider commitments were maintained. The new head, Miss Shields, was asked to join the London Diocesan Board of Women's Work, the Women's Municipal Society, the COS standing and training committees, and the Central Council of Women's Church Work.

Oxford links were strengthened when Lady Oman became vice

president; and, after a meeting at her house in November 1920, Miss Jourdain, principal of St Hugh's, undertook to speak to her students about the settlement's needs. An approach was also made to Ruth Butler, head of the Oxford Society for Home Students, for Somerville, LMH and St Hilda's were already committed elsewhere on this front. However, university allegiances continually overlap and Miss Anson's sister Gertrude, who had moved with her from Oxford to London, was then working with the Cheltenham Ladies' College Guild at St Hilda's East.

By May 1921 St Margaret's House, still in financial difficulties, was charging £2 a term for training students. It had 14 residents, five of them its own workers including the head and a bursar, four lodgers engaged on teaching or social work in the East End, two medical students and one COS worker. The head, however, reported that the shortage of voluntary workers meant that very little help could be given to the students and there was a general lack of *esprit de corps*. This somewhat depressing picture altered soon after the appointment in 1921 of her successor Miss Havergal, aged 50, who had been working in All Saints parish, Clifton, Bristol. Early in 1922 the Diocesan Council of Women's Work granted recognition to the settlement as a training centre for church workers, St Margaret's being the first settlement in the London diocese to be so recognized. Then a resident club leader was appointed and substantial support was provided from a full house in ten local parishes. The start of a club for young married women, stressing education for citizenship rather than recreation, proved immediately popular, and an international conference of settlements, held at St Margaret's House, was judged to be 'most illuminating, enlarging and educative'.

In 1929 St Margaret's House council was fortunate in securing for the first time the services of a highly trained social worker with pioneering experience, both in Britain and the USA. Eleanor Kelly, after graduating from London University, had been awarded a Pfeiffer training scholarship by WUS in 1905 and then spent 24 years as an industrial welfare supervisor, becoming in due course a founder member of the Association of Welfare Workers, forerunner of the Institute of Personnel Management. Her arrival in Bethnal Green coincided with a clear need for cooperation between women working in voluntary organizations and the growing number of official administrators in local and national government. 'Here seems an opportunity for St Margaret's to perform a most useful service in the postwar world,' she remarked. 'Students can study for their diploma in surroundings where religion and the things of the spirit are regarded as the only sure foundation on which to build.'

Among many changes now made at the settlement, the most important was its establishment as a social work training centre. It thus came into line with other influential women's settlements. Some residents attended the LSE or Bedford College, others took a recognized course in club leadership and all helped in various house activities while the head, besides taking classes at the settlement, lectured on industrial welfare for the LSE and on social administration for the Diocesan Council of Youth. St Margaret's was also by now well known as a centre for the theology lectures arranged by the Diocesan Board of Women's Work.

As Miss Kelly's students were given the opportunity to study conditions in police courts, common lodging houses, shelters, factories, laundries and other places of work, not surprisingly many came from abroad, contributing in their different ways to the life of the house. In 1930 they included the warden of the Oslo settlement, the head of the public kindergarten on a model housing estate in Copenhagen, social workers from China and Japan, and, in 1932, the warden of the Philadelphia university settlement, who came to England to study the effects of insurance and made some interesting case studies in Bethnal Green, the head's American connections proving fruitful here.

Traditional activities meanwhile flourished at the house, usually filled to overflowing. The Queen's visit to St Margaret's in October 1931 was a long-remembered highlight, especially for those involved in any way with the babies' club, the mothers' club, the 'super seniors', the little girls' play centre and the netball club, all of which the royal guest saw in action before having tea with the residents. The redecoration of the fine tall-windowed first-floor drawing room, henceforth called the Anson Room, had just been completed, made possible by Florence Anson as a memorial to her formidable sister Elizabeth who had died the previous year.

Sir Wyndham Deedes, a good friend of St Margaret's over many years, was by then a well-established figure in Bethnal Green. After joining the police on leaving Oxford and subsequently serving with the armed forces, he ended his distinguished service career as an adviser to the government in the Middle East and then, with his mother, herself a remarkable personality, moved to 17 Victoria Park Square intending not only to help at Oxford House, while his brother was pursuing political ambitions, but also to provide an hospitable centre linking east and west Londoners, in the Barnett tradition.

Among those whom he introduced to settlement work was young Barbara Murray, who had been living in the country near the Deedes family but knew something of east London as architects in her family had designed both the Bethnal Green children's museum and the spacious gardens of Victoria Park Square. Before moving to No. 18 in the square, she began her local involvement, like so many other volunteers, as a care committee worker and occasional resident at 21 Old Ford Road, 'collaborating also with Miss Bruce at the nearby St Hilda's East Settlement', as she remarked in 1984. Her valuable personal commitment to the settlement has continued for well over half a century, during which time one of her nieces, Lady Moberly, now president of St Margaret's, has been responsible for starting a children's centre there, run largely by local mothers. And another niece, Dame Rosemary Murray, a fellow of LMH and governor of several schools as well as former principal of New Hall at Cambridge and vice chancellor of the university, has shown practical sympathy for the settlement movement. During the depression of the 1930s Miss Murray, then recently elected to the council, helped much in cheering local life both through club work, dramatic productions and private hospitality to the elderly. When St Margaret's staged the *Pilgrim's Progress* under her direction in 1934, every club and section of the settlement, from members of the council to members of the newly formed unemployed men's centre, took part. This was followed in 1935 by an equally happy *Pageant of Bethnal Green*, produced by St Margaret's. All the 400 actors, scenery and costumes came from within the borough, and the community feeling thus aroused was no small achievement at that time.

The Peel Grove Hobbies Centre for the unemployed made a contribution along different lines when, after months of planning, it was opened in St John's parish hall early in 1933. Boot mending, furniture repairing and gardening were the staple weekday occupations there, the waste ground behind the hall being converted from an unsightly rubbish heap to a wealth of flowers and vegetables. Here settlement workers and the unemployed could meet happily on common ground and, as Miss Kelly remarked, 'cement friendships which are the stuff of which true settlements are built'.

In 1937 St Margaret's holiday camp was once more at Southsea for the first two weeks of August. 'At no time of the year can life at St Margaret's be regarded as a leisured proceeding,' remarked Miss Kelly that year.

> But perhaps never is it so busy for such an unbroken stretch of time as in the months of July and August when the uninitiated often think we are, if not closed, at least finding time hung heavy on our hands. There is no question as to the amount of hard work involved in arranging holidays for some hundreds of people, but it is work as rewarding as it is strenuous, and everyone enjoys the holiday season.

Besides, there were CCHF parties accounting for over 500 children.

> As usual our Holiday Bureau (to which non-club members come for help and advice), was flooded with applications and we arranged holidays for 268 people in all. Without the help of the Women's Holiday Fund and the Factory Girls' Holiday Fund we could not get along at all, and we are also indebted to many generous friends. Tired mothers, old men and women in the Cosy Club, and young boys and girls just started work, all blessed the donors for the holidays they would otherwise have missed.

Clients (except the pensioners) contributed something to the cost. 'Some pay the whole, only needing our help in the planning. Per-

ABOVE. A play centre at LMHS in 1926

BELOW. LMHS workers in 1928

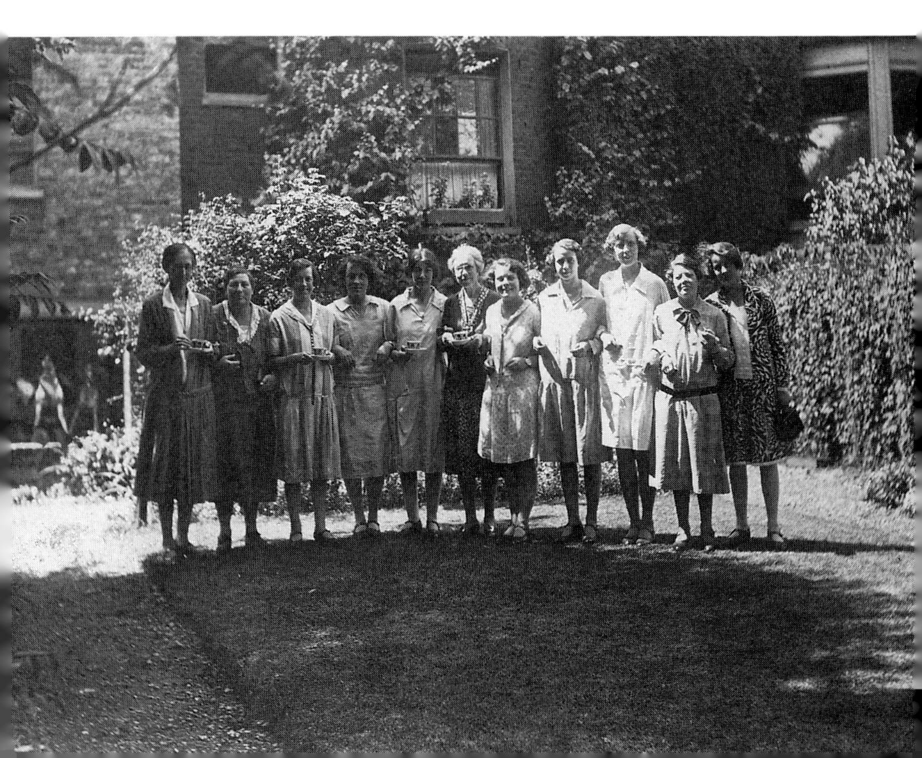

ABOVE. An inspiration for settlement work – Lambeth children in 1928

BELOW. LMHS and the Silver Jubilee, 18 May 1935, in Lambeth

ABOVE. Feeding the minds – 'Hundreds of Books'

LEFT. Feeding the minds – the Cowley Children's Library, 1963

ABOVE. Practical life skills – children's handicrafts

BELOW. Cards and a good read at the Cowley Community Centre, 1947

ABOVE. Children of the LMH Settlement

BELOW. A Settlement resident visits a pensioner in the late 1960s

RIGHT. The Lambeth Festival, 1970s

BELOW. Getting to grips with marching trainees at the 'All Sewn Up' Training Project

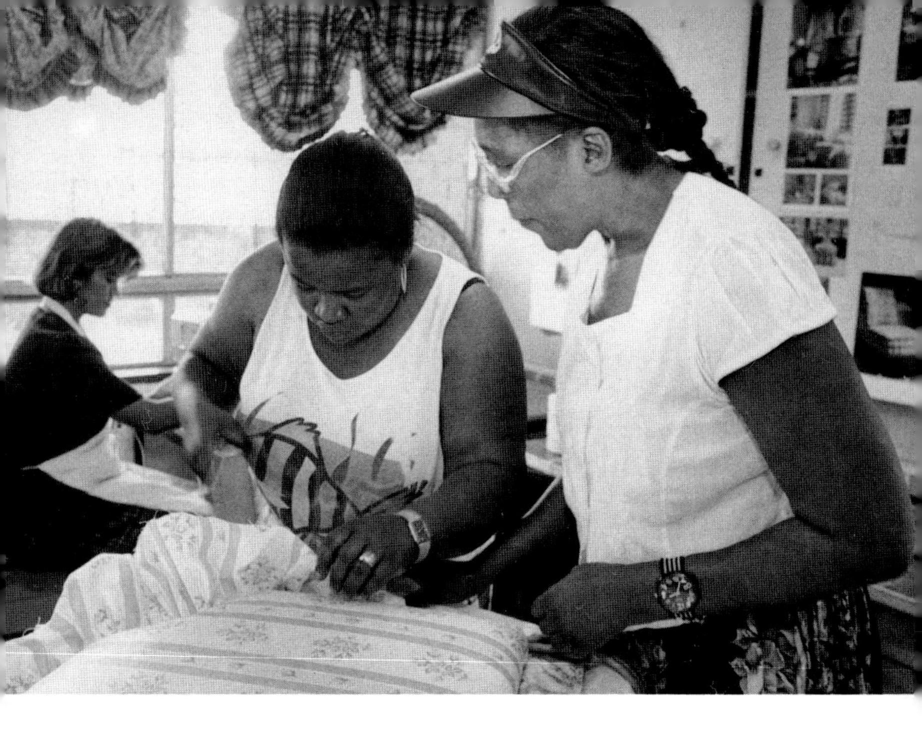

ABOVE. 'A stitch in time' at the 'All Sewn Up' Training Project

LEFT. Life skills' training 'Roots and Shoots' – YTS scheme for young people with learning difficulties

ABOVE. Homework at the After-School Project

BELOW. Time out for staff and students at ‘Roots and Shoots’

haps no one who has not done this particular piece of work can appreciate how badly it is needed. Girls from Bow, Hoxton, Hackney, Shoreditch and even Islington came here regularly last week for "holiday week" and one from as far afield as Woolwich.' She added that 'if they have any chance of a holiday through a club or other agency we do not take them when they live outside Bethnal Green, but if this is the only hope, we promise to do our best and, so far, have failed no one.'

Meanwhile, to help families staying at home:

> The Holiday Play Centre went on so smoothly that one found it hard to believe that from 80 to 100 children were spending their day on the premises. Painting, modelling, bead-threading and needlework kept the older ones happy for hours, while a wonderful 'slippery slide' (presented to us by one of our fairy godmothers as a Coronation present) provided endless delight. Soap bubbles were a pleasant variation too. The climax of a visit to the zoo was made possible for all those big enough to go.

The settlement's aim of brightening local life was certainly achieved at this time.

Pioneering extended to club work and the Cosy Club, claiming to be the first old-aged pensioners' club in London, was started in 1936 when 12 men and 12 women, recommended by the local Board of Guardians, which included more than one resident as well as the head, met regularly at the settlement. It was the forerunner of the popular Old People's Day Centre to be established there in 1957. 'But it would be wrong to think of Miss Kelly as merely a good organizer and administrator,' wrote Stella Penley, a future head. 'She was both but she was much more. From her students, and I speak as one of them, she demanded high standards, but imposed few restrictions. With her staff she was always ready to discuss problems and new forms of service. In difficulties she always did the worst jobs herself.'

Meanwhile, a complete survey on 'Recreational Possibilities for Boys and Girls in Bethnal Green', inspired by Sir Wyndham Deedes and the first of its kind to be made in Britain, was engaging settlement students and other residents, several of whom had earlier been responsible for organizing and recording a survey of two typical streets in the borough and of a housing block near-by, as well as starting a mixed club for young people over 16. An aftercare experiment for school leavers was one consequence of this survey. And, in building up a happy, busy, disciplined centre of value to the neighbourhood, a substantial contribution was made by the shop, which now replaced the jumble sales of the past. Among gifts to the house at this time was a hut, built on the small plot of wasteland behind its chapel, to serve as a store for second-hand clothes; and soon a weekly sale became a highly popular social event, all women connected in any way with the house having a 'season ticket' for the Friday openings.

Moreover, this settlement's early reputation as a mother house won further support in the interwar years when, on the initiative of its council and helped by the Pilgrim Trust, a branch settlement was established in Bow.

Two years later Sir William Deedes, who had been serving on the Pilgrim House committee, took over the chairmanship as the young settlement moved towards independence, with Miss Kelly still heading its finance committee. In 1937 it became a self-governing body with the Rt Honourable George Lansbury as chairman and Sir Wyndham, by now chairman of the London Council of Social Service (LCSS), as president. Though St Margaret's had no longer any legal responsibility, several of its members remained actively concerned, particularly with its CAB work until the local government reorganization of Tower Hamlets, when Pilgrim House was closed; and later on some of the trust money involved reverted to St Margaret's House.

7

Lady Margaret Hall Settlement in Lambeth

When LMHS opened in 1897 at 129 Kennington Road, its founder, then Bishop of Rochester, hoped it would serve as a bridge between parochial and other organizations operating in north Lambeth and Vauxhall. Friendships were important at the start and especially those between the Talbots of Keble College, Archbishop Benson's family and the Bishop of Lincoln's daughter, Elizabeth Wordsworth, first principal of LMH. Early years were coloured also by complicated local patterns of Anglican and Nonconformist influence.

At the turn of the century, Lambeth, covering an area roughly six miles long and one mile wide, was the second largest of the newly created metropolitan boroughs, exceeded only by Islington and closely approached by Stepney. Though there were then few ethnic problems, plenty of others arose among its 300,000 people, some of whom lived in slums around Waterloo station and Lambeth Palace, others in the respectable working class houses of Vauxhall, Kennington, Stockwell and west Dulwich, and others again, as Ruskin had done, in prosperous Denmark Hill or perhaps in Streatham, Tulse Hill or Upper Norwood. According to the invaluable Charles Booth's interviewers in 1899, Nonconformist chapels attracted more worshippers than did the Anglican churches if mission halls were included. The two sets of religious professionals lived in separate worlds. But the Church of England was already the traditional path out of dissent for wealthy Nonconformists.

Members of well-known local families with Nonconformist backgrounds, including the Briants, funded much of Lambeth's network of self-help organizations concerned with the indirect relief of poverty. In 1882 Frank Briant became superintendent of Alford House, a Nonconformist club for men and lads on the Duchy of Cornwall estate, still flourishing today. He also served as a Lambeth guardian for 27 years and as a member of the LCC for 13 years, before entering Parliament in 1918. T. B. Briant ran the Lambeth ragged school after 1870, founded nearly 20 years earlier by Henry Beaufoy in connection with the Brixton Independent Church; and W. B. Briant was patron of the Moffat Institute in north Camberwell, where free dinners were given and children in the neighbourhood encouraged to join uniformed organizations. The Unitarian Sir Henry Tate, of sugar cube fame, was another wealthy local philanthropist; the Quaker Barclay family supported the London City Missionaries and were patrons of mission halls; and the temperance advocate W. S. Caine, son of a Liverpool merchant and a Liberal MP, maintained two mission halls and persuaded his own Stockwell Baptist chapel to sponsor Wheatsheaf Hall in 1884, an agent of social reform which drifted into the Congregational Union.

The Liberal, Sir Henry Doulton of the potteries firm, who established the Lambeth School of Art, of interest to settlement workers in *Lambeth Tiles*, had by then, like the international banker C. E. Tritton, a name well known in T & T (Time and Talents) circles, abandoned his parent's dissent for the Church of England and the Conservative Party. Mark Beaufoy MP, an Anglican in another traditional Nonconformist family, nephew of Henry and heir to the eighteenth-century firm of vinegar distillers, initiated various educational and social projects, including the Beaufoy Institute near Lambeth Walk and the Church of England Waifs and Strays' Society, founded in 1881 at the family's home in south Lambeth.

Not surprisingly, there was considerable opposition in some quarters to the COS. Though Dr Solly, who first conceived of the idea of charity organizations, was a Congregationalist, the society had early moved towards a position in which it would have the

Archbishop of Canterbury as president. But as it tried to develop its voluntary poor law system through district committees within the framework of Anglican parishes, while striving to distinguish correctly between the deserving and the undeserving, many local COS workers were told that 'you should trust the poor'.

Mrs Dunn Gardner, a long serving member of the Lambeth Board of Guardians, was well aware of the difficulties they faced. In 1884 she put her thoughts on paper in what was later quoted in COS circles as 'the earliest available document on training for social work'. It was read to the COS general council that November and two years later the COS set up its Joint Committee for Lectures with the WUS and the NUWW. Mrs Dunn Gardner's personality comes alive in her remarks, which, if seemingly obvious, are still relevant today. She insisted that before those in charge of the district committee of the COS could be expected to devote themselves to 'the difficult and troublesome task of training volunteers', they must be really convinced that 'this is one of their chief and most important duties'.

> Trained workers are needed as Guardians, to visit the workhouse and infirmary, to act as school managers and members of Notice B. Committees, to take part in the management of School Banks and Collecting Banks, to visit in connection with the ICAA, the MABYS and the GFS, and with the many Reformatory and Rescue Societies; to work under the clergy and ministers; to act as visitors to the hospitals and as workers for the CCHF, for Evening Clubs for boys and girls, for sanitary aid committees and for many other purposes. Those in charge of our District Offices have made their control the means of training these workers. They will know whether they have hitherto made the most of the trust confided in them.

Largely as a result of this paper, the COS central training committee was appointed in June 1897, a few weeks after the start of the LMHS in Lambeth, and the committee's first report was adopted by the COS council in December 1898. By then the arrival on the scene of several young women residents, educated at

Oxford and eager to offer their services to the COS district officer, had cheered many Lambeth people, whatever their religious slant.

On coming to London as Bishop of Rochester, Dr Talbot, who then gave up the chairmanship of LMH, had promised to pay for a year's rent if suitable premises for an LMHS could be found near the Vauxhall slums where Eleanor Benson had worked before her early death in 1890. Accordingly, a formal proposal to embark on one was made by Edith Pearson at the hall gaudy in 1896. This was seconded by Maggie Benson, and young Edith Langridge was the obvious choice as the settlement's first head, contemporaries appreciating her strong sense of humour, keen critical intellect, shrewd judgement of people and gentle persuasive manner. With a Quaker background on her mother's side, she had been educated at Queen's College, Harley Street from the age of 11 and thus early influenced by the Christian Socialist ideas of its founder, the Revd F. D. Maurice, before being steered to LMH by her brother, of Corpus Christi College.

Wider support was then canvassed in London. As Bishop's House in Kennington Park proved too small to accommodate all those who wished to attend a meeting announced for 18 February 1897, it was held instead at St Mark's parochial hall in Newington. With the bishop on the platform were the rural dean, the headmaster of Merchant Taylor's School and Mr F. H. Rivington, both of whose LMH daughters were actively involved. Also among the ladies were the Honourable Mrs Pascoe Glyn, Mrs Arnold Toynbee and Miss Sewell, head of WUS. Miss Wordsworth said characteristically that women living in a community found that they must get into the habit of being cheerful, this was essential, and laughter greeted her remark that she believed the students at LMH were 'jolly'. Clearly the proposed house in Lambeth would be made as bright as possible. Lord Stamford, the Oxford educated chairman of the COS, then moved the required resolution and Edith Pearson, who had worked at both WUS and St Margaret's House, spoke at some length. Later Lavinia Talbot entered in her diary 'many came back for tea.'

An attractive house in a Georgian terrace overlooking the broad Kennington Road towards Walnut Tree Walk and owned by the Walcot Educational Foundation was vacant, and the 'settlers' were able to move in there after a few months' work. The fact that the rector of Lambeth, a relative of Elizabeth Wordsworth, was one of the Walcot trustees was to prove helpful on more than one occasion. The move took place over Easter.

> The Bishop came to bless us and give us Holy Communion after our first night at the settlement. Till we had No. 131 the chapel was the little room down the passage from the half landing of No. 129. It only held about ten. There was no address but the Bishop stayed to breakfast and talked to us. He took us very much under his wing because of his great affection for LMH and to our great advantage he got Canon Brooke of Kennington, although we were not in his parish, to be Chairman of our Work Committee.

Several of the settlement's first residents already knew the neighbourhood through serving on local committees. They and others were soon helping with the boys' and girls' clubs at the Salamanca Mission, with Sunday schools at St Anselm's in Black Prince Road, St Mary's in Lambeth and St Peter's in Vauxhall, and with work for elderly and sick people. All were made members of the local COS committee, regardless of the tension already existing between this organization and some social workers elsewhere.

Within a few months settlement pioneering had begun with the opening of a class for children unable to go to school, residents' work with the ICAA having shown the need here. The class was held in the settlement garden that first summer, and was visited by Mrs Humphry Ward, who afterwards put pressure on the government to start similar special schools for invalid children.

With the head herself living as one of this small dedicated community, it is hardly surprising that the house kept full while both the workload and the number of volunteers steadily increased.

> So we soon asked the Walcot Trustees to give us the refusal of the adjoining house whenever it became vacant, and within four years we obtained it. By then one of our residents had been elected a Guardian and we were able to

> take in one of Miss Octavia Hill's rent collectors and others whose work gave us further insight into the conditions of the neighbourhood, so that the Settlement was becoming an increasingly good centre for social study as well as for work. Fortunately growth did not in the least impair the strong sense of family life among the residents, which from the first had been a marked feature of the Settlement, just as it had been of the Hall.

The Oxford Mission to Calcutta had for some time been competing with London's East End for support among both senior and junior members of the university, and from its earliest days the LMHS provided the mission with office room. If the demand for such work overseas was later to be given as one reason for the temporary decline of Oxford House, Edith Langridge was clearly a pioneer in regarding her settlement duties as training for such a calling.

In 1902 she resigned her post as head of the settlement and went out to India as leader of the first band of women admitted as probationers of the Oxford Mission under a provisional rule adapted from the brotherhood, becoming here also a beloved figure, combining, as a London contemporary remarked, 'clear-headed business capacity with qualities which had won our hearts and lifted the settlement work into a purer higher atmosphere than mere practical philanthropy'. Eventually the pioneers took life vows and Sister Edith became mother superior. Only after 30 years did she lay down her rule and retire to the community house high up in the Assam hills. In 1928 she briefly visited Oxford for the LMH jubilee celebrations, two years after being made an honorary fellow at the same time as Mrs Arnold Toynbee, and happy to have her niece Christine Anson on the staff there. When Mother Edith died in 1959, the *Church Times* described her as 'in the true succession of the great foundresses of religious orders'. The framed photograph of her as a young woman working at her settlement desk is still a treasured possession in Lambeth.

At least one of her contemporaries realized the first head's stature. 'She is a saint. But that is a secret,' wrote Alice Lucy Holden, treasurer for the settlement before it opened and an early resident. She had taken a science degree (Class III) in 1896 and was typical of the intelligent well-educated young woman who 'is not really wanted at home and would like to study social questions and do charitable work had she not an uneasy feeling that she is both ignorant and incompetent'. In her *Letters from a Settlement* she emphasized the contrast between life there and at Oxford. 'We live in a whirl where quiet thought is almost an impossibility.' The general ugliness, sordid lodging houses and ubiquitous dirt appalled her, but there was compensation in that 'we learn to look at life from an entirely different point of view.'

At first she was taken around by a 'grey lady' in uniform. 'There are two of these ladies working in the parish and as they come from a distance they have a little snuggery at the top of the schools where they can read and write and make tea.'

Settlement work, if not yet seen as a profession, at least demanded training, although early on it was 'difficult to apply the theories of relief as taught by the COS to any of the practical cases I come across'.

Training in method included attendance at committees. 'Every case is discussed in detail, and as there are Church people, Roman Catholics, Dissenters and it may be Agnostics on the committee, you can understand there are sometimes great differences of opinion on the worthiness of the applicants and the best way to help them.'

To complete the training, 'without which no one can be left in charge of a COS office', she had to learn to 'take down a case'. This she found very difficult. 'To sit opposite a proud and sensitive man and be obliged to ask him all sorts of questions about his family and his work, his income and his debts makes me feel hot and cold all over. The temptation to skip difficult questions is almost irresistible.' In connection with this COS work Holden went to lectures on the poor law, the duties of the guardians, the dangers of outdoor relief and treatment of workhouse children, 'all new subjects to me'. She also ran clubs for boys and for girls, became godmother to one child in her district, did her share of encouraging thrift by various forms, and helped with much else, including treats and country holidays. Evening work was no problem but she did not visit in dark courts at night.

She was delighted to be asked to take mixed classes in chemistry and arithmetic at Morley College. The students were aged from 18 to 60.

> As a rule most of them wanted to do fractions. They began them at school but have forgotten all they learnt. Some are in for exams and others want to go up a step at their works. I am getting quite proud of my 'top boy' and I want him to try for some sort of scholarship; there are just a few for the Extension Course at Oxford.

She would have had Charlotte Toynbee's approval here.

After living for some years in Lambeth, Holden devoted much of her life to educational and other local government work in Wolverhampton before spending the Second World War as an ARP warden in Oxford.

Social work training at LMHS took on a new dimension with the arrival of Edith Pearson in 1902, and the settlement's long held reputation as a leader in this field dates from her time. Her responsibilities were to include service on a joint parliamentary advisory committee of MPs and social workers for four years until its meetings in the House of Commons ended in 1914 with the outbreak of war. This also thwarted her plans for linking the settlement with the Webbs' recently formed LSE. She was for many years a member of the central council of the COS and chairwoman of its Lambeth branch, and from 1910 to 1919 lectured at Morley College.

Daughter of Sir Edwin Pearson, fellow of the Royal Society, the second head of the settlement was educated at her home in Chester Terrace, Belgravia, before going up to Oxford on an AEW scholarship in 1879, winning also an LMH scholarship the following year. She read philosophy and some physics and then taught at Wimbledon High School before returning to Oxford as vice-principal first of St Hugh's College and soon afterwards of LMH.

Edith and her mother had stayed with the Talbots when they went up to the university for an exploratory visit. They opted for LMH despite the fact that they did not fit in well with the other, their hostess even using the word 'ugly' in her verdict on the somewhat severe looking young woman and her firmly controlled hair. In due course the settlement secretary was to describe her as 'shy and short-sighted, a little alarming at first sight' and no doubt 'it was not everyone who got behind the veil of her shyness.' However, over the years she became the honoured and trusted friend of many in Lambeth besides the frail and elderly women in her Bible class at the workhouse, others whom she met during her 13 years' service on the Lambeth Board of Guardians and, among public figures, Frank Briant, later to become MP for Lambeth, who found in her a kindred spirit and keen ally in developing social services locally.

Edith Pearson took a considerable part in working out plans with Professor Urwick for the School of Sociology, started in 1903 under the auspices of the COS, the NUWW and the WUS and later to be amalgamated with the LSE; she was both a member of staff and also on the council of the school. Its curriculum stressed practical work under careful supervision, usually in a district office of the COS or with rent collecting, and students visited various poor law and charitable agencies. Here the settlement could make a considerable contribution. Its head, herself a staff lecturer at Caxton Hall, also held classes on her home ground, the fully trained being then expected to stay on for at least a year and take responsibility for some aspect of local work, directing newcomers. She formed other classes for workers unable to take the full course and, since many taught in Sunday schools, lectured on the art of teaching. By 1905 two of her former pupils had posts as hospital almoners, then a new career, and pupil teachers at the local Kennington centre were coming regularly to the settlement on Saturday afternoons where 50 of them had been encouraged to form a club, run by its own committee. Thus a start was made in helping the local community to understand and meet its own needs, now regarded as the main task of present-day community workers.

Edith Pearson also played a major part in the North Lambeth Apprenticeship and Skilled Employment Committee. With no labour exchanges yet in existence, parents had for some time brought their children to the settlement for help in avoiding dead-end jobs, and several residents were involved in patient and specialized counselling. The need had long been clear. Then, shortly before the end of the settlement's first decade, Frank Briant took the chair at a conference held there which launched the new committee, of which one of the residents was appointed honorary secretary. Others embarked on such jobs as raising money for apprenticeship premiums, and Edith Pearson became a member of the Central Apprenticeship Association Council as well as vice president of the north Lambeth committee. Of all contemporary work that found a focus at the settlement for people of various interest, continuing well into the First World War, this was one of the most far-reaching in effect; and at a settlement garden party held in the 1970s an elderly visitor remarked that he had always looked on the place with affection since his parents brought him there as a boy to discuss his future. He had gone into the building trade.

A major change took place in 1907. Incorporation under the Companies Act that year meant that Edith Pearson was relieved of obligations for which hitherto the head of the settlement alone had been legally responsible, and a memorandum and articles of association defined new methods of control. A council had already been set up in 1904, Mrs Arnold Toynbee being among those who then joined, and now was added a body of regular subscribers (with a membership fee of 5/–) spread nationwide and with the power of proxy voting, which was to prove of crucial value in difficult years ahead. By April 1908, when Canon Brooke was established as permanent chairman, the settlement occupied four houses in a row on a 21-year lease, electric light had been installed during a thorough overhaul of the premises and the stables under the last house to be acquired had been reconstructed as a playroom for children on wet days. Residents' fees were then £12 a quarter; visitors paid 25/– a week.

As school care committee work developed, the residents became managers of local schools and Edith Pearson joined the governing bodies of both the Kennington Girls' High School and the Beaufoy Institute.

Soon after the formation by the London County Council (LCC) of a care committee in every school attended by 'necessitous children', both teachers and committee members had urged that the north Lambeth schools should combine to raise funds and arrange dinners in chosen centres. And, when a combined association was formed with a resident as honorary secretary, delegates from each of the care committees, which still kept their responsibilities for home visiting, met monthly at the settlement.

Attractive premises and gardens easily accessible from the main road provided an ideal meeting place for social workers and the general public. The opportunity was not wasted. In 1907 Canon Barnett came from Toynbee Hall to address an influential audience on ways to promote further interest in the Children's Country Holiday Fund (CCHF) and a few weeks later Mrs Mandell Creighton spoke there to members of Church settlements for women on the purpose and scope of the Pan-Anglican Conference. The kitchens had for some time been used by the queen's nurses for their biannual cooking demonstrations; now newcomers finding a welcome included the almoner at St Thomas's Hospital, who numbered several residents among her health visitors at their first conference. They were also currently helping in four Lambeth parishes with a mission held that year, during which the rector of Lambeth again gave Bible readings in the settlement chapel, and the Bishop of Southwark conducted a Holy Week service there as well as one of dedication of the four houses at the start of what was recognized as a new era.

Many school missions were meanwhile going ahead and these, with education and the relation of settlements to universities, were the subject of speeches by Canon Brooke and the warden of Radley at the settlement's AGM in 1907, held again in Oxford, though not under Dr Spooner's direction at New College as three years earlier but at Wadham. Men and women supporters were afterwards entertained to tea by Miss Wordsworth at LMH. Several schools were then helping the settlement, though 'many of our most diligent supporters' still came from Queen's College in Harley Street, where the LMH principal had addressed the settlement's annual meeting in 1902, and from the Francis Holland School.

Supporters had cause at this time to mourn Miss Verney, a settlement worker who over the years had invited sick children to spend happy weeks in cottages on the family estate at Claydon.

Settlement workers were also concerned with holidays for members of the Salamanca Girls' Club and with a Women's Holiday Fund, the hostesses including Lady Antonia Colet at Kemsing as well as several women's institutes, while among other efforts to brighten up the neighbourhood were picture exhibitions and entertainments given in their vacation by LMH students, encouraged by their play-writing principal.

Princess Alexandra had headed a long list of regular donors before the end of the Victorian era, helping a young invalid enjoy a country holiday and sending spring flowers from Sandringham, and now 'a message of sympathy was offered to their Majesties the King and Queen in the great national sorrow. As Princess of Wales, Queen Mary had shown frequent kindness to the settlement and interest in poor persons living on the Duchy of Cornwall estate.'

This wide net of contacts was controlled from the centre by Edith Pearson who, after breakfast while papers piled up on her desk, was usually found to be reading a newspaper in her room, considering, as she told her impatient secretary, that any resident who wanted to talk to her should have first claim on her time.

By 1910 it was clear that 'the scheme for boy and girl applicants in connection with the newly established Labour Exchanges will touch the future of our Apprenticeship Committee as well as those over all London.' And the main speech at the annual meeting held soon afterwards at St Thomas's Hospital concerned the relation of the settlement and all other voluntary work to the coming reform of the poor law.

By 1914 social work had achieved a status which brought it recognition as a form of national service. The poor man's lawyer scheme at LMHS was an early casualty at that time, this valuable service being by then well established in a room there but having to be given up when three legal volunteers who had taken on the job resigned in turn to join the armed forces. However, other workers were encouraged when the annual service was held that year for the first time in the private chapel of Lambeth Palace, Mrs Randall Davidson, like her husband, being interested in settlement work. But though Bishop Talbot had by then moved to Winchester, it was not until after his death in 1934 that the Archbishop of Canterbury became president of the settlement council. Till 1910 Mrs Talbot had 'managed, amid her many engagements, to find time to attend the meetings of the Executive Committee and has taken the most genuine interest in our well being'. The active family connection was then maintained through her daughter May, who became a member of council.

When Edith Pearson retired in 1915 to continue social work on various fronts from her new home in Wiltshire, her secretary Katharine Thicknesse was appointed settlement warden for what proved a comparatively uneventful decade. Bishop Thicknesse's daughter knew the area well, having come to work there in 1899 at the age of 23. Her main contribution was through the scheme for training Church workers, and she sat on various committees, both diocesan and inter-diocesan, to work out plans directed by the Bishop of Stepney. But when the new warden took over in 1915 her immediate task was to keep the place going with a diminished number of residents and consequent financial problems, while helping with local war work. As air raids began, residents would hurry along to local shelters to help entertain groups of children with story-telling during the dangerous hours. The settlement chapel was much used at this time by wives and mothers of men serving in the armed forces, for whom the residents ran a club. Then, in June 1918, when the end of war was in sight, the settlement celebrated its twenty-first birthday at a garden party in Lambeth Palace, the guests being again welcomed there by the Archbishop and Mrs Davidson.

Peace brought a return to the former pattern of social work and training, residents continuing their parish work with clubs, visiting, Bible classes and relief committees; their COS involvement in north Lambeth, Vauxhall and Battersea; their hours spent with hospital out-patients under an almoner's direction; their rent and provident collecting together with visiting and other detailed jobs concerned with the CCHF and the ICAA; and their help in local emergencies such as the Thames flood disaster of 1928.

By 1930 the settlement was training students for social science certificates at the LSE and Bedford College for the certificate of the Charity Organization Society (COS), for the bishop's recognition under the Inter-Diocesan Council of Women's Work, and also providing practical experience to complete what was necessary to gain the recently established Oxford University social training certificate.

The friendly personality of Olive Butler, by then in charge, found expression particularly in club work. Daughter of the first headmaster of Harleybury who, as a don at Oxford, had played a significant part in the women's educational movement, she lived at the settlement from 1911 to 1935 (with the exception of part of the First World War), spending her last ten years there in what had become the salaried post of warden. Much of the later work owed its inception to her realization of the changing needs of the district, and none was dearer to her heart than The Duke, the long since bombed out and demolished public house in Vauxhall. During her time of office the opportunity arose of securing this and other public houses as club premises. With parents away in the armed forces or working long hours, attention had been drawn to the urgent need for a club for older boys and girls. The help of the YWCA was enlisted in 1917 and, under its management, a girls' club known as the Dug Out was started with a settlement worker as its first leader. But the premises proved unsuitable and in 1921 the club was closed. About the same time the settlement undertook care committee responsibilities for the Vauxhall Street LCC school, and soon afterwards residents started an old scholars' club in a room there. Then in 1927 the adjacent Duke of Clarence public house became redundant and the settlement, helped by the Social Service Union of the Oxford Society for Home Students, took the place on. The home students had a beaver as their badge, and soon the beavers and the sallies, members of the still flourishing Salamanca Girls' Club of earlier days, were joining up for a Whit Sunday outing to Oxford.

When unemployment and its attendant miseries were dominating the bad years of 1932 and 1933 Miss Butler's vision was realized of a family club where local people of all ages would drop in for a chat, advice and recreation. Soon, besides some 300 children happy to turn up after school, there were Scouts, Guides and Brownies, a father's club, the Lambeth Players and a musical society all managing to coexist in a building which held many small rooms.

As increasing numbers brought further development of the settlement's educational work, some of the more adventurous club members, though not ready for formal LCC courses, willingly joined a class there and the children's library became increasingly popular, while delicate girls from the Lollard Street schools were taught during summer months in the settlement garden. The Lambeth flower show owed its inception at this time to LMHS. The pattern went on for years, until community work became the accepted norm.

8

Time and Talents: Peckham and Katherine Low Settlements

After university women had led the way the settlement movement soon spread among a younger age group. Thus the T & T guild, described at its start as 'a Union of Service amongst girls of leisure', was pioneered by members of the Young Women's Christian Association (YWCA) already helping poor working girls. Its influence was to extend far beyond Britain.

In 1888 volunteers at the YWCA headquarters in Russell Square decided that many West End homes included daughters 'with good hearts doing very little, who need a religious society to bring them together and offer opportunities for service'. A drawing room meeting was arranged and when a number of them, several accompanied by their maids, arrived at the chosen house in the Hyde Park area, the organizer pointed out 'the great opportunities there are for service and how it is the privilege of those who have time and talents at their disposal to use them for those who have so little'. Emphasizing work that could largely be done from home, she instanced copying missionaries' letters and helping to raise funds for a hospital in Bethnal Green and a club in Bermondsey.

Both idea and title quickly caught on. By the summer of 1889 the YWCA had a T & T department, with Lady Victoria Buxton as president and Mrs Abel Smith as honorary secretary, T & T centres having already been organized in two of the five home divisions of the YWCA.

The first T & T centre in Scotland was started that October and the following year over 100 T & T members north of the border provided a stall at their YWCA bazaar. Families of poor children had been sent petticoats, chest preservers and other garments, and help had been given in furnishing YWCA central premises newly set up in Edinburgh. Moreover, a 'young Australian lady, who was among the first to join the Edinburgh North Centre, has been the means since returning to her home of starting T & T in Melbourne and the suburbs.' Within two years Australia had over 100 T & T members. Others were at work in Ireland, where Lady Dufferin was in due course to accept the presidency, and the movement had spread also to Florence, Constantinople and Gibraltar.

In June 1890, when presidents and secretaries of 24 English centres held their second annual conference in the West End, attended by representatives from each of the YWCA home divisions, the departmental bye-laws about to be submitted by the committee to the YWCA council would, it was hoped, 'make the whole standing of the department permanently satisfactory'. And so it proved.

Work was now divided into sections for pioneers, volunteers, missionary, mutual improvement, Christian evidence and students, a subsequent literacy section proving particularly vigorous. Most members, besides giving practical help, were expected to hold Bible readings, some also deciding to study the course suggested by the society for promoting higher religious education. Among the 24 centres already established in London and southern England, the most active were in Belgravia, Cheltenham, Croydon, Dulwich and also South Kensington, where Mrs Herbert Tritton and her daughters gave an enthusiastic lead from their home at 36 Queen's Gate Gardens.

Work had also begun in London's East End with the appointment in March 1890 of Miss Flowers to take charge of a girls' club in Spitalfields. And the frequent change of premises associated with T & T adventures was soon apparent. In April 1893 the club moved to the adjoining densely populated parish of Whitechapel where the welcoming rector had offered two rooms on the ground floor of Sir George's Residence, a large building off the busy High Street and only a few minutes walk from Aldgate East station. A two-bedroomed top floor flat nearby was also available and Miss Mabel Buxton was the first T & T member to stay there with Miss Flowers. Another visitor remarked, 'Our little flat has proved a very convenient and happy abode and the advantage thus secured of having this tiny settlement of our own is most helpful.' It was at least a start, and Hampstead (Christ Church) centre was among several which supported the Whitechapel club during 1894.

A year later T & T emerged as an independent society on the departure to Adelaide of Lady Victoria Buxton after her husband had been appointed governor general of Western Australia; and Mrs Herbert Tritton now became the first national T & T chairwoman, work, however, being largely in the hands of young members including her own two daughters.

There was already a strong accent on service abroad and in 1896 Una Saunders, head of the T & T central volunteers' section, went to Bombay to help at a missionary settlement started by British university women for educated Parsee women and girls: before leaving England she spoke at the annual conference, again held that year at Mrs Tritton's home, where another speaker drew attention to the needs of the YWCA in Alexandria, asking if any T & T member would go out there as secretary. Supporters in the educational world by now included Miss Wordsworth, principal of LMH, who welcomed T & T holiday campers to the college grounds, and Miss Soulsby, head of the Oxford High School for Girls, who emphasized in one speech that 'a period of work with a settlement should be a part of every girl's education'. They both did much to help here.

During 1898 the guild was asked to befriend factory girls in Bermondsey, so corporate work moved there from Whitechapel. Canon Lewes, rector of St Mary Magdalene and soon to be Bishop of Kingston, exempted from T & T care only those already belonging to the YWCA and who, known as the 'aristocratic ones', were for the most part attending his wife's sewing classes. Presidents and secretaries of T & T centres were now told that 'The Rector has handed over the entire responsibility of the rough girls of the parish to your settlement. There are over 24,000 struggling poor in the parish and over 15 factories, some of them employing as many as 400 girls.'

They quickly responded to efforts made on their behalf. Thus 'Teacher! Got a flower for me?' was a usual greeting for Frances Bathurst, who now took charge of the work from three rooms at 33 Bermondsey Square, about ten minutes walk from London Bridge station, to which she had moved with her maid Jane, a courageous pair. Music was another attraction. Night after night the newcomer played the piano near an open window of her downstairs room and the 'wild spirits' collected outside to listen and then were lured inside until, after a few weeks, the room would hold no more and she moved to larger premises nearby. In *News from the Flat* she was soon appealing for helpers to visit factories, explaining that 'dinners, which gave our workers an opportunity to get to know the girls, are provided twice a week and will be increased as funds permit. Girls pay as much as they are able but not enough to cover the cost.' Local employers naturally encouraged this initiative.

Indeed so successful was she that in May 1899 two adjoining houses in dingy Bermondsey Street, one of them occupied on the ground floor by a tailor, were opened as settlement premises when the Honourable Mrs Pelham, as president, welcomed 80 guests including representatives from most of the English centres as well as the rector and other local clergy; and an announcement was made that classes would be held in the small front room when volunteers came forward to teach girls singing, basket work 'or any special industry'. Miss Marples, who worked the parochial branch of the YWCA, rented two rooms on the top floor, a spare room for T & T members was furnished by the Hyde Park centre and, in December 1890, news was circulated that the club was doing well.

But before long Miss Bathurst left to marry the local curate; then Miss Marples, who took over from her, married the local doctor. Another volunteer, Mrs Stewart, also married locally. Settling in the East End clearly had its attractions. The work was then carried on by the Honourable Anne Macnaughton, a gifted, sympathetic leader with a strong sense of humour, who was later to be governor of the Barnardo Homes.

A Victoria memorial fund appeal was soon launched for £1000 to build a larger club room, as many girls who applied for cheap dinners had often to be turned away: some were artificial flower makers, others shirt and collar stitchers or 'more homely chocolate and jam hands'. Then the Victoria Hall, adjoining the settlement, was opened in February 1902 by the Bishop of Rochester and, though HM Princess Victoria of Schleswig Holstein could not be there (she came instead in June), the mayor of Bermondsey and an alderman attended in their robes, hearing Dr Talbot speak on the importance of making greater sacrifices for those who needed help and sympathy. Several workers at other settlements were by now members of the T & T volunteers' section, and Miss Benson appealed to them at this time for help as watchers at the Southwark and Lambeth free loan exhibition of pictures, her particular concern at WUS. Moreover, factory owners in the neighbourhood had given active support, one of them, Mr Barron, installing a telephone at the settlement.

Violet Tritton, then in her early twenties, was already showing the character which over the next 50 years was to make her one of the most loved and respected figures in Bermondsey. And she was largely instrumental in moving the girls at Dockhead, where the Oxford Mission ran a club house, into the nearby empty White Hart pub.

A young volunteer whom she recruited to take a singing class there recalled how:

> One evening the girls were becoming increasingly unruly when a gang of boys started battering at the doors and windows, shouting and cat calling. Vi walked quickly to the door, said something to the boys and they faded away into the night. The streets were unlit and narrow, but as one walked along them with Vi, all one's fears vanished.

Another volunteer remembered 'terrifying visits to factories in the dinner hour. We seemed to enter Bedlam, and then Vi would be recognized and they would turn to listen to what she had to say. She spoke simply and directly about the Kingdom of God.' And her appeal was not only as a missioner. 'Her gift of humour saved many a tedious committee and strained situation and her enjoyment of life was shared with everyone she met.'

By 1906 cheap dinners were provided three times a week, while each visitor had a room in a factory where she held services, distributed flowers and made friends with the workers, with Bible classes, a library and country outings being also part of the scene. And a gentler mood was already apparent when the Excelsior Club at Dockhead was opened in 1907.

Bermondsey's old parish church, closely associated with the Cluniac abbey in medieval days, stood in the park with the rectory beside it and the settlement nearby. In February 1908 an historical pageant on old Bermondsey was organized to raise money and extend the work among factory girls.

Soon afterwards a new and stimulating character arrived. Sister Marjorie, sometimes still known as Miss Hobbs, was introduced by the Bishop of Southwark as the incoming head of the settlement, when the newly converted premises at 187 Bermondsey Street, adjoining the Victoria Hall, were opened. This small rosy-cheeked Irish woman, a trained Mildmay deaconess with a varied experience of work among girls in India, was to spend eight years in the area. Her somewhat prim appearance belied a strong personality. Her main pioneering was to launch a hostel for girls with no homes of their own. She found a verminous old lodging house and, against all advice, cleaned it up and converted it into one-roomed flatlets, the first of its kind in London. By 1909 she had six resident helpers, some 70 girls were regularly attending clubs at the settlement and at Dockhead, and 250 lives were influenced each day through clubs and cheap dinners.

A new Dockhead club was opened in June 1911. In 1912 Violet Tritton wrote about the real friends of the Bermondsey club who week after week pilgrimaged down there and helped to make the clubs what they are – 'the happiest and best loved places in London'. Her technique for enlisting volunteers combined happily with Sister Marjorie's more stringent approach. Now one representative from each T & T centre was invited to spend three nights at the settlement each year as a guest while all workers were asked to let the head know what was required, particularly in the way of flowers, fruit and poultry.

During the First World War T & T was kept going by the few who struggled on; then the questioning mood, characteristic of it, re-emerged with the return of peace. Soon afterwards it was decided that the guild should be interdenominational, that there should be an age limit of 35 ('older women could become associates') and that in the membership, differences of creed, nationality and class should cease to exist, all members pledging themselves to carry out the three aims of service, prayer and fellowship.

The work in Bermondsey now became the main focus for the T & T guild and, led by the warden, local club members took an increasing share of being represented on hostel and settlement committees and staffing the children's club in Dockhead.

Backed as it was by the efforts of the older associates, T & T in the interwar years came to be a real influence, a centre for pioneer work, a normal force in Bermondsey and a rallying point of friendship for many and varied people. Moreover, Violet Tritton, though often abroad or working elsewhere, still took a major part, and in 1928 was made chairwoman of the Dockhead club executive committee, which undertook to raise £14,000 and rebuild the premises.

Though T & T training for professional social work had not then the emphasis given it, for example, in Peckham, early educative efforts were maintained by the *Newsletter*, started in 1890. By now it included mention of Parliamentary bills on social questions. Missionary work abroad had long loomed large in its columns, especially in connection with the Bombay settlement and the girls' movement of the Church Missionary Society. The desired wider circulation was achieved in 1929 when T & T combined with the Girls' Diocesan Association (GDA) to issue the first number of the *Review*, edited by Ruth Bailey, who had left Oxford four years earlier: and partly through her Lyttelton family connections she had a broad view of the settlement movement. The GDA was open to 'educated girls of the Anglican Church between the ages of 17 to 35' and its members were referred to in T & T circles as 'our half cousins'. They helped in the Dockhead scheme and ran a stall at the T & T bazaar in 1930. St Mildred's House on the Isle of Dogs was also involved here, sharing the bazaar profits of £1000; for 'about two and a half years ago three of us who happened to belong to the GDA came to help and since then there has been a steady influx of people wanting to share in the Island's life.' The joint *Review* was published until the outbreak of the Second World War, when the T & T guild reverted to its original short news-sheet.

Meanwhile, Honoria Harford had succeeded Sister Marjorie as settlement head in the mid-1920s. A capable, energetic and stimulating speaker, like her sister Laetitia who was later president of the British Association of Residential Settlements (BARS), she was often away canvassing support among centres. In 1931 she moved to 225 Abbey Street as leader of the new Dockhead club formed the previous year, and Lesley Sewell, chair of the settlement's finance and housing committee, became warden at 187 Bermondsey Street. Partnership was the key to local action, and the early months of 1939 saw this settlement flourish.

Though Canon Veazey was given a mandate to start the United Girls' School Mission (UGSM), later called the Union of Girls' Schools for Social Service (UGS), it was the brainchild of Mrs C. R. Bailey, wife of the organizing secretary of the Rochester Diocesan Board of Women's Work. In May 1895, seven years after the formation of the guild at Cheltenham Ladies' College, it occurred to her that girls in many other recently established secondary schools might well undertake the corporate mission work currently attracting public school boys and undergraduates. The Baileys consulted their bishop, the Rt Revd Randall Davidson, and several headmistresses, all of whom welcomed the ideas, so a small promotion committee was set up in 1896 which included Miss (later Dame) Frances Dove, head of Wycombe Abbey, Miss Douglas of Godolphin School, Miss Williamson of the Princess Helena College and Miss Miller of St Bernard's Redhill, with Miss MacArthur as honorary secretary. They agreed on a common purpose: 'to bring brightness and hope into lives and homes; to help men and women to realize that they are children of God; and to plant and work a mission that shall be the centre of increasing sweetness and light, and health in its widest sense, to all around'. And when towards the end of that year the Edward Talbots came south from Leeds on his appointment as Bishop of Rochester, both he and his wife were immediately involved in settlement work.

Until her cousin Helen Gladstone became head of the WUS, Mrs Talbot's main link there was through its LMH supporters, including the Benson sisters, Edith Argles and Edith Langridge, though she more than once canvassed support for it at Girton and Newnham. She joined the LMHS committee at its start. The T & T settlement in Bermondsey and Mrs Humphry Ward's Passmore Edwards Settlement in Bloomsbury were soon to be well known to her. And while in the USA with the bishop in 1897 she visited 'a delightful women's settlement called after E. Denison in what looked to me an intensely quiet comfortable part of Boston but they seem to have corresponding work to ours. A nice Miss Dudley at the head.' Later she entertained the Duchess of Albany, founder and president of the settlement in Deptford.

Moreover, with three children still at school her influence was naturally exercised on behalf of the UGSM. Her younger daughter, then aged 15, was sent to the Francis Holland School in Graham Street, Westminster. And Miss M. Wolseley-Lewis, appointed as the youthful head when it moved from Eaton Terrace nearby in 1894, served for many years on the mission's executive committee: she had the support there of the daughters of Bishop Wilkinson, formerly vicar of St Peter's, Eaton Square, and was guided by its co-founder and chairman, Canon Scott Holland of Canterbury, who came weekly to give divinity lessons, for, in Canon Veazey's words, 'she quickly realized what the UGSM could be to God's poor but it could also mean much as a Mission to the girls themselves. ... Thus Graham Street had the honour and good fortune of being one of the Founders of the United Girls School Mission.'

Victorian philanthropy had recently extended to Deptford. For centuries travellers had passed over the 'depe ford' built in the marshes by the Romans to ease land transport from Dover to London. Then Henry VIII's shipbuilding industry changed Deptford from a maritime village to a prosperous small town before the industrial revolution brought in an era of mean back streets. The young Duchess of Albany, widow of Queen Victoria's fourth son, started a settlement there during 1894 and in 1898 her brother-in-law, HRH Albert Edward, Prince of Wales, laid the foundation stone of a building in Creek Road, which was to serve as headquarters for the Albany settlement for over 80 years. Money-raising was naturally important and, in June 1902, Lavinia Talbot 'went to a huge luncheon at the Mansion House to meet [the] Duchess of Albany and [her] charming little daughter re Deptford Fund, with discussion afterwards'. Later that month she was glad 'to see Edith Langridge who had Barissal of India talk with Ted, just back from seven and a half months in India, very brisk, well, thinner and full-of talk'. Then in July 'to Deptford Fund meeting with Duchess of Albany, everyone mopping in the heat'.

Settlement engagements in November 1904 included 'a great sale for UGS Mission; received the Duchess of Albany and had to make a speech. It was all a great success. £300 made. Then with Lucy to Dulwich College for temperance meeting.' Later that month she went 'to party of Helen Gladstone's at University Settlement' before going to Repton to see her daughter May, by now married to Lionel Ford; and on another day 'with Constance to UGS Mission Sale, Winny in full swing over refreshment stall.'

Mrs Talbot was elected first president of the UGSM and it was in no small part due to her enthusiasm that 41 schools had joined before it was officially launched in 1897, and that by 1906 the number of supporting schools and old girls' associations (OGAs) had risen to 140. As in her Oxford days, diary entries put settlement affairs in a wide if chatty perspective. Thus on 24 October 1896, 'Am in a nightmare over Lambeth. L. Creighton came to sleep and went on to Deptford where she spoke very well to Ladies' meeting on rescue work.' Next day there was 'a Missionary meeting close by, E in the chair'; and on 24 October she attended 'a School Mission Guild at Paradise Square. A Mr Veazey to be Missioner.' The young Harry Veazey took up his new responsibilities in Camberwell soon afterwards with a mandate both to run a mission in the St Hilda's part of St Mark's parish just off the Old Kent Road, and also to start a UGSM to work among 7000 poor people crowded together in that area.

Ordained in 1892 in the diocese of Rochester, his interest in social problems developed during two years in Stockwell and four in Woolwich, then found ample scope in Camberwell where, as vicar of St Mark's from 1902 until three years before his death in 1951, he became an outstanding figure, remarkable especially for his gift of inspiring others, whether as parish priest, rural dean or canon of the cathedral. Helped by his wife Mabel he gave UGSM its early impetus and direction and, as a borough councillor, top of the poll in local elections, pioneered much social work that has since been absorbed into the normal life of the community.

'At a meeting of headmistresses and others about a year after our start in 1896', reminisced Canon Veazey shortly before his retirement,

> I was able to announce that a large leasehold house in Calmington Road, with a tumbledown skin-drying shed in the rear, had unexpectedly come on to the market. I suggested that one would be just right for housing our first Mission staff, and the other for building an iron-roofed Mission Hall on the site of the shed, but that £300 would be needed for one and £500 for the other. There was a real health problem at the time, with no district nurse, no ante-natal or dental aids, no infant welfare, school clinics or milk supplies, no hospital savings association.

Before the end of that year the UGSM was established at St Hilda's Mission Hall in Kempstead Road, off Albany Street, with Miss Rennie as honorary secretary. Two years later Bishop Talbot drew up the UGSM's special prayer and by 1900 some 84 schools and OGAs were helping in some way.

The UGSM extended its befriending work as quickly as more schools joined. In its adopted areas both in south London and elsewhere, it was soon carrying on, in its missioner's words, 'all kinds of helpful social and religious work, for children, young people, women and men alike, through Sunday schools, clubs, guilds, classes, gymnasiums, Guides, Scouts, Brownies, Cubs, and in a host of other ways such as Mothers and Babies Welcomes, Children's Clinics and aftercare'. Though services were financed for the most part by money-raising efforts of girls while still at school, the work itself was largely done by 'old girls' as 'once in a weekers', led by trained staff.

Wycombe Abbey led the way by establishing a special link with the young ICAA. An early volunteer wrote:

> The UGS Mission in Calmington Road was just starting work with the first Old Girls from its schools, when the ICAA asked the Missioner, then Mr Veazey, if the Mission would undertake the work in Camberwell, and he entrusted it to the first batch of Wycombe Abbey seniors. A list of 80 names and addresses was handed to us, and we set to work to visit, to find out how to do our job and what was needed for our children. A large part of our work consisted in visiting and teaching children in their own homes, supplying invalid carriages and chairs and collecting 2d a week for their hire, and trying to cheer and help gallant mothers nursing TB hips and spines on chairs in the kitchen. All we could then hope for was to alleviate and bring a little interest into a dreary and miserable existence. It was a great day when we managed to get one of those children away to skilled care and nursing. We began with Camberwell, then Talbot settlement took over an area near them which was called south Camberwell, but was returned to us again in a couple of years, and in 1924 we took over Dulwich so that we now include the whole area.

Ten years after the UGSM shouldered responsibility for the ICAA in Camberwell it became a fully-fledged ICAA branch with its own committee and, by the mid-1930s, 30 UGSM members and 11 students were helping in this work, based at the settlement.

Wycombe Abbey seniors were also responsible for early experiments in school feeding before the first infant welfare centre in Camberwell was provided by mission workers in Cobing Road. Later the UGSM built premises for this centre in its own garden, while maintaining at the same time a second centre at 60a Amott Road where local women, including young expectant mothers, welcomed lectures in hygiene, health, cooking and sewing. Girls from Queen Anne's School, Caversham ran a succession of Christmas parties at these two welfare centres, while others from Putney High School concentrated on summer garden treats, with news of both centres and of the Camberwell branch of the ICAA being issued for many years as part of the UGS report.

The UGS settlement dates from 1906. That year the bishop considered it was time for the mission to extend its work and at a meeting held in the Grosvenor Gardens home of Mrs R. J. Cooper (Constance Grant-Thorold, an old girl of the Francis Holland School in Graham Street) he suggested that the proposed settlement should be sited either in Camberwell or Battersea. Eventually 19 Peckham Road was taken and work began there under the direction of Miss Gooch, with Miss de Burgho-Hodge as vice head, both well known in Francis Holland School circles.

> Anyone who helped there in those early days must remember the charm of the place, the pleasant old house with a big comfortable drawing room which always seemed full of flowers, and the friendly cheerful lunches and tea. Of course this was largely due to Miss Gooch herself. It is difficult to describe that most attractive personality, so absolutely good and possessed also of delightful humour. Alas her time there was very short, for she died the next year, having laid her foundations well and truly, and managed to secure No. 17 as an additional house.

She was succeeded by Miss de Burgho-Hodge, who carried the settlement through the difficult years of the First World War.

Within a few days of its declaration,

> hundreds of angry and tearful wives were at the Town Hall, asking what they should do as they would get no Army or Navy allowance for a month at least. The Mayor promptly sent them to the settlement, and ... the settlement committee drew out its entire balance of £300 and trusted to Providence that they would be repaid.

More money soon came in, its doors were reopened and thereafter a few workers kept up the settlement's reputation as a good friend and neighbour.

Diocesan links further developed in 1919 when the Bishop of Southwark became the settlement's warden (the title soon changed to visitor) and again three years later when Dr Herbert, Bishop of Kingston, was elected chairman of the executive committee.

During 1924 the settlement was able to expand into adjoining premises and a social services bureau was opened there for volunteers concerned with the current problems of bad housing, unemployment and adolescent troubles arising partly from the closure of the continuation schools. The name of UGSM was now changed to the UGS and thousands of pupils, past and present, responded to the bishop's appeal for a widespread corporate effort, realizing that 'Our Founders' ultimate aim was to bring the need, the interest and the joy of Social Service before all Girls' Schools and so to enlist an ever growing body of workers in our ranks.'

'The training of students was always a special favour if not the *raison d'être* of the Peckham Road Settlement,' wrote Miss Green, warden from 1923 to 1930. The benefit was mutual, for without the help of eager young students the settlement staff in all departments would not, as they agreed, have been able to cope with the work for which they were responsible.

Among many old girls helping the settlement at this time was Miss G. C. Bacchus, formerly at Godolphin School and Newnham. Then, after working for a social science certificate at the LSE, she served for two years as an assistant organizer of childcare under the LCC before taking charge of the settlement's care committee office, while also acting as assistant to the club leader. Her main work at this time was to create two orchestras, before an unexpected opportunity occurred for her in 1929 to study at the Royal College of Music. She then kept on the senior orchestra at the settlement while another student at the college, formerly at Wycombe Abbey, took the junior, spending one day a week teaching as well as conducting. Perhaps the keenest recruit was

> a boy of 14, about 4' 6" high, who left school at Christmas and became a butcher's assistant. Throughout the week he cuts up meat and makes sausages out of it (and even appears to get pleasure out of doing so) and on Monday, his free afternoon, he tramps all the way to the settlement, a walk of nearly half an hour each way, first to have his cello lesson in the afternoon, and again in the evening for the orchestra practice.

He was one of five cello pupils, 'all of whom are making real progress'.

Teaching sick children in hospital engaged several UGSM members. In 1929 four more volunteered for this work, so the settlement was able to start classes that year in a second hospital.

The broad support enjoyed by the UGS at this time is evident from its 1929 advisory council. This included Eleanor Rathbone, Elizabeth Macadam (honorary secretary, Joint University Council for Social Studies), Hilda Cashmore (warden of the Manchester University Settlement), Percy Iden (chairman of the executive committee of the British Institute of Social Services), the Revd J. Scott Lidgett DD, Miss Butler (Barnett House, Oxford), Miss Ashley (Edinburgh Council for Social Service), R. H. Tawney (LSE) and W. Melland (Manchester and Salford Council of Social Service).

The settlement had solved a major problem the previous year when the site of its three houses in Peckham Road was sold to enable building to go ahead for a housing estate; but only after weeks of anxious search did hopes centre on Stafford Street hall, formerly a Wesleyan church and at the time used as an LCC school. There was no garden, but a playground at the side gave scope for development. Negotiations were quickly completed with the Wesleyan trustees for the purchase of the hall at a cost of £3000, another £4000 being needed for alterations and repairs, and the move took place before Christmas.

Queen Mary opened the new settlement building in May 1931, Lady May Abel Smith having by then become president of the UGS. Energetic fund raising among schools and OGAs substantially reduced the UGS debt, so St Mark's church was completed and plans went ahead for a Christmas fair. Then in 1934 the whole picture was changed by the generosity of Mrs Townsend, who gave the settlement five houses in Goldsmith Road, at its junction with Staffordshire Street. Their transformation and incorporation into the settlement buildings were soon accomplished and the warden and residents were able to move in by June 1935.

Among leaders in the 1930s were the new warden, Dr Gertrude Willoughby of Paris University who, like her predecessor, emphasized social work training, and Miss Elsie Bowerman, a barrister at law elected honorary treasurer for the UGS, then honorary secretary and later president. Like Canon Veazey and others, Miss Bowerman campaigned vigorously for support among schools throughout the country.

With its feeling for tradition always strong, the Peckham settlement later welcomed as its president Lady (Geoffrey) Howe, a former pupil of Wycombe Abbey.

At least two other London settlements were started independently by staff, pupils and old girls of schools, one in Battersea, the other in Stepney.

Katherine Low, after attending the Francis Holland School in Graham Street, was treasurer of the UGSM for 15 years, and when she died in 1923 there was widespread support for a memorial to this 'delightful personality with a great desire to do all that she could for those in less happy circumstances than herself'. The initiative here was taken by Miss Morison, then head of this school and, like her predecessor M. Wolseley-Lewis, a long serving member of the UGS executive committee.

Charles Booth in his book on London had blacked an area in Battersea just off the High Street as 'irreclaimable' and the description fired the imagination of the small committee appointed to find work that would have appealed to Katherine Low. While exploring a particularly drab area of crowd tenements they saw an empty house called The Cedars at the corner of the High Street and Orville Road. Long occupied by two philanthropic ladies, Miss Nesta Lodge had lived on there after the death of her sister, to whom she had built a memorial chapel, until eventually ill health obliged her to leave, when she handed the premises over to Christ's College, Cambridge; but the only local evidence of this in 1924 was a boys' club run there by the college.

Enquiries elicited that Christ's College was willing to let The Cedars at a nominal rent provided it was used for charitable purposes and money was available to repair and redecorate the house. The challenge was accepted by Miss Low's friends and seven schools, led by the Francis Holland School. The Katherine Low Settlement at 108 High Street, sometimes then called The Cedars, was opened on 24 May 1924 by HRH the Duchess of York, who, as Queen Elizabeth the Queen Mother, was to visit it again 40 years later.

Cheering crowds and coloured banners transformed the dreary neighbourhood that opening day: a choir from supporting schools sang 'Lift Up Your Hearts' and Bishop Talbot, who had consented to bless the house, was there with his wife and Canon Veazey, the canon later remarking that, 'Graham Street splendidly became the settlement's principal godmother in addition to what it was already doing for the UGS part of south London.' It was emphasized at the start that 'training of workers under experienced guidance will be undertaken and arrangements can be made for students to attend the Social Science Course at Bedford College, or the London School of Economics'. More school leavers were thus steered towards a worthwhile career.

Miss de Burgho-Hodge, the recently retired head of the UGS settlement, who took on the job of honorary warden, gathered many enthusiastic workers around her during the next six years. Her chief assistant was Miss Gotto and, according to Lady Elizabeth Pleydell-Bouverie, who was early involved there, 'They made a comic couple, for Miss Hodge was very tall and not a little frightening and Miss Gotto was tiny like a bustling little wren.' There were four residents at the start. A popular mothers' club was opened in 1924 by Mrs Hamilton who ran it for the first 12 years, and soon lack of space prevented the inclusion of numerous children who begged to be allowed to join the various other clubs.

Miss Katrine Baird of Abbot's Hill School, one of the founders and a generous benefactor, was chairwoman of the settlement's first management committee, and when she died in 1932 her old girls decided, as an addition to the recently acquired 106 High Street, intended as a hostel for students and girls from supporting schools, to build a new and much needed club room called the Katrine Baird Memorial Hall. This was opened in December 1933 and later housed the CAB, which was started by the settlement in the Second World War. Travel problems were more demanding elsewhere for West End school supporters of the settlement movement including some in Hammersmith.

St Paul's Girls' School Union for Social Work (SPGSUSW) was founded by the pioneering headmistress, Miss Frances Gray, on 15 July 1912 and later she was to remark, 'I do not think that there was any time after I began to make plans for the school when there was not floating somewhere among them an idea that we must do something for those less fortunate than ourselves.' Members of the SPGSUSW had embarked on a local school care committee centred at two rooms in Rectory Square, Stepney. Two years later CCHF work was added and a girls' club opened in borrowed premises; then in 1916 an infant welfare centre was started with help from a local doctor and superintendent. Before the end of 1918, through the generosity of one old Paulina's father, Dame Colet House (DCH) was in action as a residential settlement. Its premises were near the People's Palace in the Mile End Road, and Miss Searle, warden until 1935, was helped at the start by another old Paulina, Joyce Field, who lived there for eight years while studying at the LSE and later teaching. During this time six Guide companies, one Ranger company and two Brownie packs were started as well as several clubs, and a woman poor man's lawyer attended at DCH once a week. But young helpers still found the long train journey from the West End a considerable disincentive to social work. However, two years later the Stepney Housing Trust was formed, and three resulting blocks of flats, named respectively Frances Gray House, Paul's House and Searle House, survived the East End ordeal of 1940, an island in a mass of rubble.

DCH was firmly established in a modern building opened in Ben Jonson Road, Stepney in 1957. The ownership of the leasehold property was transferred from the trustees of the SPGSUSW to the trustees of the Frances Gray memorial fund in 1969, after the parent school had withdrawn its involvement to concentrate on similar work near at hand. Among old Paulinas actively involved in later years were Miss Miranda Gwyer as a trustee of the Frances Gray memorial fund and Mrs Peggy Jay JP, as management committee chairwoman of what was renamed a social action centre.

Meanwhile, Mrs Heather Brigstocke, after a period in charge of the Francis Holland School in Marylebone's Baker Street, was appointed high mistress of St Paul's Girls' School and in due course became president of the nearby West End settlement in Fulham started in memory of Bishop Creighton.

9

Mrs Humphry Ward and Mrs Mandell Creighton

Mary Ward and Louise Creighton, brides together at Oxford, made a major contribution in extending settlement influence at home and abroad. And, unlike most pioneering social workers, they early became well-known figures, for Dr Arnold's Paulina soon proved herself a successful author and her friend steered the influential National Council of Women Workers in its formative years.

When Humphry Ward joined the staff of *The Times* in 1882 he settled at 61 Russell Square, an eighteenth-century house in Bloomsbury with a garden adjoining Queen Square. Mary found time to review French and German books for her husband's paper as well as looking after their children, entertaining a rapidly growing circle of friends and working on her first novel, *Miss Bretherton*. This came out early in 1884 and that November she embarked on *Robert Elsmere*, Toynbee Hall and Oxford House having just started.

The new book was intended as a study of how human life reflected the clash between older and younger types of Christianity, the rector of Lincoln College and Professor T. H. Green being among several characters mirrored in it, though both were to die before it was published in 1888. Gladstone had a long talk with her about it when she was staying with the Talbots at Keble College, as well as about charity and the 200,000 people in south

London alone, for whom, according to *The Record*, 'Christianity has practically no existence.' This number would of course be vastly increased today. Then, after a much discussed article called 'Robert Elsmere and the Battle of Belief' had appeared in the May number of *The Nineteenth Century*, she sent him a copy, the *Pall Mall Gazette* commenting at this time that 'for two and a half years the GOM had been able to think of nothing but Home Rule and Ireland, but Mrs Ward has changed that.'

The book which caused so much controversy had huge sales. Among her critics were the warden of Keble who wrote six sheets of friendly remonstrance, and Dr Creighton who, during a closely reasoned criticism of her hero's position, told her that 'Elsmere was never a Christian.' He took her to Toynbee Hall soon afterwards, and she was delighted to find in the library there a copy of *Robert Elsmere*, which 'had been read to pieces, and in a worker's club which had just started several ideas had been taken from the "New Brotherhood" with which the book ended'.

Her own effort to give them practical expression began in the autumn of 1889 when Lord Carlisle came to Russell Square for a long talk about a proposed Unitarian settlement somewhere in south London. Then, in February 1890, a group of people met in her drawing room to discuss her draft circular announcing the foundation of a 'Hall for Residents' for men on the Toynbee Hall pattern but in the St Pancras area; and the proposed 'settlement at University Hall, Gordon Square' was soon on its way in part of an old building there, with both a definite religious aim and also a considerable social side.

Its prospectus explained that there would be several large rooms suitable for lectures and social gatherings, and that 'the Hall shall do its utmost to secure for its residents opportunities for religious and social work and for the study of social problems, such as are possessed by the residents at Toynbee Hall and those at Oxford House.' Though situated in one of the west central squares 'it was surrounded on three sides by districts crowded with poor' and, being close to Gower Street, would provide its residents with easy access to any of the organizations already existing in the east or south of London for the help of the poor and for study. Moreover, a 'special effort will be made to establish Sunday Teaching both at the Hall and by the help of Hall residents, in other parts of London, for children of all classes.'

There was much argument about the religious bias. The Unitarian Manchester College in Oxford had exerted considerable effort in helping to start the settlement and Lord Carlisle, a prominent Dissenter among several others in the hall's committee, proposed that it should be unequivocally a Unitarian settlement. This idea, however, was turned down, Mary Ward herself still cherishing a 'lingering feeling for the Church of England', well aware that at the time of Keble's famous sermon her grandfather Arnold had spoken up for the inclusion of Dissenters in the national Church. Canon Barnett helped here as he approved the choice as warden of Philip Wickstead, then minister of the Unitarian chapel in Little Portland Street.

Mary Ward spoke at the opening ceremony in the Portman Room, taking the floor for the first time at a public meeting. And soon Mrs T. H. Green had been roped in to give a series of lectures on the development of English towns, later to appear as a book, and Beatrice Potter, not yet married to her Sidney, spoke to the Cooperative Movement, also anticipating a book. Other subjects included the warden's choice of Dante and political economy, though the main focus of educational plans was the Jowett lectureship intended 'to promote the study of the Bible and the history of religion, in the light of the best available results of criticism and research'. Like Henrietta Barnett when starting her unorthodox Sunday evening services, Mary Ward had long felt that 'many people are deeply dissatisfied with the whole state of religious teaching in England; either it is purely dogmatic ... or it is colourless and perfunctory.' Disappointingly, youth in the nearby Tottenham Court Road did not respond, but another effort made on their behalf at the local Marchmont Hall by a dissident group of young residents lacking sympathy with Robert Elsmere proved immediately popular. By 1891 boys' and men's clubs, meetings and concerts, with a Saturday morning play centre for children, were all flourishing there while the school of biblical studies and other programmes continued to attract educated young people of both sexes to University Hall. However, by 1893 the more intellectual effort proved too expensive to maintain, especially as Marchmont Hall was vastly overcrowded. So Mrs Ward launched a building fund. And her family was long to remember her delight when she opened her post one May morning in 1894 and exclaimed 'Mr Passmore Edwards is going to build us a settlement.'

This wealthy philanthropist, founder of the free libraries, had already visited the district to consider her plan 'to plant a Toynbee Hall in the Somerstown district' and convinced himself that such an institution was as much need in north London as in the East End. He promised to back it if someone else would provide a suitable site, whereupon the Duke of Bedford came forward with the offer of one in Tavistock Place at less than its market value and also a contribution to the building fund. Happily such windfalls are part of settlement life.

Mrs Ward now undertook a money-raising tour of northern towns despite recurrent illness and other commitments, including her third novel *David Grieve*. Then Passmore Edwards stepped up his donation, being, as she put it, 'possessed by the very passion of giving', whereupon two keen young architects living at the hall were commissioned for the work, and early in 1897 a general committee of 55 was formed representing academic circles in London, Oxford – notably the principal of Brasenose College – Cambridge and Manchester, and including also politicians and other public figures such as the Rt Honourable H. H. Asquith, Sidney Buxton, Mrs Henry Fawcett, Jane Harrison and Anna Swanwick. The new building, listed as one of outstanding architectural interest, has proved a lasting ornament to the square. It was launched informally as a residential settlement for men that October, seven years after the founding of University Hall, and was formally opened on 12 February 1898 by John (later Viscount) Morley with Lord Peel in the chair, the Duke and Duchess of Bedford and Henrietta Barnett being among those in the packed audience. Soon afterwards Mrs Ward was appointed chairwoman of a women's work committee.

Her three-pronged initiative to help deprived children now began to take shape. Clearly the Saturday morning play centre which had attracted over 100 children to Marchmont Hall each week must not be allowed to lapse under the new regime, and it seemed equally necessary to keep children off the streets on weekdays in the late afternoons while their parents were still at work. Her daughters Dorothy and Janet were involved here as well as her sister-in-law Gertrude Ward, a trained district nurse who lived with them and knew well what life was like in the slums. Hard-working teachers in the St Pancras schools were soon to cooperate and Mrs Ward herself took a class of about 30 boys between 11 and 14 who came regularly to hear her read stories by Kipling and R. L. Stevenson. According to one teacher, 'the smaller children knew her as their "fairy Godmother", and it was a pretty sight to see them all clustering around her, and her kind, beautiful face whenever she was amongst the children will haunt me for years.'

Soon the bright settlement rooms were fully occupied by youngsters of various ages attending either the play centre or the recreation school before the hour at which the normal evening activities began for their elders, and by 1901 Mrs Ward was calling it 'The Community House'. Though some people joined mainly for the social evenings while others wanted to exchange ideas or attend lectures, increasingly the associates, both men and women, offered help and service in the area. All major difficulties were referred to Mrs Ward, whether affecting the residents, associates or the warden, and she also bore the main brunt of fundraising. Lord Northbrook's contribution of £100, which followed an invitation to dinner and was used in clearing the ground and laying grass at the back of the settlement, helped forward her second initiative, which was to open a school there for invalid children in 1899.

The previous year she had set on foot an enquiry into the numbers of children in the area who spent all day at home being unable to attend any ordinary school. Other women's settlements had taken action in this field, notably WUS, and Mrs Ward had been an early visitor to the LMHS class for crippled children started in 1897. The London School Board, which included her old friend Graham Wallas as chairman of its school management committee, helped her enquiries, for their few special schools were for the mentally defective and thus did not meet her main objective. Then the ICAA and local hospitals also gave her their support. Transport was another problem. And who was to pay?

The settlement now undertook to provide rooms free of charge for an invalid children's school, to employ a nurse-superintendent and to maintain a special ambulance, Sir Thomas Barlow having in the meanwhile given one. With the groundwork thus prepared, in 1899 both the London School Board and the Board of Education gave their approval, whereupon the settlement geared itself to serve a daily dinner at the cost of three halfpence a head. The school opened in February 1899, and the devoted woman teacher, Miss Milligan, who was then put in charge of these delicate children, was still at her job there nearly 20 years later. Moreover, volunteers who were recruited both as dinner hour helpers and to superintend the subsequent play hour proved themselves forerunners of reliable care-committee workers in the years to come. This aspect of Mrs Ward's work influenced the London School Board when it began to set up similar schools in other parts of London, insisting that each must have a local committee of managers, half of whom should be women.

Then, during the winter of 1900/1, Mrs Ward, with typical thoroughness, undertook an investigation into the numbers and conditions of children not attending school in some of the largest and poorest London boroughs, employing trained workers for the purpose. Young community workers based at settlements were later to conduct similar social investigations. This one extended to nine out of the ten school board divisions of London and embraced about 1800 children of whom some 1000 were recommended to attend invalid schools. It was a figure that could not be ignored. Other children were judged fit for ordinary schools if given special care, some were too ill for any school and some were recommended for the existing schools for the mentally handicapped.

The Honourable Maude Lawrence, chairwoman of the special schools subcommittee of the school board, and a supporter of St Margaret's House in Bethnal Green, had meanwhile been working on the building problem and in 1901 sites for four centres were agreed, the first two in Paddington and Bethnal Green being opened in September 1901, with children drawn entirely from Mrs Ward's list; and here again other women's settlements were to be involved. In a letter to *The Times* she then pleaded for the extension of the movement to the provinces, and when this happened she and her helpers concentrated on the training of children for suitable employment on leaving school mainly through apprenticeship schemes, which included finding work for crippled children, helped here again by Miss Lawrence.

Her third major initiative concerned holiday schools. The settlement gardens, shaded by vast plane trees, were empty for weeks at a time during the summer holidays when large numbers of children roamed about all day in the surrounding streets. Could she not bring them in? In 1902, after hearing that vacation schools had been started in New York, she enlisted the help of Mr E. G. Holland, an assistant master at the Highgate secondary school, who supplied a list of children who might be invited and that summer 750 of them, divided into two groups for morning and afternoon sessions, were enjoying what the settlement had to offer, facilities there soon extending to the waste ground beyond the garden and, in wet weather, to the basement and other rooms. Occupations were much the same as those already popular in the play centre and recreation school. The London Education Authority (LEA), when set up in 1903, gladly left control of the settlement's vacation school in Mrs Ward's hands, helped as she was by the Highgate master who directed it for 13 consecutive summers until the outbreak of the First World War; by which time the number of children attending had risen to 1000 each day and an additional building had been brought into use.

The Browning Settlement organized a similar holiday school in 1904. Then in 1908 Mrs Ward opened two more in the East End, at Bow and Hoxton, while the success of her settlement school emphasized how much more could be done with empty playgrounds of ordinary London schools during August. In 1909 she started another experimental holiday school for delicate and sick children who were eligible for free dinners. Two years later she tackled the problem again, drawing up a scheme for 26 London schools to open their playgrounds for the summer holidays; and, after the LCC had promised to lend equipment, she herself raised £1000 and superintended the engagement of staff, later visiting the playgrounds and reporting the cheerful scenes in a letter to *The Times*. But there was still a crying need for more space, as many had by now realized. 'I let in 400 boys and the street outside was still black with them,' wrote one games master at this time. During the 1911 summer holidays and the following year the LCC shared the work with her when 40 schools enjoyed 'organized playgrounds'. She thought with some reason that the whole enterprise would now continue under council control, but sadly it lapsed at the outbreak of war, staffing being a main problem.

Meanwhile, the associates of the Passmore Edward Settlement, mainly men and women who lived nearby, had been enjoying its concerts and social evenings, a high proportion of the 250 who paid their subscription in the first year coming from the Peabody tenements in Little Coram Street (now Herbrand Street) and by 1905 the number had risen to nearly 400. But classes and discussion groups were noticeably less popular. Highly qualified teachers were available but in 1898 there was an average attendance of only 20 for three lectures given by Ernest Aves, one of Charles Booth's team, which enquired into the conditions of the aged poor and was to lead to the Old Age Pensions Act of 1908. And even Humphry Ward on 'Old Masters' was similarly not much of a draw except for residents, committee members and their friends. Music fared better, Mary Ward herself having in her Oxford days a considerable reputation as a pianist. And there was an immediate and enthusiastic response when a director of music was appointed in 1905, the young Gustav van Holst teaching and conducting an orchestra of associates at the settlement for two years, and founding the still flourishing Mary Ward Madrigal Choir before moving on to Morley College and St Paul's Girls' School.

All this time the vacation school flourished, and the children, regardless of the ups and downs of adult education schemes, continued to crowd each day into the building or its garden despite some adverse comment from those associates keen only on promoting men's clubs. These were largely placated by a compromise reached in 1903, when a new building for the invalid children's school was put up on the far side of the playground and a men's club, open until midnight for billiards and smoking, but with no alcohol allowed, was accommodated on its upper floor. But the women associates then took umbrage. Here as usual Mrs Ward had to sort out difficulties, a new mixed swimming class soon proving popular. And there was another crisis in 1907 when the Duke of Bedford threatened to withdraw his support if the Progressives in the LCC elections were backed by all the residents. Somehow she jockeyed everyone along, helped on this occasion by the otherwise deplorable fact that only ten of the 17 rooms available were let at the time. However, the children, by their enthusiasm, prepared the way for what in 1918 grew into a national play centre movement as a permanent feature of British life.

Knowledge of the American initiative for children had done much to encourage Mrs Ward. When she visited New York with her husband and Dorothy in 1908, the city education authority had only recently authorized 100 school playgrounds to be equipped and opened under its own supervision. She was the main speaker at a dinner for 900 at the Waldorf Astoria given by the Playground Association of America. She then dined with President Roosevelt at the White House before setting off on a lecture tour to raise money.

She was also concerned at this time with the anti-suffrage campaign and in 1912 resigned from the NUWW which, though bound by its constitution to favour 'no one policy' in political matters, had just passed a pro-suffrage resolution, afterwards informing the prime minister and all MPs of their decision. Feelings were running high, for Mrs Fawcett had recently transferred the allegiance of the National Union of Women's Suffrage Societies to the Labour Party, which was prepared to back to the hilt the principle of women having votes. It was a difficult time for Mrs Creighton, the NUWW president.

During the first two years of war Mrs Ward continued her efforts to procure funds for the play centres. When juvenile delinquency became an increasing problem, the Home Office complained to the Board of Education, which in turn consulted Mrs Ward, Mr Fisher being among her friends. Then in January 1917 came an encouraging announcement that:

> Grants from the Board of Education will shortly be available in aid of the cost of carrying on Play Centres. Hitherto Centres have been established only by voluntary bodies mostly in London where the LEA has granted the free use of

> school buildings. It is hoped that the powers which education authorities already possess of establishing and making such centres will be more fully exercised in the future.

The battle now seemed won on this front. *The Times* added its tribute. 'The announcement that the Treasury has approved the principle of play centres and will signify its approval in the usual manner forms a fitting climax to 20 years of voluntary effort on the part of Mrs Humphry Ward and a devoted circle of workers.'

The Board of Education regulations had been largely drawn up by Mrs Ward herself. And adventure playgrounds are now a major concern in the settlement movement, its first having been opened at Cambridge House in south London in 1948.

Life at the settlement had meanwhile undergone a radical change. At the outbreak of war when young men had left to join the armed forces, about 16 Belgian refugees were housed in part of the building, and Red Cross workers had use of the other rooms.

It seemed that a major need now was a body of trained volunteers to carry out the social legislation of recent years and that these were more likely to be recruited in peace time from the ranks of leisured young women than from young men with jobs. Not all council members were convinced by this line of argument, but Mrs Ward had a strong ally in the Duke of Bedford who offered to provide for three years about two-thirds of the money needed for a women's settlement. His offer was decisive and, in August 1915, Hilda Oakeley, who had recently left Somerville, was appointed warden of what now became a residential settlement for women, and she carried it successfully through the war years. A school for mothers was set up, forerunner of the later nursery school, and girls' clubs for the 14 to 19 age group, started by Miss Dorothy Ward and the sub-warden the Honourable Eleanor Plummer, proved highly popular with a regular attendance of about 300. Later, a day continuation school started by the LCC in 1920 was among the first and most successful, though, like all others, had only a short life of one year. At the same time the settlement cooperated with Bedford College and the LSE over social work training and was a centre for the Workers' Education Association (WEA) until the WEA secured offices in Theobalds Road.

Mrs Ward meanwhile had been engaged on various war jobs. In December 1916 Theodore Roosevelt wrote to ask this now famous woman in her late sixties to tell the USA about Britain, hoping thus to help bring his country to a declaration of war. Following a luncheon with Lloyd George and a meeting with the Foreign Secretary, Sir Edward Grey, a round of visits was arranged to munition factories, the fleet and northern France. After the publication of *Letters to an American Friend* and a small book called *England's Effort*, a second and similarly hectic tour of the British military zone took place in March 1917, shortly before her nephew Tom Arnold died at the front.

Her third journey to France took place after the armistice. The intense cold of that January 1919, coupled with her efforts to meet innumerable people and absorb the vast amount of material put at her disposal, proved too much for her, precarious as then was her state of health. Moreover, her husband too fell ill. Early in 1920 she visited him in hospital after an operation, but soon herself succumbed. She died on 24 March 1920, with her daughter Dorothy beside her. That evening people hurrying through the rain to the cheerful shelter of the Passmore Edwards Settlement found its doors closed, and posted upon them a notice of her death. The place had provided a refuge for many homeless people during the war years. Then, soon after a memorial service had been held, its name was changed to the Mary Ward Settlement, Passmore Edwards having died ten years earlier.

When Miss Oakeley retired as settlement warden in the year that Mrs Ward died, Edith Neville, as honorary warden, guided it through a prolonged financial crisis before handing over in 1924 to the Honourable Eleanor Plummer. On her retirement three years later the council decided to attach the settlement to a leading movement for adult education. Thus, in 1930, it was affiliated to the Educational Settlements Association (ESA) a year after the appointment as warden of Horace Fleming JP, founder of Beechcroft, the first educational settlement, and chairman of the ESA. No longer a women's settlement, it now became one of the early residential mixed ones, and Mrs Fleming started a training scheme for tutors and part-time workers in adult education. By 1931 about 130 people were regularly attending a university extension course on English literature, and other classes were organized by the WEA, the type of cultural education provided being in no way competitive with that offered at evening institutes or polytechnics. While music and drama flourished, there were also classes in physical training for men and women. At the same time the nursery school, the physically defective school and the children's play centre all filled a local need and the Mary Ward Boys' Club, with a membership of over 600 in 1931, was the largest in London.

Meanwhile, the settlement started by Mary Ward's Oxford friend Louise Creighton was flourishing in Fulham.

'I think the late Bishop of London was perhaps the most alert and universal intelligence that existed in the island at the time of his death,' said Lord Rosebery of the man for whom Bishop Creighton House (BCH) was opened as a memorial in 1908. A northerner by birth, he had changed little, according to his wife Louise, since his undergraduate days at Merton: 'In spite of all his brightness and humour, of his warm affectionate ways, he was in truth very stern, grim he called it – stern with himself and stern with those for whom he felt any responsibility.'

Like Mary Ward, he led public opinion in controversies later revived by the 1985 *Faith in the City* report. In September 1883, while still in the Northumbrian parish of Embleton, Mandell Creighton had spoken at the Newcastle diocesan conference on the duty of the clergy towards questions of social reform.

> Their unique position between the classes of society should enable them to know what the people want and articulate for them, but as citizens rather than as clergy, whose primary duty is to preach the Gospel. They should do their utmost to get working men to trust them, and therefore regard it as one of their duties to study economics and social questions.

And here the settlement movement, launched two months later, could clearly help.

Then, in May 1884, he was appointed professor of ecclesiastical history at Cambridge, and though coming there 'as almost complete strangers' he and Louise quickly established friendly relations in university circles, helped by having six children living at home. The impression he produced was that of 'stimulating power', though this could be intimidating. During early married life in Oxford, while she and her friends planned their higher education campaign, as late as December 1895 Creighton wrote to Professor Henry Sidgwick: 'I quite agree ... that the question of degrees for women is one that must be considered ... but all I can see my way to is an attitude of benevolent neutrality in the first instance.' Education on other fronts, and particularly for working men, had his enthusiastic support, and in 1900 he was to become president of the LSE after laying the foundation stone of the new building and subsequently attending an important dinner as Beatrice Webb's guest.

Lord Salisbury offered him the see of London on 28 October 1896, a few days after Dr Temple's appointment to Canterbury following the sudden death of Archbishop Benson. Then on 29 January 1897, the Creightons moved into Fulham Palace, where all their children joined them for the enthronement of St Paul's next day. And almost immediately the bishop was caught up in preparations for the Queen's diamond jubilee as well as for the Pan-Anglican Conference. On Jubilee Day he stood beside the two archbishops on the steps of St Paul's to welcome the Queen before preaching there in a service of thanksgiving on 20 June. By then he was already involved with the settlement world in London. In April 1897 he told his niece Winifred, 'Last night I went to dine at Toynbee Hall and talked to an assembly of Trade Unionists and Socialists about education and then we had a discussion,' and the same month, when writing to his niece Ella, 'Cuthbert and Walter have amused themselves by offering their services to the Cambridge settlement during their vacation. They spent last night in a boys' club at Camberwell, playing cards and such like things with some 40 little ragamuffins. They enjoyed it very much.' The bishop discussed with his wife the possibility of starting a settlement but nothing was done in the short time remaining to him. Cuthbert, however, like his sister Beatrice, was to become deeply involved with BCH, and he was president there for nearly 30 years before his death in 1963.

Other young men were similarly encouraged. In January 1898 the warden of Radley College heard that 'quite recently the Inns of Court have established a mission in Soho' and public schoolboys could be referred there as well as to the Eton, Marlborough and similar missions, while 'the Oxford House and Cambridge Mission in Southwark have many men connected with them who would be sympathetic.'

And now the huge garden parties, which had been the rule at Fulham since the days of Bishop Tait, included many East Enders connected with the Toynbee Travellers' Club, cheap group holidays being an aspect of education particularly encouraged by the bishop and his wife.

After his experience of strikes both at Leicester and Nottingham, he had remarked that 'the worst of the position taken up by the English working man is its entire insularity.' In frequent lectures he tried to enlarge minds and train judgements by lifting them into a bigger world, his own travels including a visit to Moscow in 1894 for the coronation of the tsar who had married Queen Victoria's granddaughter, though Louise then stayed at home. But he was in some pain when they went off to Switzerland for a fortnight after he had taken the Holy Week services at St Paul's.

'One of his first engagements on returning to London', wrote Louise after his return from a visit to Russia in 1898,

> was to preach at the festival connected with the opening of the new buildings at St Hilda's, a Ladies Settlement started by the Cheltenham College in East London. He spoke of the feeling that must lie at the bottom of all work for others. Only in the sense of the spiritual equality, of sharing the same gifts, can men meet on terms of frankness and cordiality . . . work done with the smallest sense of condescension in the heart is worthless. There must be reciprocity, the frank and full recognition that they who would teach others are also ready to be taught by them. . . . Let us bring all that we have together and look at it with common eyes; let us not regard one another as separate and apart!

This was the message of the new brotherhood, though not quite as Arnold Toynbee or Mary Ward had expressed it. The bishop had written to congratulate the author of *David Grieve* in 1892, telling her 'I think the advance on *Robert Elsmere* is enormous.'

Overwhelmed as Louise was by her husband's sudden death after only four years in London, she soon embarked on her two-volume biography, relying much here on the Talbots: 'Louise came to dinner and was afterwards closeted with E.' They had been the Creighton's first guests at the start of their ten happy years at Embleton.

A plan was also made to start a women's settlement near their last home as a memorial to her husband. Suitable property was found in Lillie Road overlooking a green open space associated in the past with flower girls on their way to Covent Garden, yet near the poorest and most overcrowded parts of Fulham and Hammersmith, where the infant mortality rate was 116 per 1000 and unemployment a major problem.

With the approval of Dr Winnington Ingram, now Bishop of London, and with the support also of the executive committee of the Women's Diocesan Association (WDA), the three adjoining houses were taken on a lease, though all in bad repair and needing many alterations, with two of them having had their ground floor room thrown into one by the currently occupying Lillie Road Girls' Club.

These arrangements had been completed before the annual meeting of the WDA took place on 23 November 1907, when a fund-raising appeal was made also to the Girls' Diocesan Association (GDA). Mrs Creighton's main helper at this time was her daughter Beatrice, then president of the GDA and later to become deaconess and head of St Faith's Mission in Madras. It was also clearly necessary to appeal to a wider circle of friends; and a small steering committee held its first meeting at the home of the Honourable Mrs John Bailey who, as Sarah Lyttelton, had been the first organizing secretary of the LMHS but preferred after her marriage to work nearer home. Besides the WDA and GDA representatives, it included three local women, Miss Curtis, founder and head of the Fulham and Hammersmith Nursing Association, Mrs Vincent, wife of the rural dean of Fulham, and Mrs Hilliard, wife of the high master of St Paul's School.

Young Catherine Wickham, daughter of the dean of Lincoln, was by then in residence as warden. Chosen for the post by Mrs Creighton, her generosity, vivaciousness and intellectual stature brought immediate recognition of the enterprise, and her family connection with the Gladstone, Talbot and Lyttelton network was a continuing source of strength. She had helped in a boys' club in her home town before deciding to devote herself to social work, then a training period at WUS had been followed by further settlement experience at St Margaret's House. Her new job provided ample scope for her exceptional talents as a leader and after her retirement as warden she was to serve on the BCH council until her death in 1973 in her ninety-ninth year. Honoured by being made a freeman of the borough she had a profound influence both on the women's settlement movement as a whole and on social work in west London.

Apart from other subscribers, supporters living in any part of London who were willing to become associates and help for certain hours each week, or remember the house in their prayers, paid no fixed sum and could obtain meals in the house and stay whenever a room was available.

According to Miss Wickham, Mrs Creighton herself gave the marching orders on how and what work should be started. Both Fulham and Hammersmith were to be served, the area being seen not as two boroughs but as a network of parishes urgently in need of workers; apart from a small domestic staff of two, the settlement was to accommodate only eight residents and these, whether experienced in social work or prepared to take such training as was available, would act as a spearhead for a regiment of part-time volunteers recruited in the West End; and thirdly, BCH was not to run organizations of its own, the clergy being assured that the Lillie Road Girls' Club, one of the earliest and best known of its kind in London and with its own committee, was only a tenant on the premises paying, however, a substantial rent.

The chairman of the Fulham Board of Guardians was then the Revd P. S. G. Propert, vicar of St Augustine's in Lillie Road. The board gave little outdoor relief except where it could get people permanently on their feet, while running good institutions for the infirm and aged, the sick and wholly destitute. Settlement workers, sympathizing with the vicar's aims, proved valuable allies here, responding to the welcome he gave to BCH as a focus for voluntary service.

The settlement also brought reinforcements to the COS offices both in Fulham and Hammersmith. Very soon the original aim was modified as the relationship with Fulham borough developed, though no similar organic commitment grew up at this time with Hammersmith, despite much voluntary work done there. The first infant welfare centre in Hammersmith was started by a settlement worker who had already given devoted service in the pioneering of the Fulham one.

The settlement's location in the West End was partly responsible for its development as a 'civic' as well as a 'neighbourhood' centre, with life there intertwining closely with that of the borough. School care committees were a case in point. The work involved concerned all settlements, but here the LCC inaugurated the system for this part of London in the same year that the settlement opened, at a meeting in one of its rooms. Here, as elsewhere at this time, settlement volunteers were also a godsend to the medical officers of health as visitors. And the settlement's door knocker seldom stood silent for long.

Civic work for education and health authorities had many ramifications. Miss Wickham spoke in 1910 at the inaugural meeting held in the town hall for a Fulham dispensary for the prevention of consumption, and she became treasurer for a branch of the WEA started in the borough at a meeting held at the settlement, when its newly formed committee was also given use of a room. The local district nurses were entertained at BCH for their annual meeting in 1911 and in 1912 a suboffice of the Fulham and Hammersmith branch of MABYS was opened there, 80 girls being helped within the year. However, though the settlement organized a meeting in connection with the white slave traffic, with Lady Frederick Cavendish as the main speaker, this was held in the town hall. Thus, apart from the well-attended 'at homes' held regularly by Mrs Creighton and Miss Wickham, when subjects discussed included the WEA, schools for mothers, Sunday school kindergartens, district visiting and industrial problems, BCH was becoming increasingly useful as a centre for social workers of all kinds. It had by now 203 associate members, and its club room was newly decorated with wall paintings in tempera by Henry Tonks and his pupils at the Slade School.

Then, shortly before the outbreak of the First World War, the long-standing Lillie Road Girls' Club of proved usefulness linked up with the settlement, BCH becoming responsible for its finance and management. With Mrs Creighton as chairwoman of council, Mrs Bailey as chairwoman of the executive committee and Miss Wickham as chairwoman of the club committee, BCH by its sixth year had reached a strong position except for the continuing money problems.

Particularly as the financial backing of the WDA and GDA had soon ceased, there was rejoicing when the recently established North Foreland Lodge, then under Miss Wolseley-Lewis, herself well versed in settlement life, adopted it in 1910 as its school mission in what proved a lasting commitment, the school's traditional hospitality of 'Daffodil Days' being particularly appreciated by countless elderly people. Downe House also gave its support until it moved from Kent to the West Country, and Belstead School at Aldeburgh proved a tower of strength until it ceased to exist in 1940. Other schools, including local ones, helped in due course and many teenagers thus learnt the value of settlements through a personal commitment, which continued in some cases for life. Not, however, until the late 1960s did the nearby St Paul's Girls' School link up with this settlement, its high mistress, Mrs Heather Brigstocke, becoming president of the BCH council.

Part III
In Britain and Abroad

10
The Second World War and the Welfare State

By 1939 women's settlements were firmly established and they certainly helped to maintain morale in the years ahead. All had been linked from their start with school children and their teachers, and as war clouds gathered problems were shared. After evacuation, other common problems arose in connection with the staffing of the new CABs, the departure of staff and residents to other war jobs, the bombing and its aftermath in human terms, and demands for the training of students especially in connection with the coming youth service.

CABs were set up in 1939 to give an emergency service of advice and information in time of war. The need for this had been shown in the First World War when people flocked to settlements for guidance in personal problems, as in Peckham. Help was needed through a maze of new restrictions and regulations, with allowances and pensions, in problems of evacuation, in contacting prisoners of war, and much else. Settlement workers were known to have experience in personal service and settlement premises were familiar to local people, so not surprisingly soon after the declaration of war CABs had become part of settlement life.

By then the great exodus from London on 31 August and 1 September had taken place. In Southwark, soon to be heavily bombed, 44 Nelson Square proved of special service on both days for local teachers and children who had to make an early start and lived some distance away. Other workers helped to solve ICAA problems and a CAB was set up, the commonest enquiries being those about evacuation, form-filling and lost ration cards.

The Women's University Settlement (WUS), partly emptied in the last months of 1939, was again filled by Easter 1940, largely by students, 'this happy state of affairs being rudely interrupted by the arrival of a bomb which forced us to turn out most of our residents at a moment's notice.' The Pfeiffer scholar of that year was subsequently allowed to hold the scholarship at the evacuated LSE in Cambridge. Then, in May 1941:

> Our next door neighbours were burnt out and we had to spend ten days and nights in a shelter in Blackfriars Road and do our work at the Square corner. However, the Baby Centre, the ICAA and the CAB were soon as busy as ever, and during the winter of 1941 an evening canteen was run in No. 47 for the members of our local ARP post and a District Warden's office on the premises was equipped by the LCC as a Third Line Rest Centre should need arise.

The settlement had then ten residents including three members of staff and six students, most of them preparing for youth work, though the Pfeiffer scholar was training as a housing manager. Only for a short time between 1940 and 1941 was this important part of the work curtailed.

During 1943 the number of students exceeded that in any previous year. The 40 who came for long or short periods included three Pfeiffer scholars, one each from Somerville, St Hilda's and Leeds University. Some 28 were engaged on definite courses of training for various social work professions and were sent to WUS, in most cases by the social service departments of their universities, for the practical part of their training. Some worked with COS committees, some with ICAA, while others obtained experience of children's care work under LCC organizers or helped in one of the borough day nurseries. Hospitals claimed almoners who had reached the specialist stage, while students learning housing management were attached to estate offices run on Octavia Hill lines. Some students came for general experience to be gleaned in the settlement's own departments and, besides seeing something of the CAB, were to share in the work of the baby centre, with its electrical clinic, and in collections for hospital savings, thrift and holidays.

Youth leaders in training were expected to take responsibility, under supervision for clubs and classes, but all students took part in one or more of them either as members or helpers.

> For it was considered important in WUS circles that those training as Almoners, Labour Managers, Probation Officers, Family Case Workers or whatever should have experience of a branch of social work in which their clients were not forced to seek their help because of special circumstances, generally adverse. The free association which we call clubs whether for children, young people or adults, invite local residents into a democratic atmosphere where views and experience are exchanged and where if you do not pull your weight you cease to count. This is an invaluable corrective to the cardinal sin of the social worker which besets both experienced and inexperienced alike and from which it is our duty to protect our students — a desire to manage the lives of others.

This candid comment was typical of settlement self-criticism in the early days of the welfare state.

For some time after the end of the Second World War, WUS was faced with the depressing threat of losing its headquarters in Nelson Square under a compulsory purchase order. However, a small band of activists who rallied round Dr Margaret Kerly (chairwoman of council for 18 years from 1952) eventually triumphed, and with the withdrawal of the order, the potential for reinvigoration and development returned. Much was to happen in the next quarter of a century, including work for discharged prisoners, to earn the generous support of the borough council, the City Parochial Foundation, the Baring Trust and other benefactors, in bringing the four settlement houses into full repair, both inside and out, by 1982.

The job of easing WUS's work into the modern world fell in the

1960s on the capable shoulders of David Collett, the second man to be appointed warden there. Other settlements, including Cambridge House and Peckham, were similarly in need of a boost and his influence was far-reaching when he became director of the South London Federation of Settlements, then funded by a Gulbenkian grant. During much of his time at Nelson Square he had the happy cooperation of Miss Aida Tennent who, remembered for her youthful service there, returned to WUS in 1958 for a decade as a part-time neighbourhood worker after retiring from a long career with the school care service. Together they generated ideas, developing them into major projects, tested, researched, clearly communicated and adequately financed. The name was changed to Blackfriars Settlement in 1961.

At St Hilda's East in September 1939 'we were plunged straight into emergency work and a maze of gas masks and evacuation plans.' This settlement, bounded by the docks to the south and the City of London to the west, would clearly be a target for bombing. So many people left the area that in 1940 a second St Hilda's was opened at St Albans. Soon a play centre and a Guide company, with clubs of various kinds meeting in hired halls there, were providing support for evacuees and children, many of whom had come from Bethnal Green.

Four full-time St Hilda's workers were established at St Albans and the settlement warden, Miss Cathcart, travelled between the two sites. During the heavy bombing of May 1941 the London settlement narrowly survived on a night when

> the fires were all around ... and we feared the house must inevitably be swallowed up in an ever increasing ring of flames. The complete lack of water was a very alarming factor against our survival and we could only wait and pray that the wind would change, which it did at the last moment, and once more we were safe and ready for work the next morning.

The SSAFA (Soldiers', Sailors', and Airmen's Families Association) was among the organizations that continued to function from its base at the settlement.

The new wave of bombing in 1943, bringing the major disaster at the Bethnal Green underground, and the flying bombs of 1944, when one landed near Shoreditch church just after midday, also involved settlement workers. Miss Cathcart, who after the evacuation to St Albans had devoted herself to the organization of St Hilda's Air Raid Relief Fund for bombed-out people, was later appointed welfare officer for the borough and did much pioneer work among old people.

It was, however, with the youth service, set up under the 1944 Education Act – 'to encourage the development of young people by helping them to broaden their interests, to enjoy recreational pursuits and to mix socially in their leisure time' – that the settlement world was to have its next call to action. During a visit to St Hilda's in 1943 an enthusiastic HMI had found its club full to overflowing with boys and girls 'keenly interested and well conducted'. Knowing of the young people outside who could not be admitted for lack of room, 'he asked us to do our utmost to secure more and larger premises, promising the full support and backing of the Board of Education for any good proposal we could make.' Almost immediately opposite the settlement, at the corner of Old Nichol Street and Club Row, were some derelict buildings then belonging to the union chapel, Islington, which, when transformed, were to become widely known as Dorothea Beale House and Bruce Hall. Old Cheltonians attending the guild diamond jubilee celebrations on 25 October 1949 found the new building completed, though Bruce Hall was still a forest of scaffolding the previous day. The Bishop of Stepney, the Rt Revd R. H. Moberly, and the rector of Bethnal Green had taken services in St Hilda's chapel earlier in the week.

Other changes that year included the appointment of an educational secretary by the Shoreditch and Bethnal Green Marriage Guidance Council which, like the Skilled Employment Committee, had its headquarters at the settlement. The premises were now increasingly in demand.

Dorothea Beale House, on a site of about 9000 square feet, was the settlement's freehold property. Miss Tredgold, who had succeeded Miss Popham as principal of the college in 1953, was nearing the end of her 11 years in office when, as president of the guild, she approved the decision to sell the remaining 15 years' lease of 3 Old Nichol Street and carry on all work from the freehold site, the settlement's address being henceforth Dorothea Beale House, Club Row. Compared with this upheaval, it seemed of comparatively minor significance that 'from April 1965 we shall be part of the Borough of Tower Hamlets and the LCC's responsibility for education, including youth work, will pass to the ILEA.'

Building later started on a new community centre and adjacent offices in Dorothea Beale House. Then, in 1968, shortly after the death of Margaret Bowley, who had served on the council since the start of Mayfield House, David Collett, director of the Blackfriars Federation of Settlements, helped the incoming warden, Brian Stapleton, to plan a new committee structure for St Hilda's with an executive formed of council members representing the main management interests of finance, upkeep of buildings and community work. Though financial and other difficulties led to resignations and a temporary cessation of youth work, full-time staff and volunteers at St Hilda's were soon afterwards happy when given a voice in its management, and the settlement, always forward looking, then abandoned the old name, calling itself a 'Community Centre'. Meanwhile, its former partner at Mayfield House had weathered its own recurring crises, often financial and seemingly endemic in the settlement world.

On the day war was declared the head's room at St Margaret's House in Bethnal Green became one of the new CABs and shortly afterwards a suboffice of the local evacuation office. Staff and an office were also provided for the SSAFA and a poor man's lawyer kept busy nearby. Some 14 of the residents evacuated with school children to the country. Others continued with the clubs and, when bombing began before the ARP took over, helped to run the Globe Road rest centre for bombed-out families, where conditions were very tough.

At a council meeting held on 13 September 1939 a letter was read from Sir Wyndham Deedes urging that, as the Ministry of Health considered the work of settlements to be of national importance, the house should be kept open. In 1940 he became a resident there for two years while chief ARP warden for Bethnal Green.

By November 1940 four out of ten houses had been damaged or destroyed in Stepney, though the tube extension at Liverpool Street was relieving the situation at Bethnal Green.

After the 1940/1 Blitz had left London for other targets, more youth clubs and play centres were opened. By 1943 hot dinners were being delivered to elderly people by settlement workers in co-operation with Invalid Kitchens and often on bicycles, though meals-on-wheels had not yet emerged as a title. In crises such as the Bethnal Green underground disaster in which some 300 people lost their lives, long official hours were stretched, and during the period of the flying bombs, when St Margaret's was in Bomb Alley, the staff worked under great pressure. However, the house was fortunate in escaping serious damage, despite much broken glass and several near misses, including an incendiary bomb which fell on the chapel roof but failed to ignite. In contrast to the First World War, St Margaret's kept full as more students than ever before applied for short intensive courses to prepare them for youth work.

That the stabilizing influence of the settlement helped to create a vital sense of community in the borough at that critical time was recognized in a tribute from the mayor. 'Particularly would I like to say a word for the work performed by the representative of the CAB,' wrote A. E. McAuliffe early in 1945. 'They have indeed rendered a service which will never be forgotten in Bethnal Green.' Meanwhile, as Sir Wyndham Deedes remarked, 'Go round to St Margaret's, they will help you is a sentence continually on our lips.'

The last months of the war brought several council changes at St Margaret's. Sir Wyndham Deedes became chairman in 1944, replacing the long-serving Mrs McClean who had hired the Albert Hall for one money-raising event. The same year Stella Penley was appointed head on the resignation after 15 years of Miss Kelly, who, however, stayed on the council and became honorary secretary the following year, replacing Phyllis Egerton.

Miss Penley had come to St Margaret's in 1930 as a student and then worked as Miss Kelly's secretary from 1932, thanks to an annual payment from St Hugh's College to cover her salary. She left in 1939 to be called to the Bar, but returned as a resident a few months later, to be mainly engaged in CAB work in Islington and at Pilgrim House before becoming head.

Immediate postwar work included coping with delays in repairs of war damage, shortages of every sort, including rationed food, and three months of unbroken frost in the winter of 1947.

Miss Egerton also knew the settlement well, for she had joined the council in 1929 while secretary of the St Bartholomew's School care committee. 'My earliest memories of St Margaret's are parties given on its behalf at 24 Park Lane, a site now occupied by the Hilton Hotel,' she remarked in 1986. After spending some years abroad and in voluntary social work, Miss Egerton combined her settlement responsibilities with a considerable WVS commitment, eventually resigning as secretary at 21 Old Ford Road in 1945 to undertake a WVS staff job in the Far East: on her return she became secretary of the settlement's general purposes committee and a trustee.

Early settlement workers had been characterized by their caring attitude towards individuals, particularly those in need of direct and patient support. Fortunate in having no specific terms of reference for their work, the volunteers had also made a contribution to the social services by initiating new schemes while also supporting existing ones. Then during the war their value to the local authorities was proved beyond doubt. With the birth of the welfare state came an increasing trend towards community involvement and a new professionalism.

Oxford interest was stimulated when Miss Gwyer, principal of St Hugh's College, became chairwoman in 1946 on Sir Wyndham Deedes's retirement owing to ill health. Other senior members of the college also joined the council, which then included representatives of the mothers' club, elected in 1945, and of the residents, besides several members of the local community. At this time 19 Old Ford Road was bought by the council and adapted into bedsitters for ordinands from King's College who came to help and to learn.

The London Diocesan Settlements' Committee was set up in 1943. Chaired by the Bishop of Stepney, it consisted of representatives of the London diocesan conference and heads of Church of England settlements who met regularly in Bedford Square. The aim was to find out whether settlements were dealing adequately with social problems in a changing world. Deaconess Souttar, head of St Mildred's Settlement in Docklands during the war, was soon a key figure here. Though not a member of St Margaret's House council until 1955, she had intimate knowledge of the daughter settlement founded by Ingram over 50 years earlier with Miss Harington's sister in charge. Moreover, she epitomized the link between women's settlements, the universities and some religious houses.

Elizabeth Souttar had come to St Mildred's in 1937 as a young woman in her twenties and, with an LMH reputation, was a popular president of the junior common room. It was a time when the hard-pressed Miss Wintour, warden for 28 years, was increasingly hampered by the lack of a salaried, reliable assistant. The impact of the newcomer was immediate and considerable, St Mildred's soon winning recognition as a social work training centre, and one where students carried much responsibility for the rapidly accelerating pace of local life before the area was devastated by bombs.

'I was there for seven years in all,' Deaconess Souttar told the author in 1982,

> the first three as youth leader and then as warden, including the Blitz. We had a housekeeper and seven residents; the ground floor was devoted to club rooms and an office, and we lived in the upper part of the house. The main pieces of work were the school care and aftercare visiting for four large LCC schools, the running of clubs for people of all ages from seven years old upwards, and representation on committees in the neighbourhood including the Red Cross, British Legion Relief and the ICAA. We normally sent away 400 children for the CCHF and in the summer the whole place was given up to the work and to club holidays, parties and outings. With the outbreak of war after the first tremendous rush of evacuation it seemed that everything had stopped, but by Christmas things were fast returning to normal.

All involved recall the brilliant weather when the bombing started.

> That Saturday was a beautiful day with such a perfect sky that I remember we talked about it at teatime. An hour later squadron after squadron poured over. Our big guns went off for the first time, the house shook with the vibration and soon fires were raging everywhere. Some blocks of flats had been demolished, and as well as the fires around us the whole of the opposite bank appeared to be alight. The barges on the water were burning even mid-stream and, helped by a tearing wind, huge pieces of fire were coming across the river increasing the flames on our side.
>
> In desperation we packed the people (there were about 100 of them) into ambulances, and took them back to the house, where we found that gas and electricity had failed. ... We emerged next day into a nightmare of devastation. The church had been demolished, windows were blasted, houses down ... the arrangements for the homeless seemed to be quite inadequate and we set about working for an improvement in that ... for many nights and spasmodically in the day the bombings continued.

Eventually, after a rocket attack, the building, with deep cracks in its walls, was declared unsafe; the few residents were housed temporarily in a flat occupied by the SSAFA staff, and they worked at the nearby Docklands settlement, before being moved to the local vicarage. With the return of peace, when it seemed possible that settlements would merge into local authority community centres, St Mildred's council steered a different course towards something like a mission house. The local curate lived there, the warden attended parish staff meetings and each resident undertook some teaching or visiting assigned for the Church, continuity being maintained by Miss Bradford, a resident before, during and after the war.

Elizabeth Souttar was ordained deaconess in 1945, two years after leaving women workers in the diocese of Rochester. She later became head deaconess at the Clapham Common centre, before being appointed general secretary to the London Diocesan Board of Women's Work. She made a unique contribution in this field, serving also for many years on the councils of the LMH and Katherine Low settlements as well as of St Margaret's House, and as president of BCH. After her death in 1983, Dame Diana Reader-Harris of the T & T settlement wrote, 'at all times her deep spiritual resources made her a very dependable person to whom many turned in time of need. Never was this truer than in the Blitz of London's docks.'

The LMHS in Lambeth, which was immediately involved at the outbreak of war in evacuating children from London, was soon recognized as a centre for information and voluntary effort. Its gardens were used as a meeting place for sick and invalid children from all over London (who were not hospital cases yet were not eligible to be sent in school parties) before members of the WVS, cooperating with the ICAA, took them by car to their country destinations. A settlement resident involved here wrote:

> Owing to the evacuation, the 'Cathedral' closed for a time and I was asked to go to Fairford and run a settlement for mothers and babies. We expected 90 babies and 50 mothers ... 76 school children arrived, however, and four mothers. The settlement consisted of a large barn 30ft by 35ft, one end of which was turned into a kitchen with five gas stoves, while the other was used as a canteen and rest room for parents visiting their children and as a play centre. The adjoining stables had been converted into bathrooms.

The phoney war brought many such 'settlements'. Clothing was an immediate problem, and other residents were asked to organize a clothing scheme for the three schools whose care committees they ran until an LCC care committee took over responsibilities here, covering 30 schools in Lambeth.

When bombing began in earnest, the settlement overnight moved into the front line of the fight against the threatened collapse of social organization and morale. Among senior members of LMH on its wartime council were Alice Johnston, in charge of the evacuation department at WVS headquarters, Elizabeth Souttar, warden of St Mildred's Settlement in the heart of Docklands and Cherry Morris, almoner at St Thomas's Hospital, whose personality contributed much in establishing the settlement's reputation during the war years as a friend for all in need.

The Blitz took its toll of settlement workers. Some of those who helped to staff shelters and rest centres were killed in the corridors of Morley College during an October raid in 1940. Next day an enquiry and evacuation bureau was set up in the settlement hut, and from this developed its much used evacuation service which helped elderly and shell-shocked people to find suitable billets. Its own premises, already extensively damaged by a bomb which fell on Walcot Square in September (making holes in the roof, bringing down ceilings and damaging all windows and doors), faced near disaster the following spring.

'On 10 May the warden and two residents were fire-watching at the settlement. About 8.00 p.m. bombs were heard to fall, and from the front garden the warden noticed a fire bomb on the empty house next door!' The resident's account ends, 'The firemen were not able to extinguish the burning house next door, but they put out a fire in the sitting room of No. 133, and with the help of our water buckets, another in the house on the other side of the fire. We went to bed at 4.30 a.m. thankful that the settlement was still standing.' And it could still offer shelter to others.

The Bishop of Southwark, bombed out in 1942 soon after Winifred Hogg had begun her six valuable years as settlement warden, moved his offices at that time to the ground floor of No. 129, where he worked until the end of the war.

As shelter life became more organized, there was a growing demand for libraries run by settlement workers, as in the large shelter at Waterloo station where a room was set aside for children and young people. The men's committee in the tube shelters at Kennington and the Elephant and Castle also asked them to help with an infant's school and a Sunday school. A start was made in one rest centre with 200 Penguins and other books given by supporting schools, Roedean among them, and from contacts thus made came discussion groups and classes in various subjects. Churches with rooms underground considered themselves fortunate, St John's by Waterloo station becoming known as St John's in the Crypt.

A typical piece of settlement pioneering was provided by the Cowley day nurseries, set up in March 1941. It was at first proposed to start a mothers' club with a crèche in the house originally intended for the Cowley Community Centre.

> [Then,] after we heard that the country needed day nurseries for mothers engaged in war work we decided to use it for that purpose. As soon as our plan was mentioned, a chorus of demand arose from the Department of Public Health, the Labour Exchange and from countless mothers themselves, who even began to bring their babies to the settlement doorsteps and threaten to leave them there. We pressed on with the decoration, only to be balked by a firebomb on 10 May, which destroyed half the flooring in the main nursery. When this was mended and the furniture in place we found that we had spent far more than we expected and were relieved to find that we could qualify for a government grant. ... However, although we applied for a grant in July, the matter was referred backwards and forwards between three committees of the borough council and the Ministry of Health in such a way that the grant was not actually paid until November, by which time the settlement was involved in an overdraft and the warden had spent many sleepless nights. In the end the settlement was only asked to contribute about £100, and was able to give the children the benefit of the nursery for nearly six months before any other nursery opening in Lambeth.

In September 1942, the financial burden of this day nursery, by then enlarged to take 60 children, was assumed by the Lambeth Borough Council. The premises were severely damaged by a flying bomb in 1944, but soon afterwards over 180 children were again coming in each week for books from its library. Miss Dorothy Case took charge that year, and both she and successive matrons held broad views about the function of the nursery in helping adults as well as children; a parents' club formed there pointed the way to settlement work in the postwar years.

With the return to London of Bedford College and the LSE came a renewed demand for field work placements for students. The international contacts were revived when the secretary of the American Federation of Settlements came to live at No. 129, to be followed in due course by a trained community worker from Canada and a youth worker from Australia. There were some keen gardeners among residents at this time and the head gardener at Lambeth Palace helped jubilee festivities in 1947 by judging the flourishing allotments on the Cowley estate. The ARP wardens' club, long held in the settlement's fine garden hut acquired at its coming of age, was succeeded by a St Margaret's club for women interested in handicrafts. School care committee work, given up during the war, was resumed, and a modest meals-on-wheels round on one day a week started in connection with the Lambeth Old People's Welfare Association, a service to be vastly extended in subsequent years.

Bomb damage repairs to settlement buildings engaged workmen for much of 1949. The Duke, which had reopened the previous year, was also in poor shape structurally, with a badly leaking roof. However, its members celebrated coronation year in 1953 by winning the Lambeth borough championships for both table tennis and football, as well as distinguishing themselves with a popular woodwind band. Then, in 1956, after seven years of delay while the necessary permission and funds were assured, building began on a nearby site leased from the Duchy of Cornwall, the old Duke having by then been gutted by local youth. The new club premises in Orsett Street were opened by the Archbishop of Canterbury, Dr Fisher, as part of the sixtieth anniversary celebrations of the settlement. Effort in this part of Lambeth now largely replaced that required for the Cowley Community Centre in the Brixton Road, which, mainly for financial reasons, had recently closed, soon after Miss Crossman's retirement, thus ending a long chapter in settlement history.

With its customary flexibility, the settlement also embarked on another legal advice centre, this time to fill a gap pending the full implementation of the 1949 Legal Aid and Advice Centre, a new development in the field of social service.

The birth of the welfare state had, however, raised some doubts about the functions of settlements. With all the new social legislation to hand, perhaps they were now redundant? 'Young Mr Beveridge' had indeed been among those who attended training sessions at LMHS in bygone days, but would young men and women interested in equipping themselves for social work now look elsewhere?

Members of council meeting under the chairmanship of the Bishop of Kingston (Bishop Hawkes retired in 1952 after 25 years to be succeeded by Bishop Gilpin) decided that work should carry on along traditional if modest lines until the path ahead was clearer. The good name of the settlement was kept up by the next three wardens (Miss Dunning, Miss Hewitt and Miss Duncan) who saw that the residential side was well run, while paying due attention to clubs for different age groups, outings, country holidays and much visiting of old people. Among senior LMH members then giving devoted service were Miss Kate Lea, vice chairwoman, and Mrs Dorothy Mattinson, honorary secretary since 1948, family connections with LMH through his wife and daughter ensuring the keen interest also of the next Bishop of Kingston, the Rt Revd Hugh Montefiore, later Bishop of Birmingham.

Men have always supported the settlement since Dame Elizabeth Wordsworth's day, not least as its honorary solicitors and treasurers. Men residents were accepted in 1963, and soon after the rector of St Mary's, Lambeth, the Revd Oliver Fiennas, later dean of Lincoln, had become chairman, one of his curates, the dynamic young Revd Simon Brown, was appointed warden. Already acquainted with settlement youth work at Bede House, his impact on the neighbourhood was considerable. A new era of expansion followed an appeal launched to enable the basements of the two centre houses to be converted from their mid-Victorian standard of low ceilings and stone floors into a modern kitchen and dining room. Then three years later the shock of a fivefold increase of rent was met by a further appeal, including a television broadcast by the actress Margaret Rawlings, a senior LMH member, as a result of which the premises were brought into line with modern standards required by young professional people wishing to combine some voluntary work with their jobs in local schools and offices.

An increase in both salaried settlement staff and volunteers was proof that cooperation with local authorities had taken a fresh impetus from the setting up of the borough's directorate of social services in 1970. Simon Brown, himself a family man, wrote:

> Undoubtedly to my mind the most significant direction in which our work is developing is in attempting to undertake preventive and supportive work with deprived families in a 'risk' situation. In addition to our Advice Centre, groups for socially isolated mothers and small group work for younger children supervised by our community worker, we now have 20 volunteers working with families under the careful supervision of an experienced caseworker recently appointed to the staff.

Among these volunteers was Mrs Wright from Philadelphia who thus began a long and happy connection between the settlement and members of the American Church in London.

The adult literacy scheme, pioneered by BARS, included several LMHS residents as teachers. Enthusiastic young community service volunteers, living for a period at the settlement perhaps before going abroad, made a stimulating impact, while other students on long-term placements often found that the internal community aspect of settlement life proved as instructive as the more objective learning done outside, in overcrowded tower blocks from which clients would later come to them as caseworkers.

Bridge building was helped at this time by monthly lunches and occasional weekend conferences held at the settlement. The director of social services for Lambeth, the chief planning officer for the Lambeth Walk redevelopment scheme, the community relations officer for the borough and officers of the Juvenile Advisory Bureau were among guest speakers to representatives of all social work agencies, the police, teachers, doctors and clergy, useful contacts being thus made between many working in north Lambeth who otherwise were liable to become acquainted only as voices on the telephone. Medical inspections for the CCHF were held each spring at the settlement, and work undertaken with the pioneering Lollard adventure playground, the usual play space for many children being among the rubble of redevelopment. Meanwhile, the three Walcot clubs for elderly citizens continued to attract enthusiasts for handicrafts, bingo and a varied programme of outings to the theatre or the country, members enjoying the warmth of personal welcome from Queen's College students and supporters of the Thursley Women's Institute, as well as the hospitality of the local Rotary Club.

The delicate aroma of stew or a trayful of apple turnovers, which later percolated up from the settlement kitchens before 11.00 a.m. each weekday, when 50 meals-on-wheels had to be ready for collection, together with the early afternoon job of washing up the 200 reappearing pieces of aluminium involved, ceased in 1971 when the local authority assumed responsibility here. But soon afterwards the kitchens were again in use to provide lunch for elderly citizens who attended the work centre set up as a joint undertaking between settlement and borough, while on Sundays residents ran a lunch club for a mentally handicapped group as well as weekday clubs for the young.

This recognized neighbourhood centre with strong pioneering instincts celebrated its seventy-fifth birthday in 1974 before embarking on another stage of its useful life, unaware that a crisis leading to near disaster was at hand.

Plans under a new director, the Revd David Rhys, for cooperation with a charitable organization to run a bail hostel were necessarily abandoned, but only after under-occupation of the settlement premises for several months had led to a crippling loss of income. Partly through a newly set up 'Friends' organization, closure was averted and, after the appointment of the next director, Jeffe Jeffers, formerly a community worker at Oxford House with specialist knowledge of housing combined with outstanding drive, confidence was restored and much new work undertaken. An employment worker became project manager of the Lambeth house, formed to train local youth in carpentry and other skills, a Kennington cleaners' cooperative for women was organized and help was given with wastepaper collection and the London home workers' campaign. Housing and social security problems were the main concern of a rights adviser, who also promoted a cooperative campaign aimed at giving people more control over their own housing. A community worker was closely involved with several tenants' cooperatives, a well as campaigning for permanent youth and community facilities, and a volunteers' organizer coordinated a unique service including two mums' workshops and an informal neighbourhood care scheme, in co-operation with social services, Age Concern and local people on various estates. Thus progress was made on many fronts including non-party education for citizenship, particularly among women.

However, a decision was now taken to move from the well-loved but rented house in Kennington Road to freehold premises in the Wandsworth Road, further from the centre of London but within the borough of Lambeth in an area of proven need.

Community work had come a long way in the last 50 years, but basic problems hardly altered. In the five new high-rise blocks of flats on Ethelread estate, tenants still relied largely on a few heavily committed individuals in their association, whose departure for any reason could make a lamentable gap in campaigning on various fronts, but on the older Kennington Park LCC estate of the 1930s, a similar association had put down firm roots. A community flat there, reminiscent of Miss Crossman's pioneering days, housed a popular mothers' and toddlers' group, a pensioners' shop with coffee mornings and a class for English as a second language, while the teatime latchkey project became well established in a bare six months.

Though the settlement no longer had its own minibus, taking the local youth on jaunts (even across the Channel) and barge weekends were similarly a memory of the early 1970s. The Monday and Thursday clubs run by residents were able to borrow transport from Lambeth Mission and Cambridge House for numerous day outings, camping holidays in Northamptonshire and youth hostelling in Devon. Mature members of the jolly Ace of Clubs meanwhile enjoyed exhilarating outings provided by Queen's College, Harley Street. The future of such clubs, like that of the settlement's quietly successful work centre, was assured by agreement with the Ethelread tenants' association to use their premises, Pory Hall, not far from the site of the earlier Duke of Clarence club.

Ongoing responsibilities with tenants' associations and mothers' and toddlers' groups were handed over to the borough, which would be appointing its own staff to cope; visiting problem-beset elderly people on residents' and other volunteers' lists was similarly safeguarded. Only current employment and housing cooperative work would move with the settlement to the new area.

A sociology graduate of Essex University was introduced as warden at the annual meeting on 21 June 1980, and Mrs Fierz, principal of Queen's College and long a member of the settlement council, brought several of her students to help at a garden party held afterwards. This was organized by 23 residents who, keen on tradition and determined to keep together, had recently formed a housing cooperative hopefully linked with the reconstruction of a spacious, dilapidated, early Victorian St Barnabas vicarage in Stockwell near the settlement's new home, a project to be realized in 1984.

Happy memories long lingered on for passers-by in the Kennington Road, and tall trees whispered among themselves of how on an earlier 21 June, at the start of celebrations for Queen Victoria's diamond jubilee in 1887, the residents of No. 129 had hung out gay flags and bunting. The original brass doorplate of that time, with its design of three daisies, shone bravely to cheer the last visitors as settlement roots and branches prepared to spread across the borough, true to form.

However, within three years handicapped people were creating a garden on nearby wasteland behind Walnut Tree Walk, part of a new and imaginative settlement project called Roots and Shoots and run from its newly bought premises at 460 Wandsworth Road.

* * *

The T & T settlement had also been able to provide some reassurance through the first critical days when the Surrey docks caught fire. Then evacuation, ARP, the blackout and the commandeering of the Dockhead club by local Territorials for a brief period all raised problems. And, as at other settlements, people moved to war work elsewhere. Lesley Sewell, the warden, after taking on a full-time ambulance job locally, left at the end of 1939 to become deputy organizing secretary of the National Association for Girls' Clubs, though keeping on some settlement responsibilities and accepting a new one as chairman of its war emergency committee. Soon Jean Marindin, another pillar of strength as chair of its organization committee, also departed for a full-time job as youth liaison officer for Kent and Sussex. However, early in 1940, Violet Tritton was back in her old place in Bermondsey, shouldering the warden's responsibilities on a voluntary basis.

As children began to return to London and the dangers of unlimited and unplanned leisure became apparent here as in other London boroughs, a school was started by volunteers at the Dockhead club, by now cleaned and redecorated after its brief occupation by the army, and by April 1940 'we have 120 boys and girls in the play centres and a further 60 in the children's clubs.' Then the YWCA, with its long experience in democratic club management, offered to help T & T members with the 16 to 18 age group for the duration of the war, so that the club's somewhat shaky future seemed assured.

When the Blitz started, carrying away most of the old landmarks in Bermondsey, both the settlement and the Dockhead club were evacuated several times as fires raged and glass was shattered. The buildings, however, stayed erect, though sadly both the hostel and the Abbey Street flat were obliterated. Sirens were wailing one morning when the Queen visited the area at the height of the Blitz, and stunned people stood silently watching, for there had been a bad incident in Abbey Street the previous night. T & T members early started a CAB, a music club and other activities in shelters and, by the autumn of 1941, were working closely with the Council for the Encouragement of Music and the Arts (CENA).

Then, in 1942, a major move to help check the rising tide of delinquency was initiated by the cheerful much loved Gwynned Richards, newly appointed settlement warden and to be remembered particularly as an enthusiastic gardener adept at rearing flowers on roof tops, in window boxes and in small yards. She embarked on a youth centre at Queen's House in Rotherhithe, where, amid river sounds and scents, many draughty shabby houses had their foundations in the Thames. A friendly unconventional atmosphere characterized popular Queen's House with its two resident workers. There were also at this time four residents at the settlement and five, including Miss Tritton, at Dockhead. Then a holiday home for war workers was started at Tunbridge Wells to be followed by a holiday house in Hampstead where 500 boys and girls enjoyed life during 1944. (And there was a happy consequence of this concentration on youth. After the war a group of girls who had never known the Time and Talent Guild, but had recently lived at one or other of the three guild houses, formed themselves into an association to link all those interested in the Bermondsey work.)

At a T & T jubilee reunion in July 1945 an enquiry was held not, as after the first war, into the guild itself, but on its future in southeast London, for this was by no means clear. One result was the coming together of all volunteers to form several groups, including one for undergraduates from Queens' College Cambridge who were interested particularly in Rotherhithe. Though only some were to survive, notably Miss Harford's Bermondsey group, they formed the basis of T & T work in the years of reconstruction. Men were now admitted as associates and married men wardens were appointed at Dockhead and Queen's. Moreover, by 1947, 187 Bermondsey Street was no longer envisaged as a residential settlement.

Miss Tritton was unanimously elected chairwoman of the newly formed Bermondsey and Rotherhithe Council of Social Service, the first to hold this office. The council was housed on the second floor at No. 187, thereby well sited to carry on the cooperation between statutory and voluntary agencies which had developed in the shelters. For its own use T & T has the club rooms, chapel, common room and two small bedrooms as well as a housekeeper's flat now built on the top floor. VAT, as she was widely known, also enlisted the valuable support of women's institutes for the West End Christmas fair, run before the war with the help of the GDA and still a main money raiser and meeting place for supporters.

Subsequent lively projects under the presidency of Dame Diana Reader-Harris, formerly headmistress of Sherbourne School for Girls, have been based at the headquarters flat in Drummond Road, SE16, and at the old mortuary in Rotherhithe.

Meanwhile, old Paulinas still involved with DCH in the East End may claim some credit for the current liveliness of the community work in Docklands.

The Albany settlement at Deptford, started by Queen Victoria's daughter-in-law, has recently undergone a major change and is a leader among local voluntary organizations. The Prince of Wales, continuing family tradition, on 1 May 1979 laid the foundation of this new community centre facing onto the pedestrian street market in Douglas Way, and it was opened by the Princess of Wales in May 1983 with the mayors and mayoresses of both Lewisham and Greenwich among those present. Queen Elizabeth the Queen Mother is patron, and the mood there is both serious and light-hearted. The building includes a large community room with several smaller meeting rooms as well as a café and bar areas. Wedding parties are held there, the disabled have special facilities and a garden is in the making. The majority of both daytime users and staff are women, and the general manager, with a democratic team and a chairwoman to support him, emphasizes that 'racism and sexism have to be confronted, though they often get neglected, if we are serious about working in all possible appropriate ways to counteract the present unequal distribution of power and access to resources.'

There is little leisure culture in Deptford, where much poverty has persisted through the postwar period, and, though the slums have largely been swept away, cheap blocks offer units of accommodation rather than homes.

The Albany is now seeking to improve local life by assisting people individually and collectively, and major projects there include health care.

During 1940 over 700 refugees were billeted in Camberwell, and the settlement ran clubs for them and classes to teach English. Early in the Blitz 60 homeless families moved into its two semi-basement club rooms, and it started a communal kitchen. Then in 1941, like most other settlements in London, it opened a CAB.

Over 80 flying bombs fell in the borough and by the end of the war only 400 out of 40,000 of its houses remained undamaged. The settlement itself, despite incendiary bombs on its roof, was relatively fortunate and, with the return of peace, members of the

British Federation of Social Workers were soon holding their monthly meetings there along with other groups. Then, in July 1945, the Camberwell housing society was started and within a year, from its registered office at the settlement, negotiations were on foot, with the LCC as ground landlord, to secure a site off Nigel Road, Rye Lane, to build 50 flats for elderly people and single women.

Jubilee celebrations held in 1946 for the 50-year-old mission included an inspiring service taken by the Bishop in Southwark cathedral, its great nave crammed with girls from the 136 schools then supporting the settlement. This tradition had been revived the previous year after a break since 1939. Then a presentation was made to Canon Veazey and his wife in the Friends' Meeting House, before Lady Eldon spoke on 'The Voluntary Spirit in Social Service'. It was the last time that many settlement workers were to see Mrs Veazey, beloved in Camberwell where she had spent all her married life, for she died the following year, the canon carrying on his work there for another brief period, still a living embodiment of his motto, 'Have faith and be cheerful'.

Princess Margaret, patron of the UGS, paid her first visit in December 1947 to what was soon to be called the Peckham Settlement. Shortly afterwards girls attending the social service week studied the needs of old people. Then, in 1948, a meals-on-wheels service was started in cooperation with the Camberwell Old People's Welfare Association, settlement workers cooking the meals and 'taking a great interest in the recipients'. And here, as in most settlement work, clearly both parties would gain. The mission extended over three local parishes.

The Peckham Settlement was also influenced at this time by David Collett, warden of the young Federation of London Settlements sponsored by Blackfriars Settlement where he had been director for five years. 'As many as one fifth of all the settlements in Great Britain are in the new London borough of Southwark. Of course there are good historical reasons for this, since the new borough includes the Elephant and Castle, the Old Kent Road, Peckham and Bermondsey, all of them relatively depressed areas a few generations ago.' He encouraged the settlement's educational urban studies project, which was to become a major part of local community work and was widely appreciated and used regularly, especially by four local schools, with boys as well as girls involved.

As Bishop Simpson, chairman of council, remarked of the settlement, 'the whole thing depends on the support and interest of schools,' and 72 of them, both in London and scattered throughout the country, then supported it, those in London including South Hampstead High School, Grey Coat School, Sydenham High School, Vauxhall Manor School and Peckham Manor Boys' School. With both the ILEA and the London borough of Southwark among its sponsors, and its feeling for tradition always strong, the settlement was soon to have as its president Lady (Geoffrey) Howe, a former pupil of Wycombe Abbey.

The Katherine Low Settlement suffered heavily in the Blitz. In the immediate prewar period five clubs were run at 108 High Street for Battersea girls and boys up to 14 years, three clubs for the over fourteens, two clubs for mothers and two Sunday clubs for mothers and girls.

Thus the settlement was a natural evacuation centre in 1939, even before the LCC Divisional Education Office sent two schoolmasters to work there with the power to issue railway warrants; and when bombing began in 1940 people from the neighbourhood poured in with every sort of problem, emphasizing that 'the greatest demand on our work is for the friendship available through the still open doors of the settlement.'

Besides being used as a rest centre, its kitchen and scullery were equipped with funds raised in New York to provide a shelter for those who were ill and the US ambassador's wife, Mrs Winant, aware that Katherine Low had been born in the USA, opened a new shelter there in 1941 for club members. This was an appreciated gesture at a time when Britain stood alone.

Then, on 18 June 1944 at 5.00 a.m., a flying bomb blasted part of Battersea and, though no one at the Katherine Low Settlement was hurt, it became temporarily uninhabitable, with long-term results. After the Christ's College boys' club had offered storage space in the chapel, while sharing its premises with the Katherine Low Settlement for clubs, a joint emergency committee was set up in April 1946. Cooperation led to amalgamation and in March

1947 the first annual report was issued of the 'Christ's College and Katherine Low Settlement'. The Cambridge committee, representing past and present members of the college, included the master, Canon I. T. Raven, with the historian J. H. Plumb as treasurer, while the joint managing committee had the Bishop of Kingston, the Rt Revd F. O. T. Hawkes, as chairman, Canon Raven and Miss Burrows as vice chairmen and Mr J. T. Wharton, head of Battersea's Sir Walter St John's School, as both honorary secretary and chairman of the finance subcommittee. This was henceforth a mixed settlement, and soon a visit of seven undergraduates resulted in one of them, after taking his degree in July 1947, joining the staff particularly for work among boys and men. Meanwhile, an old relationship had been renewed with the local branch of Toc H.

The decision to appoint fully trained staff and improve accommodation resulted in the arrival early in 1947 of Rita Clark as warden, and the creation of two flats in Nos 106 and 108. Miss Clark was typical of a new generation of social workers. At the start of the war she had been living and helping as a volunteer at the Mary Ward Settlement, but after it became a refuge for bombed-out people in Bloomsbury she applied to the Carnegie Trust for training in youth leadership.

> Eileen Younghusband interviewed me, I was accepted and sent to UGS and for two months worked with the COS. Then I went to Birmingham Summer Lane for a year with lectures at the university and practical work at the settlement. Afterwards I went to Southampton to train with Kit Russell before being appointed warden of Virginia House Plymouth to run the Astor Institute there.

During her years in Battersea, she planned the postwar work while welcoming students and other residents as a feeling of gathering momentum permeated the settlement. In particular, she promoted a free legal advice centre, which opened in September 1947 and filled an urgent need in the area at that time, run as it was for many years by volunteers. Then, as part of a renewed emphasis on training, Head Deaconess Elizabeth Souttar, who had recently joined the management committee as head of its local works sub-committee, sent students from Gilmore House to help in various clubs while preparing to become parish workers. Mission work had here a strong ally.

Soon the shattering discovery of extensive dry rot made drastic action necessary, and before March 1948 the parent bodies had handed over nearly all their assets to the management committee, which then controlled both the premises and the funds, including grants from the Ministry of Education and the War Damage Commission. But survival was still in doubt.

After three more difficult years, General Sir Frederick Pile began his long association as chairman of the appeals' committee, with the task of raising £10,000. Christ's College, though still a good friend, in due course formally transferred to the settlement its interest in the work of the boy's club, including summer camps encouraged by the general. Then a dinner club opened for old men, whom the warden encountered sitting around the dreary open space near the settlement, evolved into the local authority's old people's centre. A trustee until 1972, Sir Frederick was over 90 when he resigned as president in 1977, the year of golden jubilee celebrations attended by Princess Alice, Duchess of Gloucester. Soon afterwards Sir Eric Berthoud, an Oxford man and diplomat, completed his ten years as chairman before handing over to another retired soldier, Brigadier Hardy. It is not only women who find much in common between service in the armed forces and in the welfare state.

Bishop Creighton House (BCH) was also among settlements with war damage problems. On 8 October 1940 the premises received a direct hit; fortunately iron supports in the centre held and seven residents sheltering with the warden in the basement were able to clamber out safely from the ruins around them. Plans for rebuilding were to loom large for some time. Meanwhile, children were welcomed both in a nursery school and one for the unevaluated of school age; then four country houses lent to the settlement were opened and maintained for bombed-out families. Miss E. Dodds, warden for the remaining war years, made BCH into a popular centre for student training. Then the enthusiastic Miss Kathleen Wooster took over in 1946, receiving in due course an OBE for her work, an unusual recognition in the settlement world. Besides Lady Moberly, chairwoman for 12 years until 1948, another major contributor at this time was Katharine Troutbeck, a much-loved resident for 16 years and sub-warden from 1948 to 1958, during which time she served on many diocesan and ruridecanal committees, helping to strengthen the relationship between Church and settlement; she was long remembered for her large hearted friendliness and unquenchable sense of humour, invaluable qualities in anyone living at a settlement.

There was no doubt of the local goodwill enjoyed by BCH when two MPs, (Sir) Michael Stewart and (Dame) Edith Summerskill, representing East and West Fulham, attended a reception for the 40-year-old settlement held in the Fulham town hall in May 1948, after the Bishop of London, Dr J. C. W. Wand, had preached at a service of thanksgiving.

The mayor remarked that it was 'up to the public authority to build on the knowledge gained by voluntary workers'. Then Miss Wickham talked of the early days when BCH was 'a thorn in the side of the Fulham Borough Council. . . . One of the most representative and determined deputations ever to go to the Council Chamber was from BCH. We urged the Council to buy some vacant land and erect flats. That site is now Fulham Court.' The celebrations ended with a visit from Queen Mary on 24 March 1949, when it was emphasized that BCH was one of the first social centres in the country to open a child guidance clinic. Children in the play centre, members of the women's fellowship attending a cooking demonstration in the garden house and pensioners of the Good Companions' Club in the greenroom would not forget the day.

In 1951, another 'royal year', the newly rebuilt BCH was declared open by the Duchess of Gloucester who had already visited the settlement as president of the Invalid Kitchens of London. She now heard from Lady Bland, BCH chairwoman, that 'the Council had been very touched by the kindly thought of girls of the Fulham County Secondary School who had furnished one of the students' bedrooms.' Two years later the settlement was associated with the Fulham Housing Improvement Society and the

Fulham Old People's Welfare Association in acquiring and equipping Royston, an attractive house on Putney Hill, as a home for elderly pensioners. The Duchess of Kent visited BCH that year as president of the Queen Alexandra Rose Day Appeal.

Growing ethnic problems were now tackled. The start of an Overseas Social Centre in 1957 to meet the needs of immigrants (and not only from the West Indies) brought many new faces to the settlement. A French student resident at that time wrote 'I shall never forget a talk between an Egyptian doctor, two teachers of English from communist Russia, a barrister from Singapore, a handful of West Indians and some of the residents. Few meetings could boast such a widely international audience and none could offer a more friendly atmosphere.'

Both Church and borough authorities again backed BCH jubilee celebrations in 1958. A highlight of that year was the charity ball at Fulham Palace when Lady Doris Blacker JP, who chaired the council from 1954 to 1959, was among those who welcomed Princess Alexandra. And it was in line with BCH history over 50 years that the mayor of Fulham should chair the jubilee appeal committee. He also gave reassurance about the future of BCH.

> Not the least of the settlement's responsibilities is to advise and train the young professional social workers on whom our welfare state must be dependent. That is impossible unless the daily sympathetic contact can be maintained, and we in Fulham must make sure that our Bishop Creighton House Settlement is kept healthy and lively, always ready for the problems of tomorrow.

Indeed, during the 1960s students came from a wide area for experience of social work. The universities of Leicester, Manchester and Nottingham, Bedford College, the LSE and Gloucester Training College for Domestic Science were all in close contact, and many overseas visitors arrived from Germany, France, Nigeria, the West Indies, New York and elsewhere.

Good relations were also maintained with other British settlements. The warden of that time, previously head of the Sheffield University Settlement, had earlier attended a conference of the

British Association of Residential Settlements (BARS) and, in January 1961, BCH became the BARS headquarters, with the BCH sub-warden as its elected secretary. The following year BARS held its spring conference at Lillie Road, when the mayor and mayoress welcomed representatives of all British settlements while attending a luncheon on the premises. Soon afterwards the executive committee of the International Federation of Settlements (IFS) and of neighbourhood centres, which had held its first conference at Toynbee Hall in 1922, accepted an invitation to use BCH as its meeting place. Its spacious rooms, long recognized as a considerable asset, had been used in this connection during 1910 when the heads and other representatives of nearly all the London women's settlements attended a meeting there at Miss Wickham's invitation. In 1926 Sir Wyndham Deedes, as BARS secretary, had paid two visits, first to see the premises and afterwards to speak about the international federation conference held that year in Paris. Five years later Lord Astor, when addressing the settlement's AGM, expressed appreciation of the help given by BCH to BARS. Moreover, this feeling was reciprocated. 'Being somewhat isolated at this end of London we value our membership,' wrote one BCH volunteer.

The continuing religious basis of the settlement's work was emphasized in 1963 when Deaconess Elizabeth Souttar became president, to be followed by Dame Eileen Younghusband. The Revd Cuthbert Creighton, president since 1936, had recently died, ten years after the loss of his sister Deaconess Beatrice, and the link with the founder's family was now broken. But as their mother had also been largely responsible for starting, under the auspices of the NUWW, the Victoria settlements in Liverpool and elsewhere, it seemed a natural progression that BARS, dependent as it has often been on the hospitality of its members, should then be based at BCH.

11

Victorian and Other Settlements with the British Association of Settlements and Social Action Centre

The NUWW, precursor of the National Council of Women, was mainly responsible for spreading the settlement movement outside London. In the late nineteenth century there was hardly a large provincial town where ladies in comfortable circumstances were not forming groups to improve the health and living conditions of local poor people. In 1870 members of Birmingham's Ladies' Association for Useful Work started 'simple lectures on sanitary matters for women and girls over 15'. Action was needed to avoid overlap and by the mid-1880s Sheffield had formed a local federation of seven organizations, including the YWCA, the GFS and the British Women's Temperance Association, calling itself a 'Ladies' Union of Workers among Women and Girls'. The federating urge crescendoed and in 1887 a meeting in Birmingham resulted in a ladies' union there embracing 40 organizations concerned with women and children, having as its motto 'Union is Strength'. Three years later representatives of similar unions throughout the country met at a conference in Birmingham to discuss such topics as night shelters, work in prisons, prostitution, deserted mothers and employment for girls unfit for domestic service or factory work.

Liverpool hosted a similar conference the following year when Beatrice Webb read a paper on 'Cooperation among Women', after which a central conference council was formed as the coordinating body for the various ladies' unions. At the third conference, held in Bristol in 1892, Margaret Sewell, warden of WUS, led a discussion on settlements.

By 1895, with Mrs Creighton's help in drawing up a constitution, the central council had grown into the NUWW. The following year Mrs Creighton chaired the first conference of the young NUWW at Manchester, described by Lavinia Talbot as 'in slippery gloom for the most part', when Henrietta Barnett was the main speaker. And in 1897 Liverpool gave a lead when its NUWW branch founded the Victoria Settlement in 'a dreary district in the neighbourhood of the docks and abounding in public houses'.

The Birmingham branch of the NUWW soon followed suit. By 1898 a settlement committee of 12 members had been formed and the search was on for a house in a poor district that would accommodate 'a warden, two residents and a servant', have a large room for meetings and be near a tram or bus route. The secretary had by then been in touch with 11 settlements in London and visited WUS, St Margaret's House and Mansfield House. And after M. C. Stavely of Somerville College had been appointed warden, premises were opened during 1899 at 318 Summer Lane, where the settlement still functions. Miss Stavely, herself trained at WUS, was emphatic that she wished to make 'training of social workers the chief branch of work undertaken'. A quarterly magazine called *Women Workers*, started in 1891 and published in Birmingham until 1924, had considerable influence during these early years.

The first president of the Birmingham Settlement was Alice Beale, lady mayoress, wife of the first chancellor of Birmingham University, daughter of Timothy Kenrick and a pioneer of social service who was to guide the settlement's fortunes for nearly 30 years. She was also a vice president of the NUWW. Mrs Walter Barrow served as honorary secretary of both the Birmingham branch of the NUWW and of the settlement, and Mrs Bracey, wife of a professor at Birmingham's first medical school, after being chairwoman of the settlement's executive committee, helped there until her death in 1937. Among other supporters were Mrs George

Cadbury (later Dame Elizabeth Cadbury), Miss Clare Martineau, the first woman to be elected to the Birmingham City Council, Mrs Muirhead, wife of the professor of philosophy at the university and a sister of Graham Wallas of the LSE, and (Dame) Ellen Pinsent, a pioneer in the movement for education of the mentally handicapped. The young settlement had thus the support of leading local figures, many of them Quakers or Unitarians, as it now set out on a path that was to make it a major force in civic life.

Manchester followed a similar pattern. Its mixed settlement in due course linked up with Manchester University involving both Professor J. Stocks, after moving there from Oxford, and his wife Mary, historian of the settlement and later principal of Westfield College. Liverpool embarked on two settlements, its university one being founded in 1907, ten years later than the Victoria Settlement there.

In Scotland, the pioneering women's Grey Lodge at Dundee was followed in 1889 by Edinburgh's New College Settlement, started by theological students under the auspices of the New College Missionary Society, and then in 1905 by a non-religious Edinburgh University Settlement. Glasgow's influential Queen Margaret's Settlement, founded in 1897 by that college's students' union as a religious settlement for women, had been preceded in 1889 by a university students' settlement; and in Ireland a women workers' settlement was established in Belfast during 1902.

Dr J. J. Mallon, warden of Toynbee Hall, was mainly responsible for bringing all these and other settlements together. A two-day conference was held at Toynbee Hall in April 1920 on his initiative, when the decision was taken to embark on a national federation of residential settlements. He was then appointed president, and also chairman of the executive composed of three representatives of London settlements, four of provincial ones and one from Scotland. Those present also agreed that the essential feature of a settlement was 'the continuous association of a group of men or women for the purpose of investigating the conditions of life in an industrial area, assisting in local administration, cultivating friendly relations with their neighbours for mutual education and the promotion of a fuller understanding of life, and engaging in activities calculated to brighten the lives of neighbours'. As previously, men and women were still expected to form separate groups, but now it was stressed that 'though settlement residents might carry on their work in a religious spirit, and though as individuals they might have strong religious and political views, the object of a settlement should not be to disseminate those views.' In fact, in 1913, when settlements were categorized as either 'religious' or 'non-religious', several had been included in a list of 45 which were distinguished from missions only by being residential.

Nothing was said at this 1920 conference about social work training, still mainly the concern of women, but it was clear that association would be a source of strength in all activities. Particularly it would enable closer contact to be made with universities, thereby helping recruitment, and if encouragement were given to undertake research into social and industrial questions, it was thought that the federation might be recognized by government departments as an authority worthy of consultation and, hopefully, of financial support.

London settlements were represented at the conference by Hilda Oakeley of the Passmore Edwards (Mary Ward) Settlement, Mrs F. Crane, warden of the Canning Town Women's Settlement, started by the LSE in 1892, and Arthur Reade, warden of Mansfield House, also in the Canning Town area of the East End and founded by Oxford's Mansfield College as a men's religious settlement in 1890. However, soon afterwards, Mrs Crane resigned to work for the London Missionary Society and her place was taken by the Revd T. W. Pym of Cambridge House.

The provincial settlements sent Hilda Cashmore, then at Bristol University Settlement, Marion Boyd-Mackay from Birmingham, E. V. Purden of the Red House Women's Settlement in Leeds and Mr. F. W. Marquis, warden of the Liverpool University Settlement; Miss Banks, warden of Queen Margaret's Settlement in Glasgow, was the only Scottish representative. After Miss Oakeley had led off with a paper on the work of the London settlements and Miss Cashmore followed her on the provincial ones, speeches were made by Mr Marquis on the relation of settlements to national and local education authorities and by Arthur Greenwood MP on settlements and adult education.

However, the first item on the agenda was the adoption of a resolution that 'this conference representing university settlements in Great Britain places on record its profound grief at the death of Mrs Humphry Ward and its sense of the loss which settlements as a whole and all groups of social workers have suffered therein, and offers to her relations an expression of their deepest sympathy.' That her influence had been felt far beyond Britain was clear when the chairman read a letter from Else Feders, head of the Settlement House in Vienna and written from there in March 1920, the month Mrs Ward had died. She described the terrible conditions of postwar life among the Viennese poor and appealed for help.

> To you, the settlements of Great Britain, we turn in our bitter need. Eighteen years ago we founded a settlement in Vienna taking you, the older institution, as a model, you who have put forth your shoots throughout every civilized country. During these five most terrible years of bitter anguish and semi-starvation, the settlement was enabled to render the quickest and most serviceable help in furthering the work of the various Relief Societies.

The new federation, having as yet no income other than the £2. 2*s*. affiliation fees of settlements, agreed that it could only circulate the appeal, a job falling to the honorary secretary Mr St John Catchpool, sub-warden of Toynbee Hall.

The international note had, however, been struck and the following March 1921, Henrietta Barnett spoke to the annual conference of the federation, again held at Toynbee Hall, on 'Settlements in the USA', and she argued collaboration there. J. J. Mallon then emphasized the importance of good relations with the ESA and also with Barnett House in Oxford, its secretary, Grace E. Hadow, being keen to stimulate interest among undergraduates and distribute settlement information both in the UK and the USA.

Jane Addams, a leading figure among American settlements, came to London that April with her friend Ellen Coolidge. Hearing of the proposed visit, Mallon got in touch with Mrs Barnett and a special conference was arranged under federation auspices for September, when over 40 attended at Toynbee Hall. After the American visitors had both made speeches it was agreed that an international conference of representatives of all settlements should be held in London in July 1922.

During a subsequent discussion on adult education in relation to industry, a plea that settlements should hold classes for employers' firms brought a remark from Miss Rogers of the Manchester University Settlement that Sunday morning lectures were held there and attended by some 200 'railway servants'. Then Miss Addams spoke of the Parkes' houses organized by American settlements, and a protagonist for the Shaftesbury Society emphasized how much could be done by settlements in promoting the well-being and happiness of children, no doubt with Mrs Humphry Ward in mind. After Miss Burton of the Welfare Institute had suggested that settlements might collaborate closely with welfare workers to help young people in factories and workrooms, a resolution was passed that these subjects, with sickness, delinquency and amusements, should be considered at the first international settlement conference on 8 July. The line to be taken by the British delegation must clearly be formulated in advance, and with this in view a meeting was called at University College when Mrs Barnett spoke on the original purpose of settlements before the Revd T. W. Pym and four other men talked about contemporary ones. Miss Cashmore read a paper on residential settlements, Miss Dewar of Birmingham made a contribution on 'recruiting, training and maintenance' and Miss Oakeley led the way, followed by four men, on 'the spiritual purpose of settlements'.

Later it was agreed that Dr Mallon and Miss Cashmore should represent Great Britain on the International Continuation Committee until 1923, making up with a similar number from the ESA a joint allotment of four British members, and these attended a conference in Paris mainly concerned with education. But relations between the two groups of British settlements remained uneasy, no satisfactory scheme having emerged to embrace both, particularly as the ESA had a strong central body whereas settlements in the federation cherished their independence.

Then other problems arose through the formation in 1923 of a federation of London settlements, on the basis of an earlier association, and another for those outside London. These were now asked to consider themselves as groups within the British federation and a proportion of the affiliation fees was returned to them. When some of the men's settlements began negotiations with Toc H about recruiting in schools and colleges, it was decided that this group, chaired by Mr McGregor of the Oxford and Bermondsey Club with Mr Catchpool as secretary, should campaign here on behalf of the federation. Edith Trotter CBE, recently appointed honorary organizer for the federation, had already embarked on a recruiting campaign for the women's settlements. But problems developed here also after the warden of the UGS settlement had been asked if there were any objection to the organizer's plan to address schools in the vicinity of settlements she visited. Already Mrs Adami, wife of the vice chancellor of Liverpool University, had arranged informal meetings for Miss Trotter with heads of several girls' schools, both public and private, in the city, and seven out of eight who attended had subsequently asked her to speak to their senior girls on 'the call of personal service'. She had also spoken to the elder pupils at the high school in Dundee after addressing meetings at the Grey Lodge there.

As the UGS settlement was at that time discussing the possibility of becoming the centre of a union of girls' schools throughout the country, advice was sought from Miss Gray, president of the headmistresses' association. Eventually the UGS decided to limit itself to expanding quietly on long-established paths, though expressing the hope of future cooperation here with the federation, and Miss Trotter confined herself to schools near a few well-established settlements. She also spoke twice that year at the Mary Ward Settlement and at the Maurice Hostel, Hoxton, as well as at the Manchester and Edinburgh university settlements.

Good relations had meanwhile been established by Dr Mallon with the National Council of Social Services (NCSS) and, with its consent, the secretarial work of the federation was now carried on by Captain L. F. Ellis from 33 Bloomsbury Square, WC1. This was the start of what was to become a close link between the NCSS and the settlement world.

Women vastly outnumbered men at the weekend conference

held at High Leigh, Hoddesdon in 1923, to consider 'the settlement as community centre'. Discussion centred mainly on educational aspects of work in relation to trades unions and other workers' organizations. With 33 settlements now affiliated to the federation, two London representatives came from the UGS settlement and two from BCH, one from St Margaret's House, Miss Thicknesse (a comparatively new recruit soon to be on the BARS executive) from LMHS, and Miss Townsend from the WUS. Miss Cashmore and Miss Willoughby (Chesterfield), respectively chairwoman and honorary secretary of the Scottish and Provincial group, turned up with other women from the university settlements in Edinburgh and Bristol, Miss Banks came from Glasgow and Miss Wells represented Liverpool's Victoria Settlement with Mr Mabane from the university settlement there.

Sir Wyndham Deedes joined federation leaders at the annual conference held at the Mary Ward Settlement in 1924. The retired brigadier general, who had recently started work at Oxford House with its warden M. R. Seymour, soon shouldered responsibilities as the federation's honorary secretary and treasurer. With Dr Mallon as president, Mr W. McGregor was now elected chairman, Miss Trotter being still hard at work for one more year before going abroad. Among other newcomers from the London settlements on the executive were the Bishop of Kingston, representing UGS and LMHS, (Sir) Reginald Kennedy Cox of the Docklands settlement and Miss Wickham of BCH. It was an influential group.

Sir Wyndham Deedes early suggested that panels should be formed to advise on action the federation might usefully take on such matters as housing and juvenile employment. This brought an encouraging response from Whitehall, and Arthur Greenwood, parliamentary secretary to the Minister of Health, emphasized at a meeting of the housing panel how important it was to gain the cooperation of the local community. Then Eleanor Rathbone was soon afterwards brought onto this panel. Born in 1872 into a shipowning family, well known for its charitable work in Liverpool, she had been educated at Somerville with Margery Fry and Hilda Oakeley and later joined the committee of her local Victoria Settlement. She was the first woman member of the Liverpool City

Council and helped to establish the school of social service at the university where she worked with Elizabeth Macadam, a Scot on the staff also well versed in settlement work.

Then Sir Claud Schuster, permanent secretary in the Lord Chancellor's department, responded to what members of another panel saw as the need to extend provision for the legal assistance of people unable to pay for professional help. In June 1924, after he had spoken to them on the investigation of work under the poor persons' rules, 'envisaging the possibility of a closer local connection between those responsible for the rules and the profession as a whole, resulting in a regular system of advice to the poor', the federation set up a poor man's lawyer subcommittee, including representatives from Liverpool and Birmingham settlements as well as three from London, which resolved 'to make suggestions to the Lord Chancellor as to the scope of the enquiry into a question of the Poor Man's Lawyer'. The London Council of Social Service (LCSS) was also then concerned with this subject, and, like housing, it was to loom large at many settlements.

In April 1925 Sir Wyndham replaced Mallon as the federation's representative on the LCSS and Miss Towers was at the same time appointed representative on the Joint University Council for Social Studies, being soon involved in discussions on hospital almoners and probation officers. Work in prisons was also a matter of current concern. After a discussion with Mr Searle, organizing secretary of the British Institute of Adult Education, the executive decided in June 1925 to ask settlements if they could provide tutors for weekly classes in certain prisons, including Wandsworth and Wormwood Scrubs, as well as Pentonville where Toynbee Hall was already active. The initial response was poor, but 'we feel justified in calling attention to the importance of assisting the Home Office to provide educational services in the prisons by voluntary work', and not only in order to qualify as an approved society under the Board of Education regulations.

Astor's London house was by now the meeting place of a joint committee of MPs and representatives of London settlements and, in October, Mallon announced that Lady Astor was starting a settlement in Plymouth. Miss Cashmore was elected chairwoman of the federation at the annual conference held at Toynbee Hall the following June and, soon afterwards, read a paper on 'Settlements and Citizenship'. New horizons were opening, particularly in community work outside the inner cities, and when the executive met at the Mary Ward Settlement that autumn it was proposed that a settlement should be established in a coal-mining district. The idea was pursued at Cambridge House in December, by which time negotiations had already started with the Tilmanston coal mines in Kent. By February 1927 the first contribution of £100 from the Kent coalfields company was received, a rent-free cottage had been put at the disposal of a local settlement council and a woman appointed as warden at this pioneering enterprise linked specifically with a local industry. The federation's annual conference was held for the first time at WUS that year and soon afterwards Barbara Murray joined the executive as assistant honorary secretary to help Sir Wyndham Deedes; she was a near neighbour of his in Bethnal Green and they worked together at different times from offices in Oxford House and Toynbee Hall. 'Sir Wyndham saw to it that the conferences were well arranged with good speakers and interesting visits,' Miss Murray was later to remark: she became a vice president of BARS and its representative on the National Council of Girls' Clubs.

The NCSS had recently started rural community councils in many counties and, early in 1929, Sir Wyndham reported the federation's cooperation in extending the number of such councils in towns. This brought a comment from Dr Willoughby that in Chesterfield, where a settlement had been started in 1902 by Violet Markham, the NCSS was already doing what it has now proposed to embark on nationally, Miss Markham having lately restated her involvement here through an article in the *Nineteenth Century*.

Professor Stocks, a close friend of Dr Mallon, took over as president of the federation in 1929. Another new source of strength from the provinces was (Sir) George Haynes of Liverpool University, later to be chairman of the ICAA. The London representatives at this time were Sir Reginald Kennedy Cox of the Docklands settlement, Miss Calkin of WUS, Miss Butler of LMHS, Miss H. Harford of T & T and Miss Kelly of St Margaret's House; while the Scottish representatives were Miss Drysdale of Edinburgh and

Miss Cullen of Grey Lodge, Dundee. As the federation clearly relied largely on women at this time, it was not surprising that recruiting in girls' schools was again to the fore, Miss Kelly reporting that the UGS council had asked for concrete proposals for cooperation with the federation. Dr Mallon said that it would only be charged by Toynbee Hall for heating and telephone – though a shorthand typist was now engaged part time to help Miss Murray – and, in 1934, when Miss Kelly was elected president at the annual meeting held that year at the YWCA central club in Great Russell Street, Sir Reginald Kennedy Cox agreed to be treasurer, but only if given strong secretarial and office support. A BBC appeal was accordingly launched, but as this was found to conflict with appeals made by individual settlements, it was decided early in 1935 that a small percentage of every money-making scheme embarked on by any settlement should be handed over to what was now called the British Association of Residential Settlements (BARS) and that an appeal should be made both to the Pilgrim Trust and to Dame Elizabeth Cadbury, soon to be a vice president.

Problems of industrial insurance and the ability of the poor man's lawyer to cope with clients' difficulties had by now been brought to the attention of the BARS executive by a former Hull agent in one of the big companies who felt that some such organization as BARS should tackle abuses. Miss Kelly said that work along the lines he suggested to claim monies legitimately due to people was already being done at St Margaret's House, both by the poor man's lawyer there who had sent cases to the Board of Trade, and by Miss Penley, their legally qualified staff member. And Miss Penley subsequently reported on her visit to Hull, where she saw 'a steady stream of people making enquiries and lodging complaints against Insurance Societies'. It was then agreed that the new BARS organizing secretary, Miss Taylor, should make herself familiar with this aspect of the work and encourage the poor man's lawyer service in settlements.

Sir Wyndham Deedes meanwhile had been attending the third international conference on social work, arranged to take place in Hungary, but later switched to London. Social work in the community and special social services in relation to the community were the main topics, and study groups had already been set up in Britain, France, Germany, Italy, Switzerland, the USA, Czechoslovakia, Greece, Poland and Sweden. Sir Wyndham Deedes was keen to link all the settlements in the USA and Europe with this international movement.

Some progress in social work training emerged in 1935 involving two calls for BARS participation. One was from the Women's Employment Federation, which was planning a conference of societies dealing with social work among girls with a view to putting forward a united policy to the council of King George's jubilee trust on using part of its funds for training, providing adequate salaries for social workers and extending the work. This was judged highly worthy of support so Misses Kelly and Taylor were given a mandate to represent BARS. The other was an invitation for a BARS representative to join the Central Council for Education and Training in Social Work (CCETSW) among women and girls, Miss Taylor being appointed for this job. She had recently produced a pamphlet called *Legislation on Children*, which had a wide circulation among settlement workers, and, though later resigning as organizing secretary when there were no funds available to appoint a successor, she helped as vice president. Miss Murray, soon also to be a vice president, now agreed to represent BARS on the National Council of Girls' Clubs and Miss Escreet on the Central Council of Welfare for women and girls in London.

When Dr Mallon had seen the influential Dr Tom Jones of the Pilgrim Trust, known also to Miss Kelly from her years in the USA, hopes rose that money would be forthcoming so that BARS could be reorganized as an effective instrument of cooperation among settlements. Toynbee Hall's golden jubilee celebrations helped at this point. Referring to an appeal launched for an extension of the work there, the prime minister, Stanley Baldwin, wrote to the Archbishop of Canterbury in December 1935, 'You will be glad to know that ... the Pilgrim Trust has with great heartiness voted £10,000.' The young Cosmo Lang, later Bishop of Stepney, had been one of Arnold Toynbee's original supporters at Oxford, and from 1933 to 1945 was chairman of Toynbee Hall.

Miss Laetitia Harford, dynamic warden of the LMHS for four years until 1939, was the next BARS president. In January 1937

Dr Mallon, Sir Wyndham Deedes, Dr Scott Lidgett of the Bermondsey settlement (started under the auspices of the Wesleyan Methodist Church in 1891) and Sir Reginald Kennedy Cox were among those who heard her outline a scheme whereby, through their wardens, settlements could study in detail the major social problems of the day. The subjects then chosen were malnutrition (with Dr Gertrude Willoughby in charge), settlements and their relation to the churches (Miss Towers), housing under the three headings of slum clearance, life in flats and new housing estates, and unemployment, considered particularly from the angles of the unemployment assistance board, leisure and industrial transference (Mr Hodgkinson). A training scheme for non-professional social workers to be run at Mansfield House was commended by the president and, soon afterwards, a planning and extension subcommittee was set up to enlarge the number of settlements.

Then contacts abroad were fostered at this time when Miss Eleanor Ross, a bursary holder at LMHS with experience of the Edinburgh settlement, was able to visit several US settlements while her father, provost of Oriel College and a firm supporter of Toynbee Hall, was lecturing at Columbia University. Later, as Mrs T. Sinclair CBE, she was to be chairwoman of LMHS. In June 1937, when the BARS executive met at LMHS, discussion centred on a planned conference to be chaired by Sir Ernest Barker, to consider the changing circumstances of voluntary work with special reference to the effects of recent and impending legislation.

Settlement morale was now high. At a reception held by Lady Astor in January 1938 for wardens and BARS council members, Dr Mallon said:

> The world realizes that the settlements we have in this country are unique. They represent sanity and balance, good temper and good feeling which we like to think are characteristic of England. In the settlements we have trained workers to do the social work of the area. At Toynbee Hall we can speak when necessary for the whole East End Community.

The same month Miss Herford steered constitutional changes

for BARS at an executive meeting held in Edinburgh. Negotiations with the Educational Settlements Association (ESA) had been hampered partly because BARS had no council and one was now set up, to include honorary officers, vice presidents and representative wardens of affiliated settlements (six from London, six from the provinces and two from Scotland) with co-opted members including representatives of the WEA and ESA. At the same time she insisted that a permanent office must be found and an organizing secretary appointed. When the executive next met, at 26 Bedford Square in September 1938, rooms had already been leased at 1 Museum Street for three years, substantial financial support having been given both by Lady Astor and the Pilgrim Trust.

Despite the war clouds now gathering, Miss Murray reported in November that it was proposed to hold the next international settlement conference in Brussels in 1940, at about the same time as the international conference on social work. She was long to remember earlier lively meetings of this sort in Germany and Holland and the 'outstanding hospitality of the Norwegians'. Miss Escreet of WUS undertook to report to BARS on the problem of German Christian refugees, Miss Murray being also involved here. Then in April Miss Drysdale, the incoming chairwoman, raised the question at a Manchester executive meeting of the evacuation of children in wartime from non-municipal nursery schools and, within a few months, LMHS was to be the assembly centre for sick and invalid children from all over London who were not hospital cases yet not eligible to be sent in school parties.

All settlements were soon in the front line, and at a conference called by the Home Office a week after the start of heavy bombing, Sir Wyndham Deedes, by then chief air-raid warden for Bethnal Green, was the main speaker on the contribution being made by them.

Soon after the war started the BARS organizing secretary joined the Ministry of Labour, Miss Kelly remarking that 'the best way to thank her is to carry on.' Not the least of her jobs had been to represent settlements on many national organizations and this work was continued by her successor.

Then George Clutton Brock took on the chairmanship of BARS from Miss Drysdale and at the same time Sir David Ross of Oriel

College became chairman of a newly set up grants committee composed of Sir Wyndham Deedes, Letty Harford and Miss H. Escreet. This met for the first time in January 1940 with Miles Davies standing in for Sir Wyndham. Soon BARS was in the happy position of being able to subsidize individual settlements as well as support itself, for the Pilgrim Trust had by then given £2000 and grants had come in from the Board of Education and also from the National Council of Girls' Clubs, to be augmented by donations from the Carnegie Trust, the Goldsmiths' Company and a BBC appeal.

The first seven settlements to benefit in March 1940 were the two at Birmingham, one at Middlesborough and four London women's settlements (LMHS, St Margaret's House, Stafford Street UGS in Peckham and WUS). Some of these had further grants in the coming months and 46 received financial help from the grants committee up to the end of 1942. They included Bristol (both University and Corner Cottage), Liverpool (both Victoria and University), Manchester University, Plymouth (Astor Institute), Spennymoor, Canning Town Women's Settlement, St Anne's, St Mildred's, St Helen's House, St Hilda's East, Talbot House, T &T, St Francis House, Maurice Hostel, BCH, Chesterfield, Edinburgh, Bede House, Katherine Low, Beauchamp Lodge, Grey Lodge, Dundee, Cambridge House, Oxford House and Toynbee Hall itself, besides some others less well known. The sums were not large, but certainly helped BARS and the corporate feeling of settlements generally in those difficult days of bombing and its aftermath.

Valuable support was also given by Sir William Beveridge. He became president of BARS in 1940 and continued as such for over a decade while the welfare state legislation he had planned was passed by Clement Attlee's government in the immediate postwar period. The two men had both worked at Toynbee Hall in their youth. And when in January 1950 Dr Mallon was host there for a weekend conference of over 100 settlement workers, Major Ellis, chairman of the executive committee, was able to report not only 'the very satisfactory financial position of the Association' but that Beveridge had sent a message of good wishes and 'was happy to continue as President'. At a time when many settlements were facing grave doubts about their future, this was encouraging news.

Mary Stocks, principal of Westfield College, called herself an 'elder statesman' when speaking to the conference on that pre-eminently women's topic, training for social work.

> I have been out of social work since 1939 and much has happened since then. In the early days settlements were populated largely by amateurs who worked with great gusto, taught and interfered with people's lives without being told how to do it. Today you meet at settlements either trained professional social workers or students in training for professional work. That is the main difference, I think, in the settlements today.

Her own experience was typical. She had left school in 1908, aged 17, after failing the school certificate examination and,

> like most of my contemporaries, took up social work in my spare time having no need to earn a living. I became an LCC School Care Committee secretary in Finsbury, walking about with a case of papers. For training, I was invited to tea by the Vicar's daughter who showed me how to write Minutes, then handed over to me a lot of paper headed LCC and sheets of stamps. [She was fortunate here for many voluntary secretaries had to buy their own.] So I started, but what I got was a worm's eye view. I knew there was someone called the Education Officer and gradually I got the hang of the work, chiefly by contact with other social workers and with my maiden aunts, and with one worker in particular who was conducting an enquiry for Mrs Sidney Webb and who used to go in her spare time to the LSE.

In due course she went there herself, taking a B.Sc. economics degree which covered some public administration.

The question she raised about professional social work, rather surprisingly at that date, was 'have we gone too far?' Not, it seemed in technical efficiency. She was, however, emphatic that 'the administrative civil service has always believed in all-rounders, and settlements should see that it is not necessary to have the right certificate, and that amateurs have an abiding place. Settlements have something very precious to maintain in the traditions they enshrine.' Pioneering Dorothea Beale would have been pleased that arrangements were then in hand to hold the next weekend BARS conference at St Hilda's College in Oxford.

If the leading contemporary protagonist of social work training was Dame Eileen Younghusband, it was Lord Beveridge who defined settlements as 'centres for the development of authoritative opinion on the problems of city life'. One such problem has been illiteracy, and settlements made a major contribution here in the 1970s, with Cambridge House as the spearhead of a national literacy campaign. By the early 1980s, the British Association of Settlements and Social Action Centres (BASSAC) had 46 members and its director, Clive Jordan, worked from offices in Stockwell near the problem-beset area of Brixton. Much was to happen here in the years ahead.

12

Dame Eileen Younghusband and Community Service Today

Dame Eileen Younghusband, for many years a vice president of the T & T settlement, was the most influential woman on the social work scene during the first 30 years of the welfare state. Born in 1902, she spent her early years in India with her mother and father, Sir Francis Younghusband of Himalayan fame. Later she escaped from the London social round planned for her and, already a lively outgoing personality concerned with the less fortunate members of society, embarked on a Bible class for girls in Stepney; and it is indicative of the long-lasting impression she made on people that 60 years later a member of this class would attend her memorial service. A move into the settlement world soon followed. Having been educated by governesses, she had no special links with a school or university, and with time and talents at her disposal naturally gravitated to the settlement in Bermondsey run largely by young women in similar circumstances. She worked there for five years, then in 1925 joined the LSE, first as a student attending lectures by Beatrice Webb among others, and later as an academic and field work tutor.

Over the next decade she also served as a magistrate, becoming chairwoman in 1933 of the Hammersmith juvenile court. Years afterwards a children's officer remembered how sympathetically she had dealt with one particular child just before going abroad on a long working assignment, and how, typically, she immediately rang up on her return to find out how the boy was faring. During the war she was principal officer for employment and training with the National Association of Girls' Clubs and director of the British Council social welfare course, then in 1944 returned to the LSE for 13 memorable years.

'Give a man a fish and he will eat for a day. Teach him to fish and he will eat for the rest of his days.' This Eastern proverb expressed, she thought, the function of a social worker. Many others had said that it was to make people self-reliant rather than merely to provide first-aid and temporary solutions, but it fell to her to change the concepts and institutions of social work training both in this country and overseas. And as a university colleague remarked: 'She never ceased to encourage the young, enabling them to discover resources in themselves that they did not know they had got; as a teacher she was forthrightly critical of slipshod work and jargon but never disparagingly, always liberating and always ready to welcome students as friends if that was what they wanted.'

Her vision and leadership had already made their mark in the institutions she served before her outstanding intellectual gifts reached a wider public through two reports financed by the Carnegie United Kingdom Trust, the first in 1947 on the *Employment and Training of Social Workers* and the other in 1951, which together laid the groundwork for a united profession. Like Octavia Hill, Henrietta Barnett, Beatrice Webb and many other women, Dame Eileen influenced events by her writings as much as by her personal leadership, and her last, which she referred to as 'the albatross', is a classic in two volumes on *Social Work in Britain from 1950 to 1975*. It is hardly surprising that many saw her death in 1981 as the end of an era.

'Social work in this country is still regarded as a woman's occupation,' wrote Dame Eileen in 1947.

> The war has artificially accentuated this, but in the permanent pattern it is hoped that men will be employed not only as at present as personnel managers, probation officers, youth leaders, settlement and community centre wardens

> and as secretaries of councils of social services, but that they will also enter certain casework fields.... There is a deplorable tendency to think that though a woman social worker needs training a man has acquired all he needs to know through some all-sufficing experience of life which is a substitute for and not an enhancement of training.

Changes were already on the way. The 1944 Education Act had made it a statutory duty for local authorities to provide adequate leisure time activities for all those over school age who might wish to take advantage of them, whether or not they had jobs, and Dame Eileen rightly predicted that 'the Settlement Warden's new brother, the Warden of a community centre, will as often be employed by a local authority as by a voluntary organization.' Training for community centre and settlement wardens was then given under the auspices of a joint committee of BARS, the community association committee of the NCSS and the educational associations' association, mainly on a residential basis at Selly Oak, Birmingham. Some lectures were arranged independently, some held at Birmingham University or at the Selly Oak Colleges, and Birmingham Settlement was to be among the leaders in bringing others up to date when the National Health Service Act of 1946 caused major upheaval among those responsible for administering the complex machinery of statutory and voluntary services. Then, after the old poor law had been repealed and the National Assistance Board set up in 1948 at the same time that the Children's Act also came on the statute book, even more women than men found a vast new horizon opening before them.

Wartime evacuation had been largely their concern and the experience thus gained was one reason for the appointment of a large number of women children's officers, usually with chief officer status under the new act. They were often new to local government and joined their male counterparts there at a time when the medical officer of health and the director of education was each inclined to think that the new children's service should have been given to his department. Thus, when appointed as children's officer in one northern town, a trained woman almoner with a classics degree and a social science diploma found herself offered a desk in the typists' room, though after protesting she was allowed to join the health visitors before eventually acquiring her own staff.

It was a time when settlements felt that a great deal of their work was passing to a variety of specialized bodies. Moreover, as Dame Eileen remarked:

> Their wardens have been some of the outstanding figures in social work, both in this country and in the USA. The head of a settlement was, and often is, a power in the land, suffering the minimum of restrictions and given the maximum opportunities for tilting against social ills, whether local or national. They often gave their services voluntarily and a few of them are still national figures, but they are not perpetuating themselves in the second generation. It is with the greatest difficulty now that suitable fresh appointments are made when a warden leaves. Of the 51 salaried wardens, 13 are men and 38 women. The majority of the women are trained social workers, the majority of the men are not.

Then, despite the fact that in a BARS survey made in 1950, 36 out of 112 settlements gave social science students experience of normal life in a poor neighbourhood, in the social work field as a whole at that time few people of either sex had any training. This was largely because no opportunities then existed, apart from the small intake on social science university courses, the mental health, medical social work, childcare, probation and moral welfare training, and various *ad hoc* specialized courses, including those for NSPCC inspectors and home teachers of the blind.

Professor Richard Titmuss, newly appointed to the chair in social administration at the LSE, came to see Dame Eileen in 1950 and borrowed her second Carnegie Report (*Social Work in Britain*) when it was still in typescript. But although he supported her proposal for generic casework courses at the universities, and a memorandum was sent to the Carnegie Trust, the project was turned down as too costly. However, the trust did agree the following year to help finance a postgraduate non-specialist course at the LSE, with teaching of an acceptable level and the ensured support of the Home Office (regarding childcare and probation), the Ministry of Health, the Institute of Almoners and the Family Welfare Association (FWA), for what became known as the 'Carnegie experiment' to lower the barriers of specialization.

The first applied social studies course, based on the two Younghusband reports, started at the LSE in October 1954. Thus the demonstration was made that the common ground for casework was more fundamental than the differences, that generic training could be followed by opportunities to specialize, and that the same standard of professional education long enjoyed by mental health students was now available to other social workers, based on a close partnership between the universities and field work agencies, including of course the settlements. Then three years later the first student unit financed by a local authority was set up by the Essex children's department for students on this course, though not for another decade would Home Office funds be made available to a number of voluntary organizations able to offer students case, group and community work experience, Blackfriars Settlement being immediately involved here.

Not surprisingly, a shortage of social work teachers was soon a growing problem as new attitudes about the nature of social need resulted both in more services and better career prospects, while the earlier image of officials administering regulations changed to one of social workers giving a professional service. Then 'clients' began to dominate the scene, only gradually losing their inverted commas, though not for some years more would those engaged professionally try to help them cease to be called officers, except in the probation service.

More changes were steered by Dame Eileen when she chaired the Ministry of Health committee on social workers in the local authority health and welfare services. Her report in 1959 stressed the importance of preventive work directed towards families, and much of what was subsequently produced for training purposes is dominated by this approach. By then the universities could no longer cope alone with the increasing pressure of demand for generic courses for social workers, and a new form of training outside the universities was instituted. The LCC took action on its own by starting a two-year polytechnic course, then the Council of

Training for Social Work, set up in 1963, offered a social work course as a national qualification for those completing a two-year approved programme of study and field work, usually at a polytechnic or college of further education; and though students emerging from such a course were mainly destined for the health and welfare sides of local authority social work, settlements made a contribution here.

But, as Dame Eileen remarked:

> They have fewer local supporters in finance and in voluntary service than in the past, while their all-purpose activities do not attract State grants. Unless, therefore, they perform some service for which their neighbours are willing to give them both financial backing and voluntary service, their future is by no means clear. In some places they are, however, tending to become a form of Community or Neighbourhood Centre.

They took on a new lease of life when the Children's and Young Persons' Act was passed in 1963. Besides recommending the setting up of family advice centres it laid a new duty on social workers 'to advise, guide and assist' local authorities in such matters as playgroups, crèches, discussion groups for mothers and leisure activities for young people, including the provision of adventure playgrounds.

Settlement workers had considerable expertise here and Octavia Hill's vision came nearer realization on a wide front, while holiday schemes for mothers and children emerged as one way of easing problems caused by stress, as Henrietta Barnett had realized before starting the CCHF. Settlement work for the under fives was vastly strengthened by the preschool Playgroup Association (PA) set up in the early 1960s; by 1975 only a quarter of the existing playgroups were grant aided by local authorities, though in 1983 the government stressed their importance by appointing not only inspectors to oversee local authority social work but a Minister for Children's Play, a move which would surely have pleased Mrs Humphry Ward.

Thus, necessary services to meet the needs of deprived children were discovered step by step. Moreover, for the aged and infirm a broad range of daycare services developed, including home helps and meals-on-wheels, largely pioneered by WVS, and meals were often cooked in settlement kitchens until the town hall or Old People's Welfare Association was ready to cope.

The relation of volunteers to the growing army of professional social workers has, however, not always been easy. Fortunately, when the amateurs were ousted from direct work with clients as trained full-timers were appointed to voluntary organizations, there was always a wide variety of good neighbour services to welcome their help. And it was only for a limited time that many of the volunteers by experience and natural talent had more skill than the newcomers on the scene. Community service volunteers were established in 1962 and, like the largely voluntary CAB staff dating from 1939, soon became part of the scene at most settlements. Moreover, the Aves Report of 1969 recommended that there should be continuous clarification of appropriate tasks of voluntary social workers and active recruitment of them, and the resulting changed attitude was reflected in 1973 when the British Association of Social Workers (BASW) raised funds for a three-year project to examine the relations between these two groups. Then the National Association for the Care and Resettlement of Offenders (NACRO) pioneered a new career scheme under which selected ex-offenders worked with current offenders and others in partnership with social workers, though this could put a strain on some middle-class volunteers living in the vicinity of the settlements.

By the mid-1970s, despite the large numbers of part-timers active in the public as well as the voluntary social services, only a few voluntary organizations, settlements among them, still provided training for volunteers, supposedly liable to over identify, impose solutions and moral judgements, create dependency, expect quick results or lose heart. Sometimes a new volunteer, impressed by the long queue of men, women and children outside a caseworker's room, might ask how one person could be bold enough to advise on all their problems and be told: 'They provide the answers themselves. It's my job to ask the right questions.' But what were the right questions? The much needed Social Work

Advisory Service, set up in 1967 with a Gulbenkian grant, soon proved its worth at a time when increasing numbers, both of men and women, were becoming interested in social work as a career.

In 1968 the Seebohm Committee, with which Dame Eileen Younghusband was also concerned, began its enquiries into both the professional and management problems of the social services; and two years later the local authority social services departments came into being, representing the culmination of postwar developments in this field. During the subsequent reorganization of local government during 1974 an attempt was made to rationalize the provision of social services and the administration of social work. For example, medical social workers were transferred from the National Health Service and put under local authority personal social services, despite protests from many concerned; and with the exception of probation, social workers employed in the public sector, including those in the childcare service long concerned with such matters as the training of residential staff, were brought under one administrative authority.

That some, while belonging to the National Association of Local Government Workers (NALGO), or to the more professionally geared BASW, or to both, were politically minded radicals out to bring change was a fact that had to be accepted by directors of social services and councils of settlements, particularly after the youth service was set up following the Albemarle Report of 1969. However, in 1974 the director of LMHS, with seven full-time workers and another 24 engaged on various projects, remarked: 'I feel great pride in their achievements for they have developed methods of work with a sharp cutting edge, which deliver practical benefits to people and yet challenge the status quo, an approach which starts from the needs of the individual and generalizes without sentiment or romanticism.' It was one which fortunately appealed to many benefactors and trusts.

By 1975 there were 33 university departments of social administration and social work, virtually all such education being generic except for psychiatric and probation work.

Dame Eileen's contribution was as effective abroad as in Britain. She served as adviser for the United Nations and to various governments and national organizations, herself travelling widely, and for over 30 years was actively involved with the International Association of Schools of Social Work, for some time as a board member, then as president.

At her memorial service held at St Martins in the Fields on 2 October 1981 tributes were paid both by Professor Roger Wilson, formerly of Bristol University, and Dr Armaity Desai of the College of Social Work in Bombay University; and among the prayers conducted by the canon of Westminster was one 'for members of the religions of the world, and in particular for the World Congress of Faiths, founded by Francis Younghusband'. Others who took part included Professor Dahrendorf, head of the LSE, and Mr Peter Barclay, chairman of Dame Eileen's brainchild, the National Institute of Social Work.

At an informal gathering held afterwards in the founders' room of the old building of the LSE in Houghton Street, many settlement workers and others spoke of their respect, admiration and affection for Dame Eileen. They included Letty Harford, a former president of BARS and settlement warden who was herself to die a few weeks later. The Dame Eileen Younghusband memorial fund appeal was launched soon afterwards by Mrs Sheridan Russell and others to help students at the LSE and to encourage social work education, particularly in the developing countries.

'The classic pattern of a settlement is a large house in a poor neighbourhood,' wrote Dame Eileen in 1947. The nature of their premises has naturally determined to some extent how the former women's settlements have reacted to changing social conditions, but most have now given up their residential character and instead let office space to small local charities. All seek a happy balance between their caring and campaigning roles. They are widely recognized as a valuable focus for experiment and this is reflected in their funding.

The demise of the ILEA and Greater London Council has raised new problems as London boroughs debate at some length whether or not to fund settlement staff and projects; and the recession, compounded by public spending cuts, has further hampered settlement enterprise.

However, the remarkable expansion of the British Association of Settlements and Social Action Centres (BASSAC) helped fill the gap here, with women playing a leading role. By 1992, under its chairwoman of council, Elspeth Ryle, and operating from offices in Stockwell, BASSAC had 32 London members with 21 out of London and five associate members, and an LMHS supporter, Melanie McRenzie, as treasurer. BASSAC's innovative approach to many areas of work in the social care field is evident as members continue to initiate work of national significance locally. Though only a quarter of London settlements were started by women, they far outnumber men on the BASSAC executive committee, chaired by Polly Dickinson.

Multipurpose community centres, as most settlements now see themselves, present a unique strand in the voluntary social work sector. Moreover, the Ministry of Health's Opportunities for Volunteering (OFV) scheme, now in its tenth year, helps BASSAC to support its members in the health and social care fields. Thus, LMHS, describing itself as 'an enabler of local community action', has recently provided a much needed service for parents and children locally, and also brought into action a newly built nearby community centre which was due to be closed through lack of local authority funding. Of the £6 million annually available under the OFV scheme, BASSAC is able to channel a quarter of a million directly to its own members for settlement work in the health and social care fields.

BASSAC's membership development officer, Vashto Ledford, recently spoke at LMHS's open day on the importance of multipurpose centres. Mrs Elizabeth Parker, who has been on the settlement's council for many years, is adamant about there being no discrimination in its work on grounds of race or sex. Since moving to Stockwell this popular settlement has laid firm roots in a new area, which are now bearing valuable fruit under its director, Rosemary Toussaint-Giraud, before its centenary in 1997.

But BASSAC members have long suffered from a lack of secure funding, and difficulties have been enhanced by pressure recently put on local authorities to cut back on their grants to voluntary agencies. Settlements can no longer engage in social pioneering with any certainty of its being continued. LMHS recently lost all its funding for its women and work project and also one for home workers, both of which, though popular, have had to stop.

However, its Roots and Shoots initiative to train young people with learning difficulties has now become independent.

BASSAC is one of only two independent national OFV agencies represented on the consortium managing the Ministry of Health's schemes. A parallel source of support is the Voluntary Service Unit (VSU) run by the Home Office. Here also BASSAC is closely concerned, particularly in coordinating members of groups that are thus funded. Some 30 organizations are involved here and considerable progress has been made since the first meeting in 1988. Regular meetings of the VSU groups now take place at least twice a year, and are usually held in the BASSAC national office.

Moreover, BASSAC has long maintained its international connections. Birmingham still houses the secretariat of the International Federation of Settlements (IFS) and a member of the Edinburgh University Settlement is treasurer for the IFS. Women have played a considerable part here since Mrs Humphry Ward's day, and their international contribution continued when the IFS met in Canada late in 1992.

At Blackfriars new workers have recently volunteered, enabling almost every project and service to be maintained. Moreover, the Bengali advice services have multiplied, 'being desperately needed in the local community we serve'. This settlement, in at the start of the BASSAC literacy campaign, now aims to provide educational support for local adults in literacy, numeracy and ESOL (English for Speakers of Other Languages). It is also responsible for in-service training of volunteers including about 30 who help here. The ILEA, which has funded the scheme since 1976, gave a final £6000 to this settlement for the purchase of up-to-date computers. And recently the Blackfriars literacy scheme joined the Bede House educational unit, Cambridge House and the Bookplace to form a consortium called SCREN (Southwark Computer Resource in Education Network) for which the London Education Computing Centre promised free maintenance and advice.

When Blackfriars' first Bengali neighbourhood worker left in 1989 for a more financially rewarding post in Tower Hamlets, the Southwark council agreed that its grant aid here should be maintained. Moreover, the South Bank family rights project has had several success stories, such as providing practice placements for social work students funded by the Central Council for Education and Training in Social Work (CCETSW). Though the Waterloo adventure playground, which occupies a major site near the Old Vic, has been dogged by staffing problems, it has considerable potential, with a new senior play leader and two assistants.

The Blackfriars Work Centre, started in 1963, is now seen mainly as a mental health resource for Lambeth and Southwark, and the settlement's youth project provides a range of services for different age groups. Meanwhile, the Cruso Blind Club flourishes with support from several well-known firms, including Harrods, Marks and Spencers, and Tesco. At Christmas the Queen and Queen Mother send greetings, maintaining a long tradition; and the Helen Barlow Club continues to meet on Tuesdays at Waterloo Action Centre. Continuity is as important as enterprise at Blackfriars.

Responding to the Community Act of 1990, the director of Blackfriars Settlement, Barry Hedges, emphasized 'change' as the theme of a recent report. He found it ironic that the government should urge greater involvement of voluntary agencies in care in the community and other aspects of social provision while simultaneously cutting local authority funding services. However, the new reliance on voluntary work was of course itself a tribute to the settlement movement.

One reaction in Nelson Square was to produce a survey focusing on the settlement's links with neighbouring communities and new or expanding areas of work. This was made over a period of six months by two social workers in training. The sample of over 200 people selected in one area was representative of a diverse local community; of those interviewed 79 per cent were white, 14 per cent black, 5 per cent Asian and 'others' including Cypriots, Turks and Greeks, the majority having lived there for at least ten years. The most popular settlement activity was the advice centre and the main local concern was the lack of facilities for children and young people, particularly preschool playgroups and after-school and holiday care. A high percentage of elderly people welcomed the suggestion of a pensioners' 'drop-in' and several residents offered help with the education centre and youth project. One recommendation was that the settlement should provide an office on its premises for the local authority, but finance was a major problem. Only recently one of the settlement's four houses in Nelson Square was sold to give its balance sheet a more reassuring appearance to possible donors and grant-aiding institutions.

St Hilda's East community centre in Shoreditch has long since been concerned with education, the relief of poverty, ethnic problems, and recreation for youth and the elderly. Now it is among other BASSAC members recently deprived of expected funding, and this despite a recent statement by Peter Shore MP that it is 'a model of its kind'.

The immigrant population of a century ago has been replaced by others, the city is spreading northwards and eastwards and residents of the Boundary estate face many problems. Meanwhile, the settlement director, David Kitchen, has ambitious plans for building and developing on its present site. These include housing 12 key personnel including teachers, health and social workers, with some space for existing activities and the community groups based there, as well as for employment training. Several influential local people are now closely involved in deciding what is needed in the area and how St Hilda's can help.

St Margaret's House in Bethnal Green faced centenary celebrations in 1989 with considerable anxiety about its future at 19 and 21 Old Ford Road. However, a heartening story of vision, enterprise and hard work has changed the climate to one of well-founded optimism. The appointment as administrator of Murray Bracey of the Chalice Foundation proved crucial here. He soon established a reputation as both fundraiser and planner. Thus before illness struck him settlement policy had radically changed, and in future its rooms would be let to small local organizations concerned with social work.

The first charitable organization to move in under the new letting plan was the Rathbone Society, which works with and on behalf of children, young people and adults with learning difficulties. Soon Tony Hardie (its area manager and later director of St Margaret's) had established an office in the basement, where gas and electrical supplies and other changes helped in the creation of the settlement's popular community café. Substantial support here was received from the Globetown neighbourhood and Tower

Hamlets inner area programme under a policy which targeted monetary appeals to particular work. Thus the Georgian Society was a main contributor to refurbishment of the impressive Anson Room on the first floor. Then activities in the spacious day centre opening onto the garden were suspended for a few months while leaking pipes, rotting wood and other troubles were dealt with before the newly named Mulberry Rooms were opened by Councillor Sue Mitchell as a youth club with a strongly educational flavour. The settlement's president Lady Moberly and its chairwoman, Mrs Linda Ransom (formerly a student in residence at St Margaret's House), were both present that day.

The Rathbone Society's employment action programme now operates from a house adjoining the settlement and about 20 of its young people are employed in the community café, always full at lunch times and which on certain evenings also serves as a youth club. Long established work for the elderly has been maintained, and one new initiative is a Saturday morning dancing class for children. Meanwhile, a centenary appeal, intended to form the basis for a permanent endowment, has helped this popular settlement to survive and flourish.

Bishop Creighton House (BCH) has long been a thriving multipurpose community centre in Fulham. It offers a wide range of activities for residents in the whole borough, regardless of sex, race and colour. Some of its groups are specifically for women or people with disabilities and certain rooms are available for hire to community groups. Those now housed there include the Fulham Good Neighbouring Service, the Bangladesh Association for Cukryre and Education and the west and northwest London Vietnamese Association. The Creighton Café is open to the public for three hours each weekday from 11.00 a.m. to 2.00 p.m. It is run by volunteers and 'we are looking for more people to join us'. Other projects include one for local employment advice, counselling is offered to all pensioners and a group of volunteers seeks to ease the problems of those who are housebound.

Katherine Low Settlement in Battersea has recently provided an example of rescue by legacy from threatened bankruptcy, not unknown in settlement history. Wandsworth Borough Council had assumed financial responsibility for both full-time and part-time staff, though not of the overall management post. Increased help had come from the Francis Holland and other schools; the settlement had relinquished its long-time interest in the Katrine Baird Memorial Hall, and nearly £15,000 had resulted from an appeal to various trusts. Nevertheless the management committee realized that by the summer of 1991 the cash would run out. Then 'quite unexpectedly we learnt of an amazing stroke of good fortune. John Payne, a leading London solicitor, had left us a share in his estate.' The donor had been involved in the free legal advice that was to be part of the settlement's work before the growth of the CAB and had introduced to the settlement its present chairman, John Wates JP, who had been articled to him.

When the Prince of Wales sponsored a charity for inner city aid in 1986, compassionate people throughout the land registered the existence of a new need.

Seven years later a national newspaper headed its New Year home news page, 'Major sees 1993 as the year of charity and help thy neighbour.' The prime minister had recently ordered a study of ways to increase the role of voluntary groups, charities and the private sector in easing the problems of the sick, needy and homeless. The aim was to improve the delivery and efficiency of services and to extend them beyond areas presently covered by the state.

'Beveridge would be spinning in his grave', remarked the social security secretary in a broadcast made the same week. He was referring to the fact that 12 million people in Britain were living at or below the poverty line, and this at a time of celebration for 50 years of life in the welfare state. But in 1942, with Britain then at war, unemployment was no problem for Beveridge.

It is now 90 years since Barnett offered the young graduate from Balliol College, then studying law at Oxford, the salaried post of sub-warden at Toynbee Hall. Letters to his beloved parents record their doubt about the wisdom of accepting such a move. But Beveridge, recognized as architect of the welfare state, was to ascribe all his subsequent jobs to the 'special knowledge' he had acquired during his two years in Whitechapel. Now the nation faces the challenge of bringing his work up to date at a time when modern problems are dominated by unemployment, for long a main concern for community workers at settlements.

When plans were recently made for reforms in the National Health Service, 1 April 1993 was fixed as the date for 'community care' to become the rule in supporting the aged and infirm; and a woman, Virginia Bottomley, was appointed health secretary. Fortunately, the British Association of Settlements and Social Action Centres has long been geared to help here. And community centres, which developed within the settlement movement, can again lead the way.

Moreover, an emphasis on liberty for the individual, whether in planning his pension or in other matters, provided he does not thereby hurt his fellow men and women, the encouragement of diversity in society even at some cost to social unity, and of philanthropy and the 'caring' instincts whatever the problems of the 'free rider' and the closed shop, are all enduring strands of national life.

Fortunately, Mill's doctrine still holds good that 'participation in politics teaches the individual to weigh interests not his own and feel an unselfish sentiment of identification with the public.' Though party politics are traditionally barred in the settlement ethos, local campaigning by workers, paid and unpaid, for improvements in living conditions has naturally a political dimension.

Appendices
BASSAC Members

Out of London Members

l Saints Institute, Nottingham
hram Community Service Project, B'ham
th Place Community Venture, Leamington
rmingham Settlement, Birmingham
istol University Settlement, Bristol
rley Lodge Centre, Leeds
mmunity Links (North), Sheffield
rt, Plymouth
stpoint Centre Limited, Southampton
inburgh University Settlement, Edinburgh
ll Lane Community Centre, Leeds
nction 7, Northampton
co Ltd, Coventry
verpool Domestic Mission, Liverpool
verpool Settlement, Liverpool
anchester University Settlement, Manchester
ineaton Social Activities Centre, Nuneaton
dham Resource & Information Centre
f-Help Neighbourhood Project, Leicester
uthwick Neighbourhood Action, Sunderland
rginia House Settlement, Plymouth

Associate Members

nic Minorities Leadership, Lewisham
anor Gardens Centre, Holloway
e Markfield Project, Haringey
dent Community Action Scotland
Development Unit, Edinburgh

London Members

The Albany, Deptford
Beauchamp Lodge, Paddington
Bede House, Bermondsey
Bishop Creighton House, Fulham
Blackfriars Settlement, Waterloo
Cambridge House & Talbot, Camberwell
Catford Centre for the Unemployed, Catford
Caxton House, Islington
Centre '70, West Norwood
Charterhouse-in-Southwark
Community Information Centre, Westminster
Community Links (South) East Ham
Coppleston Centre, Peckham
Dame Colet House, Stepney
Evelyn 190 Centre, Deptford
The Factory, Stoke Newington
Family Friends, Brixton
Fern Street Settlement, Bow
Katherine Low Settlement, Battersea
Lady Margaret Hall Settlement, Stockwell
Mansfield House Settlement, Plaistow
North Lewisham Project, Deptford
Oxford House, Bethnal Green
Peckham Settlement, Peckham
Pitt Street Settlement, Peckham
Response Community Centre, Earls Court
St Hilda's East, Shoreditch
St Margaret's House, Bethnal Green
Telegraph Hill Neighbourhood Council, New Cross
Tottenham Community Project, Tottenham
Toynbee Hall, Aldgate

urce: *BASSAC Report 1991*

Women's University Settlement

45, NELSON SQUARE, BLACKFRIARS ROAD, S. E.

Honorary Members

MR EDRIC BAYLEY
MRS BENSON
REV W. COPELAND BOWIE
MRS ARTHUR JOHNSON
MR C. S. LOCH
MISS MINET
CANON SCOTT HOLLAND
MRS HENRY SIDGWICK
THE PRESIDENT OF TRINITY COLLEGE, OXFORD
MR BERNARD BOSANQUET

Warden

MISS HELEN GLADSTONE
(*Coming into residence in September, 1901*)

Acting Warden

MISS K. V. BANNATYNE

Vice Warden

MISS F. C. PRIDEAUX

Honorary Secretaries

Secretary to Association—MISS BEATRICE CUST, 13 Eccleston Sq., S.W.
Secretary to Committee—MISS M. FLETCHER

Honorary Treasurer

MISS E. G. POWELL, Long Wall, Walton-on-Thames
(*Please note Honorary Treasurer's change of address*)

Committee

*MISS M. FLETCHER (Girton College, Resident Members)
MISS FLORENCE WARD (Girton College, Non-Resident Members)
*MISS M. SHARPLEY (Newnham College, Resident Members)
MRS LAMB (Newnham College, Non-Resident Members)
MISS SHEAVYN (Somerville College, Non-Resident Members)
*MISS ELEANOR G. POWELL (Somerville College, Non-Resident Members)
*MISS CONSTANCE BARTLETT (Lady Margaret Hall)
MISS CLARA E. COLLET (London University)
*MISS E. M. GUINNESS (Royal Holloway College)

MRS MINET (Elected by General Meeting)
MISS BEATRICE CUST (Co-opted by Committee)
MRS C. S. LOCH (Co-opted by Committee)
MRS MARSHALL (Co-opted by Committee)
MISS SEWELL (Co-opted by Committee)
MISS M. K. BRADBY (Co-opted by Committee)
*Re-elected March, 1901

Bankers

CAPITAL AND COUNTIES BANK, LIMITED, 39 Threadneedle Street, E. C.

List of Residents during 1900

Name	*College*	*Entrance Date*	*Date of Leaving*
Miss C. R. Bartlett	Lady Margaret Hall	May 1889	To present time
Miss F. C. Prideaux	Non-College	5.10.1891	"
Miss M. G. Boord	"	5.10.1893	"
Miss G. A. Brownrigg	"	21.9.1894	"
Miss F. Eardley-Wilmot	"	1.10.1895	1.9.1900
Miss E. Macadam	"	19.4.1889	To present time
Miss E. H. Bell	"	25.4.1898	1.9.1900
Mrs Miles	"	11.11.1898	23.3.1900
Miss M. Moser	"	16.1.1899	To present time
Miss J. van Isselmuden	Newnham College	18.1.1899	"
Miss E. Miller Jones	Non-College	22.4.1899	"
Miss G. Fergusson	"	1.5.1899	5.4.1900
Miss L. Latham	"	23.5.1899	To present time
Miss Bannatyne	"	6.11.1899	"
Miss M. Rutherford	"	15.11.1899	17.11.1900
Miss K. L. Long	"	1.1.1900	10.9.1900
Miss G. S. Lewis	"	23.3.1900	31.12.1900
Mrs Rowley	"	12.5.1900	13.11.1900
Miss G. Frith	"	14.5.1900	10.9.1900
Miss M. Elliot	"	27.9.1900	To present time
Miss S. E. Dewe	"	1.10.1900	"
Miss F. E. Crook	Somerville College	1.10.1900	"
Miss F. Hindley	Non-College	14.11.1900	"

Settlement Members of BASSAC in 1984

Founded	*Name*	*Address*
1884	Toynbee Hall	28 Commercial Street, London, E1
1884	Oxford House, Derbyshire Street	Bethnal Green Road, London, E2
1884	Charterhouse-in-Southwark	40 Tabard Street, London, SE1
1887	Blackfriars Settlement	44 Nelson Square, London, SE1
1889	St Hilda' East (1898)	18 Club Row, London, E2
1889	St Margaret's House (1893)	21 Old Ford Road, London, E2
1889	Liverpool Institute and Mission	377–401 Mill Street, Liverpool
1889	Glasgow University Settlement	33 Peel Glen Road, Glasgow
1894	The Albany	Douglas Way, Deptford, SE8
1895	Manchester University Settlement	St Vincent's School, Manchester
1897	Lady Margaret Hall Settlement	460 Wandsworth Road, SW11
1898	Mansfield House Univ. Settlement	30 Avenue Road, London, E11
1899	Birmingham Settlement	318 Summer Lane, Birmingham
1899	Cambridge House and Talbot	131 Camberwell Rd, London, SE5
1902	Croft House Settlement	Garden Street, Sheffield, S14
1905	Edinburgh University Settlement	Briste Street, Edinburgh, EH8
1906	Peckham Settlement (UGSM 1896)	Staffordshire Street, London, SE15
1908	Bishop Creighton House	378 Lillie Road, London, SW6
1910	Dame Colet House	Ben Johnson Road, London, E1
1910	Pitt Street Settlement	181 East Surrey Grove, SE1
1911	Bristol Settlement	48 Ducie Road, Bristol
1912	Liverpool Settlement	Box 27, Liverpool, L69
1924	Katherine Low Settlement	108 Battersea High Street, SW11
1925	Virginia House Settlement	Peacock Lane, Plymouth
1930	Bede House Association	151 Southwark Park Road, SE16
1940	Beauchamp Lodge Settlement	2 Warwick Crescent, London, W2
1940	Caxton House Settlement	129 St John's Way, London, N19

Neither the T & T centre (1889) nor the Mary Ward centre (1897) belong to BASSAC, which includes 17 multipurpose social action centres formed since 1970 to run clubs, literacy schemes, and so forth.

Bibliographical Note

Settlement workers in the past who wrote for the *Charity Organization Review* included Miss K. V. Bannatyne of the WUS, whose essay on 'The Place and Training of Volunteers for Charitable Work' appeared in 1902 at a time when C. S. Loch and the Bosanquets were among other contributors. Helen Bosanquet's *Social Work in London 1869–1912: A History of the COS* was published in 1914 (Murray); Elizabeth Macadam's *Equipment of the Social Worker* in 1925 (Allen & Unwin); and Mary Stock's *Fifty Years in Every Street* in 1945 (Manchester University Press).

Other books on or by settlement workers that have proved useful reading include Henrietta Barnett, *Canon Barnett: His Life, Work and Friends* (John Murray, 1918); Louise Creighton, *Letters of Oswin Creighton* (Longmans Green, 1920); Emily Davies, *Questions Relating to Women: 1860–1908* (Bowes & Bowes, 1912); Gertrude Toynbee (ed.), *Joseph and Arnold Toynbee: Reminiscences and Letters* (A. G. Glaishen, 1841); Beatrice Webb, *Beatrice Webb's Dairies* and *My Apprenticeship* (Longmans Green, 1952 and 1929); and Elizabeth Wordsworth, *Glimpses of the Past* (Mowbray, 1913).

Among other useful biographies are Georgina Battiscombe, *Reluctant Pioneer* (Constable, 1978); Margaret Cole, *Beatrice Webb*, (Longman, 1945) and also *The Life of Beatrice Webb* by Kitty Muggeridge and Ruth Adams (Secker & Warburg, 1956); E. Moberly Bell, *Octavia Hill* (Constable, 1942); N. Boyd, *Josephine Butler, Octavia Hill and Florence Nightingale* (Macmillan, 1983); Arthur Sidgwick and Eleanor Mildred Balfour, *Henry Sidgwick: A*

Memoir (Macmillan, 1906); Vera Wheatley, *Harriet Martineau* (Secker & Warburg, 1957); G. M. Trevelyan, *Mrs Humphry Ward* (Constable, 1956); Quentin Bell, *Ruskin* (Hogarth, 1963); Kenneth Clark, *Ruskin Today* (Murray, 1964); E. Collingwood, *Ruskin* (Methuen, abridged 1911); and Betty Askwith, *The Lytteltons: A Family Chronicle of the Nineteenth Century* (Chatto & Windus, 1975).

Eileen Younghusband's relevant work includes *Report on the Employment and Training of Social Workers* (Constable, 1947), *Report on Social Workers in the Local Authority Health and Welfare Services* (HMSO, 1958) and her *Social Work and Social Change* (Allen & Unwin, 1964) with the follow-up story 1950 to 1975 (Allen & Unwin, 1976).

John Ruskin's *Sesame and Lilies: Three Lectures* (George Allen, 1893) and Mrs Humphry Ward's *Robert Elsmere* (Oxford University Press, 1887) are essential reading. Other relevant books are:

ACUPA Report, *Faith in the City* (Church House Publishing, 1985)

Briggs, Asa and Ann McCartney, *History of Toynbee Hall* (Routledge, 1984)

Bruce, Maurice (ed.) *Rise of the Welfare State* (Weidenfeld & Nicholson, 1978)

Clarke, A. K., *History of Cheltenham Ladies' College* (Faber, 1953)

Cox, J., *The English Churches in a Secular Society: Lambeth 1870–1930* (Oxford University Press, 1983)

Denny, B. (ed.), *Graham Street Memories* (Hazell, Watson & Viney, 1931)

Fishman, W. I., *East End* (Duckworth, 1884)

Harrison, Brian, *Peaceable Kingdom* (Oxford University Press, 1983)

Harrison, Paul, *Inside the Inner City* (Penguin, 1983)

Kitson Clark, G., *Churchmen and the Condition of England: 1832–1885* (Methuen, 1973)

McWilliams-Tullberg, Rita, *Women at Cambridge: A Man's University – Though of a Mixed Type* (Gollancz, 1975)
Picht, Werner, *Toynbee Hall and the English Settlement Movement* (Bell, 1913)
Pimlott, J. A. R., *Fifty Years of Toynbee Hall: 1884–1934* (Dent, 1935)
Prochaska, F. K., *Women's Philanthropy in Nineteenth-Century England* (Oxford University Press, 1980)
Richards, Denis, *History of Morley College* (Routledge, 1958)
Skye, Elaine, *History of Queen's College, London: 1848–1972* (Chatto, 1972)
Smith, B. A., *Dean Church* (Oxford University Press, 1958)
Smith, Marjorie, *Professional Education for Social Work in Britain* (Allen & Unwin, 1965)
Soldon, N. C., *Women in Trade Unions: 1874–1926* (Gill & Macmillan, 1978)
Titmuss, R., *The Gift Relationship* (Penguin, 1970)
Vincent, A. and R. Plant, *Philosophy, Politics and Citizenship* (Blackwell, 1984)
Walton, R. G., *Women in Social Work* (Routledge, 1975)
Wiener, M., *English Culture and the Decline on the Industrial Spirit: 1850–1980* (Cambridge University Press, 1981)
Young, S. and P. Wilmott, *Family and Kinship in East London* (Penguin, 1956)

Index